Globalizing the Sacred

GLOBALIZING THE SACRED

Religion across the Americas

MANUEL A.
VÁSQUEZ

MARIE FRIEDMANN
MARQUARDT

RUTGERS UNIVERSITY PRESS
New Brunswick, New Jersey, and London

Library of Congress Cataloguing-in-Publication Data

Vásquez, Manuel A.
　　Globalizing the sacred : religion across the Americas / Manuel A. Vásquez and Marie
F. Marquardt.
　　　p. cm.
　　Includes bibliographical references and index.
　　ISBN 0–8135–3284–1 (alk. paper) — ISBN 0–8135–3285–X (pbk. : alk. paper)
　　1. America—Religion. 2. Religion and sociology—America. 3. Globalization—religious aspects. I. Marquardt, Marie F. 1972– II. Title.

BL2500 .V37 2003
306.6'097—dc21

　　　　　　　　　　　　　　　　　　　　　　　　　　　　　　2002152411

British Cataloging-in-Publication information is available from the British Library.

Manufactured in the United States of America

Contents

Acknowledgments

Completing this book would not have been possible without help from family, friends, and colleagues. Foremost among them is Anna Peterson, whose careful readings of multiple drafts proved invaluable. Manuel A. Vásquez also expresses his deepest gratitude to Anna and Gabriel for their patience and understanding throughout the lengthy process. Thanks are also due to the members of the Rockefeller reading group on religion and globalization at the University of Florida, especially to Patricia Fortuny, David Hackett, Lois Lorentzen, Milagros Peña, and Philip Williams. Participants in the UF graduate seminar "Globalizing the Sacred" also allowed Manuel to try out some preliminary hypotheses.

Marie would like to thank Chris and Mary Elizabeth for providing love, encouragement, and much-needed diversion. Her profound gratitude goes to Elizabeth Friedmann for the many sacrifices she offered to make this project possible. Thanks also to those who have carefully read and responded to chapter drafts and presentations, including Nancy Eiesland, Elizabeth Bounds, Steven Tipton, Sarah Mahler, and Carlos Garma Navarro, and to faculty and colleagues at Emory, especially Jon Gunnemann, Carla Freeman, Karey Harwood, Barbara McClure, Melissa Snarr, and Bradley Schmelling. Marie would also like to thank the Social Science Research Council, the Lilly Endowment, the Louisville Institute, and the Graduate Division of Religion at Emory University for funding portions of this project. Finally, we both thank the communities and individuals who so generously shared their experiences with us, our anonymous reader for the insightful comments, and David Myers at Rutgers University Press for his unwavering support throughout the production of the book.

Globalizing the Sacred

INTRODUCTION

The origins of this volume date to an apparition of the Virgin Mary in 1996. Just a few days before Christmas, she appeared in iridescent shades on the windows of a bank building nestled between strip malls and gas stations amid the suburban sprawl of Clearwater, Florida. Taking advantage of the image's appearance in our "backyard," we traveled to the site to study the phenomenon (Vásquez and Marquardt 2000). Once there, we joined not only residents of the Tampa–St. Petersburg area and the occasional curious out-of-towner but also members of the national and international media, including the major U.S. television networks, and volunteers working with the Shepherd of Christ, a lay Catholic organization based in Cincinnati, who were dedicated to interpreting and spreading Mary's messages through their Internet site. Also there were transnational Mexican immigrants, many of whom saw the Virgin reflected in the bank windows as Our Lady of Guadalupe. They were joined by French, German, and Australian pilgrims and tourists who had just come from other pilgrimage sites like Medjugorge and Conyers, Georgia, or who were on their way to Disney World in Orlando. In the midst of this bustling and polyglot crowd, we understood that we could not conduct a traditional ethnographic study of the site, providing only a thick description of local beliefs and practices. We were witnessing the production of new local, transnational, and global sacred spaces in interaction with multiple "secular" spaces. Grappling with the apparition at Clearwater, we began to wonder if the complex dynamics at play in this site were not also evident elsewhere. We decided to embark on a more sustained study of the changing face of religion in the Americas, our area of expertise, in the context of globalization. The result is this book.

We approach the study of religion and globalization with some trepidation. This is ironic, given that, as Rudolph (1997: 1) notes, "religious communities are among the oldest of transnationals: Sufi orders, Catholic missionaries, and Buddhist monks carried word and praxis across vast spaces before those places became nation-states or even states." Notwithstanding this long history of religious globalization, it would be theoretically naive and strategically dangerous not to acknowledge the ideological baggage that has become associated with globalization in recent years. Globalization is often understood in purely economic terms, as an ineluctable and monolithic process that, for better or for worse, determines every aspect of social life. Economic elites have promoted a view of globalization as the triumph of open markets against state-controlled, protectionist economic regimes. This triumph, we are told, goes hand in hand with the advancement of liberal democracy and individual rights and the fulfillment of material and spiritual needs worldwide (Fukuyama 1992).

Critics on the Left, in contrast, tend to see globalization as an insidious form of U.S. imperialism—as the homogenization and exploitation of local cultures and communities. In their view, the crisis of the welfare state and the weakening of the working class as a collective agent make resistance to the steamroller of globalization ever more precarious. In this context, globalization functions as a "conservative sociodicy" disseminated by the economic elites to justify their privilege and bolster the inevitability of neoliberalism. As Bourdieu (1998: 38) sees it, globalization is above all "a justificatory myth" that, while offering utopia, leads only to "the extension of the hold of a small number of dominant nations over the whole set of national financial markets."

We share Bourdieu's concerns, and we add to them a further concern: in their attempt to reject economic reductionism, some scholars have presented a "radical" view of globalization as the erasure of all borders and power relations—globalization as utter fragmentation, fluidity, and ephemerality. When social scientists speak of the world as becoming a "global oecumene" (Hannerz 1992) or "single place" (Robertson 1992), or as defined primarily by decentered networks (Castells 1996) or global flows (Appadurai 1996), there is a danger of glossing over the contested, uneven, and situated impact of globalization. Abstract readings of globalization risk obscuring the conflict-laden relations among global, regional, national, local, and individual actors and processes. This is why we prefer to talk about "anchored" or "grounded" globalization (Fox and Starn 1997; Burawoy et al. 2000). Using case studies, we explore how specific religious communities and institutions experience globalization in its multiple manifestations.

The best antidote to hegemonic readings is to see globalization as a complex, historically contingent cluster of processes involving multiple actors, scales, and realms of human activity. These processes have contradictory effects for local life and for religious organizations, discourses, and practices. Globalization is not just about domination and homogenization. It also involves resistance, heterogeneity, and the active negotiation of space, time, and identity at the grassroots, even if these negotiations occur under the powerful constraints of neoliberal markets and all-pervading culture industries. This is what Appadurai (2000), Mittelman (2000), and Keck and Sikkink (1998) refer to as "globalization from below" or "grassroots globalization."

The proliferation of theories of globalization reflects the polyvocality of the phenomena at hand. In this light, globalization can neither provide a new theoretical grand narrative nor be seen as the only path to economic development. We see theories of globalization above all as a framework to deal with social complexity (Mittelman 2000). Within the globalization framework we find a host of analytical tools, such as the dialectic between territorialization and deterritorialization, and the concepts of transnationalism, hybridity, and borderlands, which provide a more nuanced picture of the changing face of religious and cultural life in the Americas. Given the time and space compression induced by the recent episode of globalization, traditional and emerging approaches to religion and society, such as secularization theory and the so-called New Paradigm, show significant limitations in making sense of the contemporary status of religion in the Americas. These limitations stem from a reliance on a modernist epistemology that, while emphasizing difference and change on the surface, remains primarily interested in retrieving unchanging facts, essences, and laws governing society. Globalization, as the loosening of spatiotemporal arrangements and the relativization of collective and individual identities, poses a serious challenge to this essentialism. This book represents our attempt to develop and test conceptual tools to study religion and social change in the Americas through a mixture of theory and case studies. Our primary aim is to bring the discipline of religious studies into dialogue with emerging theories of globalization and transnational migration, and into debates about identity, postcolonialism, media, and the fate of modernity.

RELIGION, THE SOCIAL SCIENCES, AND CULTURAL AND AREA STUDIES IN CONVERSATION

This dialogue will no doubt generate sparks, given the prejudices involved. Operating under Enlightenment-based notions of history and agency, many social scientists have tended to dismiss religion's capacity to shape social life. The Enlightenment construed religion as its Other, as misguided, even ignorant and irrational, beliefs and practices bound to disappear as rationality penetrates every sphere of human activity. This understanding explains why religion's enduring vitality has always posed a thorny problem for the modern social sciences. Without denying the heterogeneity of sociological thinking, the dominant impulse within sociology has been to see the persistence of religion as, at best, the result of desperate defensive, often private, responses to inevitable structural processes of modernization and secularization. At worst, religion is nothing more than an ideology, a false consciousness, that reflects and obscures more foundational social realities. Globalization theorists have also reproduced this understanding of religion. To the extent that religion appears in their writings, it is either as anti-modernist "fundamentalist" movements that seek to assert local identity and tradition against the cosmopolitanism and "tyranny of the market" brought about by globalization, or as thoroughly rationalized and privatized spiritualities that individuals purchase as commodities in a "religious market." A case in point is Jean Comaroff's and John Comaroff's introductory chapter in *Millennial Capitalism and the Culture of Neoliberalism* (2001). The essay offers a valuable critique of the millennial and messianic pretensions of neoliberal capitalism. However, it fails to see that contemporary religious phenomena are not limited to or even typified by "economies of the occult" (e.g., spirit possession, fortune-telling, witchcraft, etc.) and "prosperity gospels," which are the "spectral," fetishized expressions of speculative capitalism. While they recognize that religion offers resources for creative resistance to capitalism at the grassroots, the Comaroffs see the rapid growth of religious movements such as Pentecostalism, which link the material and spiritual world tightly, as purely a response to social pathologies generated by global neoliberalism. These religious movements are, for the Comaroffs, today's cargo cults, built on the despair produced by the exclusion of vast sectors of the world's population and on the desire for immediate gratification created by mass-media consumerism. There is no question that religion and global capitalism are connected. Nonetheless, the connection is far more complex than that imagined by the Comaroffs.

Despite their limitations, sociology's founders understood the role religion can play in the articulation of social epistemologies. Durkheim (1995), for example, saw religion as the source of "collective representations," foundational categories that order our perceptions, structure our actions upon the world, and cement social relations. Similarly, Weber (1958) referred to the role of various religious worldviews in shaping practical, social ethos. And while Marx (1978) saw religion as the expression of a world in which labor is alienated, he also acknowledged that "religion is the general theory of that world, its encyclopaedic compendium, its logic in popular form, its spiritualistic *point d'honneur*, its enthusiasm, its moral sanction, its solemn completion, its universal ground for consolation and justification."

We argue that when accorded its proper epistemological status, religion can provide important insights into the new cartographies produced by globalization. Religion has always provided complex strategies for conceptualizing self, time, and space. This means that it must be taken seriously as an independent variable in the present episode of globalization, which poses serious challenges to our traditional maps of reality. This attention is particularly important in the Americas, where religion continues to constitute a major interpretive horizon for vast sectors of the population. Moreover, the study of religion cannot be limited to institutional dynamics or overt behaviors of elites, data that can be readily quantifiable and reducible to formulas. Religion is also, in Appadurai's words, the "work of the imagination"; it is also about shifting identities and hybrid cultures, about theodicies and utopian aspirations that might make for messy theories.

Prejudices cut both ways. Reacting to the reductionism of social scientists, many religionists have sought refuge in theories and methodologies that view religion as a "sui generis, unique, and sociohistorically autonomous" reality grounded in an irreducible human essence (McCutcheon 1997). Paradoxically, by asserting that religion is about a universal subjective feeling of dependence (Friedrich Schleiermacher), awe (Rudolph Otto), or existential dread (Paul Tillich), theologians and historians of religion reaffirm the implications of social scientific reductionism. They define religion, above all, as an interior private matter. Thus, as Talal Asad (1993: 28) puts it, in Western modernity "strategies of confinement" are entwined with "strategies of defense" of religion.

A good example of this entwinement is Mircea Eliade, who played a central role in the development of religion as a sui generis discipline. Eliade reaches back to the "primitive man" to capture the essence of *homo religiosus*. For the primitive man, says Eliade, the sacred stood apart because it was absolute reality, not only transcending this world but also grounding it ontologically. The sacred is not the reflection of social dynamics, as Durkheim and Marx claimed, but reality itself. By contrast, "modern man" has desacralized existence, a process which "has sometimes arrived at hybrid forms of black magic and sheer travesty of religion"; Eliade clarifies: "We do not refer to the countless 'little religions' that proliferate in all modern cities, to the pseudo-occult, neo-spiritualistic, or so called hermetic churches, sects, or schools; for all these phenomena still belong to the sphere of religion, even if they almost always present the aberrant aspects of pseudomorphs" (1959: 26). Globalization, with its relentless dislocation and relocation of cultural forms, poses a sharp challenge to Eliade's elitist and dehistoricized understanding of religion. We argue that it is precisely the "little religions," those hybrid forms that Eliade sees as "pseudoreligions" or "degenerated myths," that are the vital and public face of religion in the present context.

A second strategy religionists have used to deal with social scientific reductionism has been to retreat to a narrow focus on sacred texts. As Orsi (1994: 142) observes: "To study religion in the United States today is to study texts. The briefest review of papers given at meetings of the American Academy of Religion over the last two decades shows how few studies are empirically based. The written and spoken word, rather than engaged behavior studied in its place, are what occupies the practitioners." We do not mean that sacred texts are not worth careful study or that textual approaches to religion are always ahistorical. After all, it is now standard in the discipline of religion to contextualize texts and discuss the dynamics of canon formation and maintenance. The rise of feminist and postcolonial theories has also contributed to a recovery of the "little texts" at the margins of the great traditions. Rather, we challenge the tendency to read all social reality—religion included—as nothing more than a text. This tendency, which gained legitimacy with the "linguistic turn," has become greatly exacerbated by deconstruction and some strands of postmodernism. We have found Derridean deconstruction to be extremely helpful in disclosing the power effects of dominant theories, especially those built on binary thinking. In fact, our critiques of secularization and the so-called New Paradigm in sociology of religion draw from Derrida's attacks on representationalism. We see religious identities not as fixed unitary essences but as complex and shifting dynamics, always mediated by multiple forces. Nevertheless, we do not subscribe to the strong version of the Derridean dictum that "there is nothing outside the text."

An example of the pitfalls of the linguistic turn is Mark C. Taylor's *About Religion* (1999). *About Religion* insightfully shows how religion operates in the most unexpected, "secular" places—in popular culture, mass media, and at the heart of global capitalism. Taylor might well approve of the Comaroffs' focus on the enchanted reality that accompanies global capitalism. However, what the Comaroffs critique as the mirage of the new economic (dis)order, Taylor celebrates as reality itself. In *About Religion*, Taylor engages in a hyperaesthetization of all social reality: "As the real becomes image and the image becomes real, the world becomes a work of art and our condition becomes transparently virtual" (5). In Taylor's view, Las Vegas, the mirage par excellence, has become the master metaphor for "our current sociocultural situation." Las Vegas embodies the "realized eschatology of the virtual kingdom," a "terminal place" where "high becomes low, low becomes high, foundations seem to crumble and everything becomes unbearably light. In light of this darkness, there appears to be nothing beyond this city—absolutely nothing and nothing absolute" (201). Here, Taylor moves dangerously from acknowledging that all reality is symbolic in the broadest sense to claiming that reality can be reduced to the play of signifiers. Certainly globalization and recent technological changes have the potential for redefining our epistemologies. However, it is premature to claim that, for all people in the world, image and reality have collapsed into each other due to the virtualization of culture and society.

Taylor reads his case studies as texts that illustrate his overarching philosophical claims. Extrapolating from these cases, he gives us a "god's-eye view" of our present age as realized eschatology. The overall effect is to freeze time and space, to enervate resistance against an ineluctably virtualized world. Despite efforts to erase space, time, and the body, computer-mediated communications still operate within social contexts, contexts of access, reception, and production, which are not the mere effects of virtuality. Instead of looking at social phenomena as texts illustrating a movement from Hegel to virtual reality, we might explore the ways in which particular people and institutions negotiate global capitalism, the culture industry, and the Internet. A far more heterogeneous and contested picture of the present age would emerge out of this exploration.

Our critique of semiotic reductionism goes hand in hand with our attempt to rematerialize the study of religion in a nonreductive fashion. As such, it bears a strong affinity to "the spatial turn," recent efforts to shift the point of reference in cultural studies, critical theory, and in the study of religion "from text to territory" (Soja 1999; Tweed 2002; Hervieu-Leger 2002). We believe that scholarship can and should go beyond the unproductive modernist dichotomy that posits religion as either a totally autonomous essence or the epiphenomenal manifestation of material reality. It is possible to preserve Eliade's anti-reductionist impetus without denying that religion is inextricably entwined with social and historical processes, particularly those connected with the production of space and embodied subjectivities. As Orsi (1997: 6– 7) writes, religion "cannot be neatly separated from other practices of everyday life, from the ways that human beings work on the landscape, for example, or dispose of corpses, or arrange for the security of their offspring. Nor can 'religion' be separated from the material circumstances in which specific instances of religious imagination and behavior arise and to which they respond."

In contrast to Geertz (1973), we are not interested in setting a transcultural definition of religion. Instead we study how religion is imagined and experienced by individuals, groups, and institutions embedded in multiple realms of activity. To study the complex ways in which religion is lived today, we draw from multiple methodologies across disciplines, including sociology, anthropology, history, philosophy, geography, and political science. Our focus on lived religion does not lead us to forsake the study of religious discourses and texts. Rather, we argue that cultural studies and ethnographic approaches must be in constant conversation with textual methods in a way that challenges all claims to offer the definitive view of the world. For, if textual approaches carry the danger of semiotic reductionism, ethnography is prone to what Malkki (1997: 61) calls "a sedentary metaphysics," a tendency to view cultures as pre-given, self-contained, and territorially rooted wholes whose organizing logics can be retrieved through "thick description." It is precisely the volatile interplay of discursive and nondiscursive practices that interests us, for globalization has blurred boundaries among realms of human activity, allowing traditional religious expressions long considered to be waning to take center stage alongside commodified consumer culture.

Finally, we wish to cross the border between American studies and

Latin American studies, which has been sustained by the primacy of the nation-state in our conceptions of space, identity, and culture. The United States is unique, we are told, in its pluralism and sectarianism, in having immigration as its core experience and making progress its main motto. Latin America, on the other hand, is seen as a patriarchal, corporatist, and deeply traditional region that has never fully succeeded in making it to modernity. This narrative ignores the entwinement of U.S. and Latin American histories, a link that globalization has tightened through increasing economic integration, post–1965 migration, and the rapid growth of the U.S. Latino population.

OVERVIEW OF THE BOOK

Within the larger topic of religion and globalization, we focus on the Americas. This focus allows us to draw strategically from our experience as scholars of Latin American and U.S. Latino religion to produce an ethnographically and historically grounded view of globalization. Our focus enables us to maintain specificity, capturing the richness of local phenomena while placing them in their proper regional and global context. We do not purport to provide an exhaustive view of the Latin American and U.S. religious fields. For example, we do not offer case studies from South America or the Caribbean. We also focus heavily on varieties of Christianity, skimming only the surface of the range of religions that permeate the Americas today. We have selected our case studies because, besides being compelling in themselves, they offer poignant illustrations of the complex interplay of religion and globalization in its economic, political, and cultural dimensions. Our case studies, moreover, raise crucial epistemological questions, pointing to the limitations of dominant theories of religion and social change and highlighting some of the challenges sociology of religion must tackle as it seeks to theorize complexity.

The first two chapters of the book lay out the theoretical context for the project. Chapter 1 examines dominant and emerging theories of religion and social change, while Chapter 2 focuses on globalization theories. Rather than provide a comprehensive review of the literature, both chapters concentrate on the theoretical and methodological issues at stake in the sociological study of religion. We will see these issues at work in the case studies that make up the rest of the book. Chapters 3 and 4 address the themes of border making and border crossing. Chapter 3 takes a historical approach, challenging both the notion that globalization is an altogether new phenomenon and the assumption that religion plays only a peripheral role in it. Chapter 4 focuses on the "future" of religion as it enters the "electronic frontier." Both chapters, however, highlight the tension between, on the one hand, physical migration and pilgrimage across political borders and, on the other, the nomadic practices facilitated by mass media and the Internet. We shall see that the Internet does not lead to total disembodiment and the erasure of locality but instead sustains contradictory relations with historical patterns of migration and community building.

Chapters 5 and 6 focus on grassroots religion and transnational migration. Drawing from fieldwork among Salvadoran gangs in El Salvador and Washington, D.C., and from a study of two congregations in Atlanta, we explore how Latino migrants negotiate globalization. The role of religion in the articulation of oppositional identities and alternative public spheres at the margins of society is central in these chapters. These identities and public spheres often make it possible for Latino migrants to assert agency and locality in the face of powerful deterritorializing forces. However, as with any social reality, oppositional identities and alternative public spheres are contradictory, sometimes even reproducing exclusionary logics.

Chapters 7 and 8 explore globalization "from above," looking at how religious institutions handle the pressures of globalization and are themselves vehicles for global processes. According to Stout and Cormode (1998: 64), many theologians and religious historians "associate institutionalization with spirit-sapping mechanization and lifeless ossification. In this framework, religious institutions are human creations standing in the way of pure spiritual 'movement' and extra-institutional 'dynamism.'" By underscoring the paradoxes and contradictions generated by institutions as they seek to reorient themselves amid rapid flows of peoples, ideas, capital, and commodities, we offer a more nuanced understanding of institutional dynamics. Like popular religion, religious institutions are dynamic, polysemic, and open to conflict. In fact, in both of these chapters, popular religion and religious institutions are engaged in a complex, if asymmetrical, interplay that leads to innovation, ambiguity, and heterogeneity. Even when institutional elites seem utterly at odds with "unruly" locals, trying to discipline and co-opt them, there are always unintended consequences, which globalization only accentuates. Just as we cannot assume that grassroots religion is always emancipatory, we cannot presuppose that the institutions are static and monolithic and that the outcome of institutional behavior will always be conservative and repressive.

We conclude the book with a brief discussion of the methodological implications of a globalization approach to religion in the Americas. As a final note, we should explain the collaborative nature of this project. Marie Friedmann Marquardt was the principal author of Chapters 1, 3, 6, and 8, while Manuel Vásquez was responsible for Chapters 2, 4, 5 (with Salvadoran sociologist Ileana Gómez), and 7. However, we have read multiple drafts of each other's work, offering extensive comments. The introduction and the conclusion are coauthored.

1

THE LIMITS OF DOMINANT
AND EMERGING MODELS

French and German tourists alongside Mexican migrant workers vener-
ate the image of the Virgin Mary in a strip mall in Florida; Latino gang
members, deported from the United States to "home" countries they
barely know, find Jesus in transnational churches; U.S. Evangelicals use
electronic media to preach a "neoliberal" gospel of wealth and health
to remote indigenous villages in Guatemala. These are some of the striking faces of religion in the Americas today. While seemingly disparate,
all these expressions reflect the complex ways religion intersects with
the economic, political, and cultural dimensions of globalization. In this
book, we seek not only to describe religious change in the Americas but
also to theorize it. This poses an especially difficult challenge, as
the dominant paradigms in the sociological study of religion fail to
make clear sense of the cases we have gathered. The religious forms we
explore here are not stripped of their supernatural referents or hopelessly privatized and inconsequential, as many secularization theorists
would predict. Nor are they mere products of instrumental calculations
in which culture, norms, tastes, and power take a back seat to the workings of a religious marketplace, as rational-choice theorists would suppose. In other words, our cases challenge both the "old" and "new"
paradigms (Warner 1993) on which scholars have relied to study religion in the Americas. More fundamentally, they question many of the
epistemological bases of modernist sociologies of religion.

The material we gather in our case studies shows that modernization and the entry to postmodernity do not automatically translate into secularization. In fact, we document how the appearance of miraculous and supernatural religious events and practices is often mediated by characteristically late- or postmodern mass media, technology such as the Internet, and the global penetration of flexible forms of capitalism. Our cases show, moreover, that as people, ideas, media, and capital transgress national boundaries, or become deterritorialized through multiple processes of globalization, the religious field in the Americas becomes increasingly complex and fluid, defying attempts at one-dimensional descriptions. People in the Americas today are presented with a dizzying array of religious forms, many of which are detached from their original context of production. Globalization has precipitated an overabundance of religious meaning that both challenges the rational-choice view of the religious marketplace as characterized by a scarcity of religious goods and points to the emergence of multiple, overlapping, and heterogeneous religious fields that individuals and institutions must negotiate as they go about practicing religion.

Our task in this chapter is to analyze prevalent theoretical approaches to the study of religion in the Americas to highlight their limitations and set the stage for the alternative, more flexible, conceptual tools we introduce in Chapter 2. We do not purport to offer new or exhaustive critiques of the dominant paradigms. Rather, drawing from some key ongoing debates about secularization and religious pluralism, we aim to give a general overview of the sociology of religion and to situate our own approach within it.

CONFRONTING THE "OLD" PARADIGM

In its simplest form, the secularization paradigm claims that modernization results in the progressive decline of religion's social significance. This decline gathered significant momentum with the Enlightenment's critique of ideology in the quest to affirm human autonomy. Enlightenment views of society set themselves against tradition and religious dogma, particularly against the search for the foundations of human practice on suprarational, divine sources. Explaining the social by the social meant a break from the misconceptions of the past, a progressive movement toward full rationality. In fact, Kant (1991) referred to the Enlightenment as the "coming of age" of human analytical faculties. As reason displaced faith and human history replaced sacred time as the grounds of legitimation, various spheres of human action became autonomous. Of these spheres, science, understood as the pinnacle of human rationality, achieved special influence. This proved particularly corrosive to the enchanted world constructed by religion, a world redolent with magical forces and baffling supernatural events. Threatened by the rigor of scientific rationality, religion withdraws from the public sphere, becoming nothing more than personal piety, a "residue" handed down as legacy (Gauchet 1997: 4).

Most versions of the secularization theory rest on two pillars. The first is Durkheim's claim that religion is the "womb of civilization." Working with the "elementary forms of religious life," Durkheim came to see religion as a foundational set of beliefs and practices that unite individuals into moral community. He perceived the church as a model for all social institutions and religious ritual as a model for all social interaction (Durkheim 1995). According to Durkheim, the earliest communities are characterized by "mechanical solidarity," that is, by a lack of individual differentiation or division of labor and by the ever-presence of religion as the powerful collective effervescence that holds the group together. With urbanization and technological development, mechanical solidarity gives way to industrial societies with deeper, more "organic," forms of solidarity, characterized by a greater division of labor and the development of individual consciousness (Durkheim 1984). Since these emerging modern societies are inhabited by interdependent autonomous individuals, religious institutional forms, values, and rituals can no longer exert the same overt cohesive power as under mechanical solidarity. Rather, religion must become increasingly abstract and generalized, becoming either collective moral sentiments or philosophies of human development. Thus, in Durkheim's evolutionary scheme, entry to modernity increasingly removed religion from the domain of the supernatural, turning it into an invisible but overarching value system that integrates and pervades secular institutions.

Building on Durkheim's legacy, Parsons (1968) and Bellah (1970, 1980) argue that as individuals become increasingly autonomous, society becomes more deeply integrated through normative or "axiological" principles that may have a religious origin but have become secularized. Perhaps the most well known formulation of this approach is Bellah's short article on "civil religion." He argues that although Americans certainly do not share a unified religion, they are held together by shared symbols and rituals that take on the characteristics (and the characteristic power) of religious symbol and ritual. In so doing, they unite into moral community (Bellah 1970). This "civil religion" provides the morals and standards according to which we judge our collective actions. Bellah argues that even in times of profound crisis, such as the Civil War and the Vietnam War, civil religion provides a lingua franca to critique perceived injustices and reweave the social fabric.

The second pillar of secularization theory is Weber's thesis of disenchantment and rationalization. Weber understood history to be marked by the increasing dominance of instrumental rationality and the demise of traditional, charisma-based authority. More specifically, rationalization meant the ascendance of science over religion as the key source of legitimation. With the loss of religion's prominent place in society, spheres under its tutelage, such as politics, the arts, ethics, and law, became increasingly autonomous and began generating their own rational foundations and rules (Weber 1946). As religious values and norms became incommensurate with those of competing spheres, religion lost significance in the modern world. More specifically, religion lost its normative power and became rationalized. Thus, studying the development of Western calculative rationality, Weber observed how religion evolved from a naïve otherworldly mysticism toward a stern this-worldly asceticism that eventually contributed unintentionally to the rise of the spirit of capitalism. Weber linked this-worldly asceticism to the Protestant Reformation, which "took rational Christian asceticism and its methodical habits out of the monasteries and placed them in the service of active life in the world" (1958:235). Moreover, by undermining the Catholic Church's claim to universality, stressing individual conscience, and widening the gulf between God and humanity, the Protestant Reformation contributed to the "disenchantment of the world." As Berger explains, it removed "mystery, miracle, and magic" from this world and made the "umbilical cord" connecting the sacred to the profane a very tenuous promise of divine grace (1967: 111).[1]

Building on Weber's rationalization and disenchantment thesis and cross-fertilizing it with the Durkheimian notion of differentiation, Berger (1967) and Luckmann (1967) argued that modernization means not that the sacred is bound to disappear but that religion will be dislodged from the public sphere and forced to change in response. As the decline in church attendance and affiliation, especially among mainline churches, shows, religion has become both "privatized"—its proper scope reduced to a personal and, at most, local relation with the sacred—and more rationalistic, stripped of its supernatural referents and bound to the logic of the market. As secular options proliferate and as the sacred canopy fragments in the face of differentiation, a religious market emerges in which traditions become nothing more than products to be purchased as emblems of individual lifestyles.

For all of their coherence, the Weberian and Durkheimian versions of the secularization theory do not find much empirical support. As Berger himself has acknowledged, full secularization—the evolution of a world "no longer ongoingly penetrated by sacred beings and forces"—has not occurred: "I think what I and most other sociologists of religion wrote in the 1960s about secularization was a mistake. Our underlying argument was that secularization and modernity go hand in hand. With more modernization comes more secularization. It wasn't a crazy theory. There was some evidence for it. But I think it's basically wrong. Most of the world today is certainly not secular. It's very religious" (1997: 974). In the United States, arguably the most advanced industrial nation, "beliefs in God and beliefs in afterlife are remarkably stable. Levels of religious participation and rates of membership in religious organizations remain high compared to other nations and other voluntary activities" (Sherkat and Ellison 1999: 365–366).[2] In fact, religion is lived so publicly—in the Internet, on TV, on the covers of *Newsweek*, *Time*, and the *New York Times Magazine*, and at the Mall in Washington, D.C. (as in the case of the Million Man March and the Promise Keepers)—it seems counterintuitive to talk about privatization.

The recent proposal by the Bush administration to fund faith-based and community initiatives provides one of the clearest examples of the high profile of religion in the U.S. public arena. What is most remarkable about this proposal is not the creation of an executive-level office to oversee the transfer of funds. After all, the Clinton administration had paved the way by encouraging private nonprofit organizations to fill the void left by welfare reform. The real surprise is in the relatively muted public reaction to a potential breach of the First Amendment.[3] This may indicate that people recognize the failure of secular initiatives to deal with intractable social problems. As secular politics come to be perceived as hopelessly corrupt, unable to offer and sustain individual and communal good, leaders and citizens alike turn to "old-time religion," to the power of the sacred to renew self and transform society. With this return to religious sources of legitimation, it seems as if religion has turned the tables on modernity, showing the latter's failure to fulfill its own utopian illusions.

But the "pulsating ubiquity" of religion is not apparent only in United States. The vitality of religion is also evident in Latin America, Asia, and Africa. As Berger (2001) recently argued, secularization seems to apply only to central and western Europe and among a small but influential international cadre of intellectuals trained in Western-style higher education. Turning the old wisdom of U.S. exceptionalism on its head, Berger writes that the United States "conforms to the world-wide pattern" of religious vigor, while "Europe is, or seems to be, the big exception." The task then is no longer to gather evidence to support the theoretical contention that secularization is "the direct and inevitable result of modernity, . . . the paradigmatic situation of religion in the contemporary world," but to study historically contingent cases such as those of "European exceptionalism."

If the privatization component of the Weberian thesis is not tenable, could one argue that rationalization and disenchantment still carry explanatory power? Can the contemporary flourishing of vocal and affective religion and the revival of old traditions be a case of spiritual backlash, in the face of a world that has become, as Weber (1958) feared, an "iron cage"? This is in fact the hypothesis that Juergensmeyer (2000: 225) proposes in his study of the rise of global religious terrorism. In Juergensmeyer's view, "the notion that secular society and the modern nation-state can provide the moral fiber that unites national communities or the ideological strength to sustain states buffeted by ethical, economic, and military failures" has been challenged by "a global market that has weakened national sovereignty and is conspicuously devoid of political ideals. The global economy became characterized by transnational businesses accountable to no single governmental authority with no clear ideological or moral standard of behavior." In this context, religious terrorism represents a violent attempt to reinject traditional authority and meaning structures into the vacuum left by secular modernity.

As the attack on one of the most visible symbols of U.S.-based global capitalism on September 11, 2001, demonstrates, Juergensmeyer's reading carries considerable weight. However, as we will argue in the next chapter, religion's relation to globalization is far more complex. Global religions are very often not in conflict with late modernity. Indeed, our case studies show that modern mass media, the global tourism industry, capitalist enterprise, and the Internet have become the very means through which many "anti-rational," supernatural religious phenomena flourish in the Americas.[4] Chapter 8 discusses the case of an "angel" that saved a suicidal Guatemalan man's life by appearing not in a vision but on a radio commercial funded by the Christian Broadcasting Network. The Pentecostal gang member profiled in Chapter 5 encountered the Holy Spirit through transnational congregations set up partly as a result of U.S. cold-war policies. In all these cases, "magic, miracle, and mystery" penetrate everyday life by means of distinctively modern media and through processes associated with globalization. Rationalized capitalism, urban migration, and technology can be the carriers of sacralization rather than secularization, and the gods certainly remain in business.

In recent years, some theorists have attempted to reformulate secularization theory by lowering its epistemological ambitions. Casanova (1994) argues that, while the claims that public religion is declining and that it has become privatized are unwarranted, secularization's stress on increasing social differentiation remains legitimate. According to Casanova, differentiation "remains the valid core of the theory of secularization. The differentiation and emancipation of the secular spheres from religious institutions and norms remains a general modern structural trend. Indeed, this differentiation serves precisely as one of the primary distinguishing characteristics of modern structure" (212; cf. Lechner 1991; Tschannen 1991; Chaves 1994). Religion continues to have a public role despite social differentiation because of the disestablishment made possible by secularization. For Casanova (1994: 213), "established churches are incompatible with modern differentiated states and . . . the fusion of religious and political community is incompatible with the modern principle of citizenship." This does not mean that voluntary congregational religion is irrelevant. On the contrary, it plays a key role in strengthening a pluralistic civil society. In other words, secularization qua differentiation opens the door for multiple "deprivatized" religious movements that, among other things, defend the "traditional life-world against various forms of state and market penetration" and articulate the principle of "common good against individualist modern liberal theories that would reduce the common good to the aggregated sum of individual choices" (228–229). More modest still is Dobbelaere's (1999) reading of secularization. Focusing on the European experience, he argues that "secularization is situated on the *societal* level and should be seen as resulting from the process of functional differentiation and the autonomization of societal subsystems" (231). In other words, the impact of secularization is restricted to the macro-level, affecting primarily institutions and religious forms of authority. Dobbelaere makes no claims about the micro-level, that is, about how secularization has affected individual consciousness (the privatization thesis). "The religious situation at the individual level cannot be explained exclusively by the secularization of the social system: other factors—individualization of decisions, de-traditionalization, mobility, and utilitarian and expressive individualism—[are] at work. Consequently, the religiousness of individuals is *not* a valid indicator in evaluating the process of secularization" (239). Stark and Finke (2000:

57–79) question the usefulness of Dobbelaere's narrow reading. If secularization is just "de-institutionalization," and "if we limited discussion to Europe, there would be nothing to argue about. Everyone must agree that, in contemporary Europe, Catholic bishops have less political power than they once possessed, and the same is true for Lutheran and Anglican bishops (although bishops probably never were nearly so powerful as they now are thought to have been). Nor are primary aspects of public life any longer suffused with religious symbols, rhetoric, or ritual." Nevertheless, according to Stark and Finke, if secularization theory makes only minimal and obvious claims about the separation of church and state and the emergence of autonomous spheres of human activity, it loses all its predictive and analytical power as the overarching paradigm in the sociology of religion. In "Secularization RIP," Stark and Finke go so far as to declare the death of secularization theory.

We disagree with Stark and Finke. It is one thing to argue that secularization is not a teleological grand narrative and quite another to reject it altogether. Secularization as structural differentiation is still a valuable analytical tool. For one thing, it tells us a great deal about the aspirations of the social sciences, their need to set themselves apart as autonomous and objective disciplines vis-à-vis religion construed as primitive knowledge, ideology, or false consciousness. This need explains why religion occupies such a central place in the early writings of sociology's founders. In this sense, secularization is not just a tool to describe changes ushered in by modernity but also a normative narrative through which the social sciences have constructed their genealogy and established authority. This narrative worked in tandem with the ascendance of scientific rationality, the formation of bureaucratic states, and the expansion of international capitalism to redefine the nature and place of religion. The impact of this narrative, however, is far more uneven and contradictory than traditional secularization theories are willing to admit. Modernity is characterized not just by differentiation but also by dedifferentiation (Heelas 1998; Luke 1996). For example, the rise of the modern nation entails not only processes of individuation and specialization but also standardizing discourses and disciplinary practices that sought to manage populations and turn them into a unified people (*Volk*) with a culture and territory (Anderson 1983; Foucault 1978; Gellner 1983).

Since secularization theory is also a modern product, it carries the "dialectic of differentiation and de-differentiation." Indeed, while the secularization paradigm is about differentiation, difference is grounded and "disciplined" within the framework of foundational dichotomies such as tradition versus modernity, faith versus reason, religion versus science, *Gemeinschaft* versus *Gesellschaft*, traditional versus instrumental authority, ideology (superstructure) versus economy (base), and mechanical versus organic solidarity. Within this lattice of asymmetrical hierarchies, understanding differentiation becomes an exercise in tracking the movement from the inferior/primitive to the superior/advanced terms in the dichotomies.

The dialectic of differentiation and dedifferentiation undermines Casanova's claim that differentiation is a "general modern structural trend," that is, that modernity entails a necessary movement toward higher levels of differentiation, whereby religion, although not privatized, is forced to conform to demands of rationality if it is to survive. Religion and modernity are not necessarily involved in a zero-sum game in which if one wins the other must lose. Rather they have been engaged in multiple relations, including outright conflict, accommodation, cross-fertilization, and mutual reenforcing. In the next chapter, we will see that as globalization challenges established spatio-temporal arrangements, such as the nation-state, and undermines the separation among economic, political, and cultural spheres of action, the relation between the religious and the secular becomes even more complicated, pointing us beyond difference toward hybridity. Attempts to rework the secularization paradigm to highlight differentiation and disestablishment bring us to the so-called New Paradigm in the sociology of religion, which has risen as one of the most cogent critiques of secularization theories.

EXPLORING THE NEW PARADIGM: RATIONAL-CHOICE THEORIES

The New Paradigm (NP) distinguishes itself from secularization theory by depicting a much brighter future for U.S. religion as it encounters late modernity. Taking religious disestablishment and pluralism as their point of departure, NP theorists argue that religion's public vitality does not shrink in the face of structural differentiation. Instead, religion thrives because a pluralistic setting requires religious creativity and specialization.

As we discussed earlier, for most secularization theorists the only recourse for religious institutions that hope to stay in business is either resistance or accommodation, either privatization or extreme generalization. Berger (1967: 134) explains: "Religion manifests itself as public rhetoric and private virtue. In other words, insofar as religion is common, it lacks 'reality', and insofar as it is 'real' it lacks commonality. This situation represents a severe rupture of the traditional task of religion, which was precisely the establishment of an integrated set of definitions of reality that could serve as a common universe of meaning for the members of a society." New Paradigm theorists dispute readings both of secularization and of the transformation of the sacred canopy. The canopy neither collapses nor goes underground, but instead reconstitutes itself as "small, portable, accessible . . . sacred umbrellas" (C. Smith 1998: 106).

The *locus classicus* of the New Paradigm is R. Stephen Warner's 1993 essay "Work in Progress toward a New Paradigm for the Sociological Study of Religion in the United States." Warner argues that the old paradigm of secularization was developed to analyze Europe, where it can be argued that religious monopolies once existed. Secularization, however, cannot account for U.S. religious history, which is "constitutively pluralistic." Warner (1993: 1047) explains: "Religion in the United States has typically expressed not the culture of the society as a whole but the subcultures of its many constituents; therefore . . . it should not be thought of as either the Parsonian conscience of the whole or the Bergerian refuge of the periphery, but as a vital expression of groups." Warner and other New Paradigm theorists agree with the Durkheimian view that religion creates social solidarity, but they stress religion's contributions in the articulation of the myriad of particular collective identities that characterize U.S. civil society. This, in turn, accounts for the vitality and visibility of religion in the United States. Like race, ethnicity, and language, "religion itself is recognized in American society, if not always by social scientists, as a fundamental category of identity and association, and it is thereby capable of grounding both solidarities and identities" (1060). Religious organizations have become spaces in which culturally particular groups can be free to create associations, and this contributes to the fact that "eleven o'clock on Sunday morning is the most segregated hour of American life" (1069). Indeed, according to Warner, the "master function" of U.S. religion is to provide a "social space for cultural pluralism" (1058). This "space" emerged in the United States as a result of the disestablishment assured by constitutional separation of church and state. As Anthony Gill (1999) argues, such space is currently emerging in Latin America, as the established Catholic Church loses hegemony and state-sanctioned legal protections.

Following Rodney Stark and William Bainbridge (1985), some NP theorists have adopted rational-choice models to understand the dynamics of religious pluralism.[5] According to the rational-choice versions of the NP, highly regulated religious monopolies create lethargy and indifference among consumers and suffer shrinking influence in the market. In contrast, an unregulated religious marketplace, filled with entrepreneurs who compete for consumer loyalty, grows and expands. NP theorists thus challenge the old-paradigm claim that open markets encourage a "standardization" of religious products or automatically result in mass marketing, thus weakening religious institutions (Witten 1993: 135). Instead, an open market can lead to increasingly flexible, particularized, and vital religious expressions. This is because the unregulated marketplace encourages suppliers to compete for market share and ensures that monopolistic religions will falter and entrepreneurs will thrive. Warner explains that "what is important about religious markets from this perspective is not so much the diversity of alternatives available to consumers as the incentive for suppliers to meet consumers' needs." This incentive is maximized "when the religious economy is wide-open to energetic entrants, none of whom has a guaranteed income" (Warner 1993: 1057).

Typically, rational-choice theorists explain the practices of religious actors, be they consumers or producers, according to cost-benefit analyses that can be applied across cases. In other words, the religious actor is a variety of *homo economicus* understood as a self-sufficient unit that behaves rationally, "making the most of what s/he has" (Elster 2000: 20), that is, seeking to maximize gains and minimize losses.[6] The religious goods at play may range from purely material commodities, such as economic mobility (for consumers) or increased market share (i.e., church participation, for the producers), to "supernatural compensators," such as rewards in the beyond or coherent theodicies. Supernatural compensators are particularly risky investments, since they cannot be guaranteed. Therefore, religious consumers must diversify their "portfolios" of religious investments to spread the risk. This leads to greater religious pluralism. Supernatural compensators also make it possible for certain religious practices and institutions to thrive in pluralistic environments. By presenting supernatural compensators as scarce, open to only a select group whose members are willing to invest all their resources in risky goods, religious institutions solve the problem of "free riders," individuals who want to enjoy all the benefits of group membership while contributing very little. Thus religious institutions that impose costly demands on their members—in the form of sacrifice and stigmatization of secular practices such as drinking and dancing—attract only individuals with a high degree of commitment, which, in turn, strengthens group morale and solidarity, producing more collective benefits for each member. As Stark (1996) argues for the rise of Christianity, the people most attracted to these high-risk religions are those who have nothing to lose and much to gain by forsaking the status quo.[7]

The New Paradigm is better equipped than the secularization model to explain the evolving religious dynamics in the Americas. The increasing differentiation of the religious field has not led to a decline of public religions.[8] The rapid growth of evangelical Christianity among the urban poor, the rearticulation of Catholicism among movements such as the charismatic renewal and the neocatechumenate, and the resurgence of African-based and native religions around the recovery of suppressed racial and ethnic identities show how disestablishment and open markets have raised religion's visibility in the hemisphere. The New Paradigm, however, provides only a partial explanation. First, the NP is provincial, assuming that the United States, as a self-contained nation-state, should be the unit of analysis and model for sociology of religion. We contend that a global and transnational perspective would provide a richer view of sources of increasing religious pluralism in the United States and the rest of the Americas. Rather than a single predictable market characterized by scarcity, there are multiple overlapping religious "markets" defined by the abundance and cross-fertilization of options. Because markets are deterritorialized by globalization, choices can become more volatile and complex, as individuals enter multiple markets at once and consume seemingly contradictory products. Pentecostal churches, such as those we discuss in Chapter 5, illustrate how religious practices and institutions do not remain static, but often enter transnational circuits in ways that rejuvenate both "host" and "home" societies. However, such processes do not lead to a global homogenization of religious forms, as some theorists of globalization have argued (Brouwer, Gifford, and Rose 1996; Poewe 1994). Rather, we see a flourishing of hybrid religious forms.

A second limitation of the NP, particularly of its rational-choice versions, is its "methodological individualism," which holds that "structures and systems possess no independent causal weight and are conceived best as behavioral constraints" (A. Gill 1998: 199). This impoverished notion of choice and practice fails to account for how decisions are patterned among particular groups of people. Stark and Finke argue that preferences and tastes are subject to variation sometimes "so idiosyncratic that people have no idea how they came to like certain things. As the old adage says, 'There's no accounting for tastes'" (2000: 38). However, Stark and Finke acknowledge that "culture in general, and socialization in particular, will have a substantial impact on preferences and tastes." But for all their stress on analytical rigor and empirical corroboration, they fail to specify what they mean by "culture," "socialization," and "substantial impact."[9] Pierre Bourdieu (1977) offers a richer way of looking at how religious activities are shaped by the consumer's enduring yet flexible dispositions molded by his or her trajectory and position in various meso- and macrocontexts, including class divisions and racial and gender formations. This is what Bourdieu calls *habitus*: embodied perceptual and motivating schemes that produce and reproduce the social structures in which individuals are located and that explain not only creative activity but regularities in social practices.

Finally, most rational-choice theorists reduce complex religious fields to the behavior of elites, or "religious entrepreneurs." And in a further reductionist move, these theorists assume that these elites act as one unitary agent, in accordance with a universal rationality of cost-benefit calculation. The result of these simplifications is a one-dimensional view of religious practices and institutions that is at odds with the increasing complexity and fluidity engendered by the recent episode of globalization (Vásquez 2000).

SUBCULTURAL IDENTITY THEORY

Most studies of religious markets have focused on institutions and elites, or "supply-side" analyses of the producers of religious goods. However, in his 1998 study of U.S. Evangelicals, Christian Smith builds on the New Paradigm to develop a nuanced approach to the choices and actions of ordinary believers who consume the products and services provided by entrepreneurial religious elites. This focus corrects many of rational-choice theorists' shortcomings by examining the sociocultural context in which consumers operate.

Smith labels his theoretical approach to religious consumption a "subcultural identity theory of religious persistence and strength." He argues that the most persistent religions—those organizations whose products are consistently consumed over time—embed themselves in subcultures that construct a collective identity and give members unequivocal moral meaning and a powerful sense of group belonging. The strongest religious groups are "genuinely countercultural," that is, they are structured in such a way that they distinguish themselves clearly from other subcultural groups and demand a high level of commitment from their members (1998: 118–119). However, these groups are not sectarians who cordon themselves off from the rest of society. Rather, they are directly involved in contesting the broader society. Thus Smith concludes that Evangelicalism in the United States thrives "not because it has built a protective subcultural shield against secular modernity, but because it engages passionately in a direct struggle with pluralistic modernity" (88).

Smith distinguishes his approach from that of secularization theorists in at least two ways. First, he argues that the most persistent and successful religious groups are not those that retrench to enclaves of privatized piety or that accommodate by subscribing to an abstract, rationalized religion, but those that engage modernity while also clearly distinguishing themselves from modern secular culture. Second, he contends that cultural pluralism encourages the strength and persistence of religion as a means by which religious consumers can create satisfying social-psychological frames that make sense of the world. Pluralism does not generate "cognitive dissonance," radically undercutting "the social support necessary for maintaining subjective adherence to a body of beliefs" (Hunter 1983). Rather, pluralism offers individual religious consumers multiple fragments of the shattered "sacred canopy," which they can use innovatively to construct their own "sacred umbrellas." These umbrellas are "small, portable, accessible relational worlds—religious reference groups—under which [individuals'] beliefs can make complete sense" (C. Smith 1998: 106). Here, Smith challenges the secularization theorists' view of religion as a force for either macrosocial integration or purely privatized affect. Religion continues to have a public role, but it is closely connected with diverse local expressions that characterize civil society. Echoing Warner, Smith sees religion in the United States as part and parcel of the "new voluntarism." Increasingly, individualized religious identification is understood to be a personal choice rather than an effect of participation in a particular collectivity (e.g., a church or synagogue). Philip Hammond (1992) describes this as a move from collective-expressive to individual-expressive religious behavior, which shifts religious identity from being an immutable core of personality to being transient and changeable, or from being involuntary to being voluntary.

Smith's stress on the individual-expressive consumption pattern also fits well with the conception of an open religious market place in which consumers shop for fragments of their personal "sacred umbrellas." However, Smith eschews the most reductive tendencies in rational-choice theories. In addition to focusing on ordinary believers, Smith introduces history and culture to rational choice's formulaic account of religious practices and choices. He explores "how ordinary people utilize their religious traditions' cultural tools more or less efficiently to construct distinctive, meaningful, satisfying social identities" (1998: 119). Smith argues that when we turn our gaze from the "normative views of historical religious elites" to the actual practices of contemporary religious believers, the notion of a zero-sum game between religion and modernity becomes less tenable. Instead, "religious traditions have *always* strategically renegotiated their collective identities by continually reformulating the ways their constructed orthodoxies engage the changing sociocultural environments they confront" (99–100).

With subcultural-identity theory, the Enlightenment rationality of sameness behind secularization theory that made modernity/science and tradition/religion mutually exclusive gives way to a perspective that recognizes difference and religion's multiple roles in constituting it. Nevertheless, subcultural-identity theory still exhibits some of the weaknesses associated with other embodiments of the NP. More specifically, it shares with rational-choice models the notion that religious actors are fully self-legislating rational consumers and producers, acting strategically to select and produce religious goods that contribute to the articulation of desired identities. In other words, despite the richer focus on the differentials in cultural resources available to religious producers and consumers, subcultural-identity theory still depicts religious actors as essentially atomic and fully intentional agents who weigh the outcomes of their decisions unencumbered by structural and systemic constraints.

In Smith's account, the process of piecing together coherent localized worldviews, or "sacred umbrellas," entails a conscious individual decision to embed oneself in a particular "relational network of identity" (1998: 218). Yet Smith does not clarify how individuals choose among the dizzying array of networks that exist in the contemporary pluralist Americas. While individuals do choose and create their sacred umbrellas by sorting through the religious fragments available to them, we contend that they do so *already embedded* in sociopolitical and cultural power dynamics operating at multiple levels, including the local, the regional, the national, and the global. As the religious actors construct new umbrellas, their choices are both limited and expanded by their position in interacting spheres of human activity.[10]

Subcultural-identity theory's most significant limitation, though, is that it understands culture (and religion within it) statically. Subcultural-identity theory operates under what we may call a "horticultural model" of culture and religion. In this model, "the activity of culture, as suggested by the etymological links to 'gardening', has been conventionally associated with the cultivation of a territory. Every culture is supposed to come from somewhere, to have its place in the world" (Papastergiadis 2000: 103). In this conventional understanding, cultures are construed as "being formed in particular territorial relationships with carefully established borders, separating one from another. They are created systems of beliefs amongst their members that [secure] a homogeneous, coherent and continuous sense of affiliation." In the context of globalization, this conventional understanding of culture exhibits serious limitations. "What is obscured by this perspective are the porous boundaries between groups, the diffuse notions of identity, the deterritorialized links between members of groups, the globalizing patterns of communication and the hybrid process of cultural transformation" (105).

Our case studies show people easily negotiating multiple, sometimes even contradictory, forms of religious identification and affiliations. In Chapter 3, for example, we will encounter a Catholic priest who models his preaching style after a Pentecostal televangelist, notwithstanding the engagement of evangelical Protestants and Catholics in a fierce competition for the Latino "religious market." Similarly, in Chapter 8, we discuss Guatemalan Catholic-school teachers who use evangelical tracts disseminated by the U.S.-based transnational Christian Broadcasting Network (CBN) to teach their students about the Bible, while CBN adopts elements of the local Catholic culture to produce context-sensitive soap operas. These are but two examples of the many ways that people combine religious forms to create frameworks for meaning—making that need not be embattled to thrive, as Smith argues. Our cases challenge Smith's functionalist assertion that religion provides, above all, solidarity in the form of tight-knit groups threatened by the outside world. Rather, we see people crossing fluid borders of religious meaning adeptly and without overt cost-benefit calculations.

BEYOND THE NATION: PLURALISM AND HYBRIDITY IN THE LATIN AMERICAN "MODEL"

For subcultural-identity theory, religion is essentially about boundary creation. Subcultural-identity theory "normalizes" difference by attributing to it the univocal role of creating and sustaining Otherness. That is to say, difference operates under the exclusionary, dichotomous logic of modern sociology of religion. Just as Warner showed how secularization theory· emerged from the European experience to become a dominant paradigm, it could be argued that the NP offers a U.S.-centric approach in its stress on pluralism and open markets. In our view, Latin America provides yet another model, where the historic institutional dominance of the Catholic Church as a state-sanctioned church (the Royal Patronage) did not translate into total orthodoxy. As Griffiths (1999:1) puts it: "The interaction of Christianity with native American religions in the colonial era (and indeed subsequently) was character-ized by reciprocal, albeit asymmetrical, exchange rather than the uni-lateral imposition of an uncompromising, all-conquering and all transforming monotheism." The popularity of the cult of the saints (with its home and town altars), lay brotherhoods, and other local lay religious specialists like *benzedeiras* (blessers-healers) and *rezadoras* (prayer specialists) demonstrates that people at the grassroots practiced multiple ways of being Catholic, which were often in a tense relation-ship with the official Church. At the same time, popular practices were defined by high levels of syncretism that blended elements of Iberian Catholicism, native and African-based religions, and European Spirit-ism. Even now, after the rapid expansion of evangelical Protestantism, which has increased competition for the souls of poor and working-class Latin Americans, religion in the region continues to enter new, flexible recombinations. As we argue in Chapter 3, the "pentecostaliza-tion" of Catholicism is increasingly transcending organizational bound-aries and becoming a style of being Catholic shared not just by charismatics but even by progressives still involved in base communi-ties and liberation theology. Similarly, Pentecostalism, with its strongly dualistic view of world, has in many parts of Latin America become highly indigenized, incorporating the practices and beliefs of native re-ligions in ways that shock U.S. missionaries.

Why should Latin American cases be of interest to U.S.-based New Paradigm theorists? As we will discuss more fully in the next chapter, the rapid circular flow of ideas, people, goods, and capital between Latin America and the United States compels us to go beyond nation-based models of culture and religion and to take into account regional (i.e., hemispheric) and global dynamics. The explosive growth of the Latino population in the United States, sustained transnational migration from Latin America, and increasing economic integration of the Americas challenge us to transcend the limitations of modernist social science, which has privileged the nation-state and area studies (as a by-product of the cold war) as the central organizing spatio-temporal scales. A hemi-spheric approach would allow us to see that religion in the Americas today is not just promoting "the formation of strong and potentially 'deviant' identities, including religious subcultures and identities" (Smith 1998: 107). Certain religious beliefs and practices thrive at the grassroots because they are a source of hybridity. In other words, many ordinary believers and institutions find in religion resources to bridge the multiple identities and functions that they must perform in an increasingly complex world. More importantly, religion helps to link realities that modernity dichotomized and that globalization has now destabilized: the global and the local, tradition and modernity, the sacred and the profane, culture and society, and the private and the public.

We are certainly not claiming that the Latin American "model," with its interplay of institutional dominance, pluralism, and hybridity, should be taken as the new universal norm.[11] Nevertheless, Latin American experiences relativize the thesis of "U.S. sectarianism and pluralism," which we would argue is a version of U.S. exceptionalism. Postcolonial studies have shown that the birth of the modern nation out of the remnants of colonial rule entailed the development and application of disciplinary and homogenizing techniques that attempted to fix the boundaries of collective identity (Bhabha 1990: 1–7, 291–321). The aim was to constitute the nation as an organic "imagined community" with a shared culture and a given territory defended by the state apparatus, thereby obscuring internal and external differences and excluding as "Other" impurities and primitivisms, which does not fit modern classificatory schemes. As Peter van der Veer and Hartmut Lehmann observe, the social sciences informed this process of nation building by setting up a dichotomy between religion and nationalism. Religion was one of the anachronistic impurities that the nation had to overcome as it marched into modernity, since "nationalism is assumed to be 'secular,' since it is thought to develop in a process of secularization and modernization. Religion, in this view, assumes political significance only in underdeveloped parts of the world—much as it did in the past of the West" (Veer and Lehmann 1999: 3). Challenging this reading of history, Veer and Lehmann show how religious themes like the divine election (the chosen people), rebirth, martyrdom, and the coming of a messiah have played an important role in building the modern nation.

Veer and Lehmann's work demonstrates that the relation between religion and modernity is more complex than teleological readings of secularization theory would allow. At a deeper level, their work shows that the repression and exclusion associated with the birth of nations do not succeed in eliminating the Other, which is always contesting the drive toward homogeneity. In Bhabha's (1994: 111) words: "Produced through the strategy of disavowal, the *reference* of discrimination is always to a process of splitting as the condition of subjection: a discrimination between the mother culture and its bastards, the self and its doubles, where the trace of what is disavowed is not repressed but repeated as something *different*—a mutation, a hybrid."

The point of this excursus into religion and nationalism is to show that binary oppositions such as self-other, identity-difference, and modernity-tradition, as well as anxiety about hybridity, are at the core of claims of national exceptionalism. By preserving national exceptionalism in relation to the United States, the New Paradigm and subcultural-identity theory reproduce the homogenizing techniques of modern social sciences, failing to see "impure" hybrid forms that operate under the principle of nonexclusionary difference.[12]

Recent comparative work shows that in the United States, identities have been construed as fixed, "autonomous unities" (García Canclini 1999). Arguably, this exclusionary view of identity is connected to a racial formation built around the notion of hypodescent, that is, a binary racial system buttressed by legal and physical segregation.[13] The notion of segregated identities grounds contemporary views of U.S. culture and social policy in the form of multiculturalism (culture as a mosaic of ethnic essences) and affirmative action. It also shapes U.S. sociology of religion, which tends to privilege religion's sectarian role, its contribution in "promoting exclusivist self-affirmations" (García Canclini 2001: 11). In contrast to hegemonic conceptions of identity in the United States, the dominant logic of difference in Latin America, while still hierarchical and Eurocentric, is open to "the possibility of various different affiliations, circulating among identities and mixing them" (García Canclini 1999: 117). This openness is rooted in Latin American understandings of race as a continuum constituted by various degrees of mixing rather than by rigid dualities. Of course, race and identity are also inflected by power in Latin America, where whiteness and all things European continue to be normative. However, in Latin America, identities are not primarily self-contained essences legitimized by legal discourses and institutional practices. Rather, identities tend to be negotiated in everyday life and crisscrossed by domination and resistance.[14]

Bringing the Latin American "model" to the fore thus destabilizes the discourse about differentiation and pluralism at the heart of the New Paradigm. The Latin American model helps refocus our attention beyond the hegemonic discourses of exclusionary identity, toward a discovery of the pervasiveness of hybridity in the U.S. religious field. This discovery is already underway among some U.S. sociologists of religion. Studying religion among baby boomers, Roof (1999: 4) argues that "boundaries separating one faith tradition from another that once seemed fixed are now often blurred; religious identities are malleable and multifaceted, often overlapping several traditions." While Roof uses the concept of subcultures to characterize the moral and spiritual enclaves in which baby boomers operate, he stresses that on the ground, "religion is also process, movement, aspiration, quest. These liminal qualities point to its effusive and creative potential; its recurrent capacity to combine elements into new forms, its bumptiousness, or ability to reinvent itself on location" (296). Although theorists may wish to fix religious practices in shorthand formulas, "in the contemporary United States, fluidity within religious groups and institutions is extraordinarily high. Boundaries are porous, allowing people, ideas, beliefs, practices, symbols, and spiritual currents to cross" (44).

Robert Wuthnow (1998a: 1–18) observes a post–1950s shift in U.S. religion from a "spirituality of dwelling [which] requires sharp symbolic boundaries to protect sacred space from its surroundings" to a "spirituality of seeking" marked by "images of those who have left home: the migrant worker, the exile, the refugee, the drifter, the person who feels alienated or displaced." This new spirituality of journeying has posed serious challenges to churches that offer unchanging goods to tightknit geographically bound communities. Believers, for their part, must negotiate among multiple "complex and confusing meanings of spirituality," as they seek to deal with an increasingly chaotic and globalized world.

New Age and other "postmodern" U.S. religions are not the only ones to exhibit high degrees of flexibility and hybridity.[15] African American religions, including Vodou and the Zion churches, have always involved cross-fertilization as much as "Othering." The same can be said of Pentecostalism, which is a mixture of African American musicality and orality and Wesleyan/Holiness piety. And, as Simon Coleman (2000: 24) observes, new Pentecostal waves, such as the Faith Movement, only intensify this mixing further, competing with and borrowing from "a post-modern world of healing movements, the New Age, materialism and pluralism." Because of the modernist bias toward purity, all these traditions have been seen as corrupt pathological responses to dislocation, alienation, and poverty. They have never been considered as potentially representing the prevalence of hybridity in U.S. religion.

Latin American and U.S. Latino experience foregrounds the pervasiveness of hybridity in the Americas without ignoring the presence of institutional and structural boundaries. It is not that difference, competition, and conflict do not matter. In fact, some of our case studies show how religion in a globalized setting can serve to reaffirm a strong sense of locality against macroprocesses, to reinforce the exclusion of the socially marginalized sectors by religious and political elites, or to form solidarity at the grassroots level on the basis of ethnic identity. Rather, because globalization challenges the modernist narrative of increasing social differentiation, we need to rethink and supplement New Paradigm approaches. Subcultural-identity theory tells us only part of the story: religion is not just about difference and marking boundaries (territorializing), but also about mixing and blurring boundaries (deterritorializing).

Some New Paradigm theorists have begun to nuance the stress on exclusionary difference, boundaries, and competitive religious markets. In a recent lecture, Warner (1997: 233–235) pointed toward a "new theory" that moves beyond the traditional U.S. alternatives of assimilation versus multiculturalism. He described the United States as a society with "a multitude of particular communities but also with multiple bridges between them." Recognizing that U.S. culture is "gloriously impure, even at its Protestant core," Warner appealed to the Hispanic notion of *mestizaje*. Warner's move, however, is still tentative: he presupposes ethnic differences and language boundaries, which he must then reconcile through affective and bodily aspects of religion such as ritual, music, and food (in a Durkheimian fashion). While we applaud this step, we also agree with Nancy Ammerman that the NP needs more radical work, directed toward its epistemological roots. Ammerman (1997: 213) argues that

> the context for that new paradigm is nothing less than the decentering of modernism as our primary interpretive frame. Modern frames assumed functional differentiation, individualism, and rationalism as "the way things are." Modern frames looked for bureaucratically organized institutions with clear lists of members and tasks. Modern frames looked for a clear line between rational, this worldly, action and action guided by any other form of wisdom. Modern frames looked for the individualized "meaning system" that would be carved out of differentiation and pluralism. I hesitate to invoke the word postmodern, given all its baggage, but it seems to me a useful concept here. The root of our problem with the either/or concepts with which we work is that we now live in a both/and world.

Affirming our both/and condition, Orsi (1997: 11) suggests that we adopt a "hermeneutics of hybridity." According to Orsi, "the analytical language of religious studies, organized as it still is around a series of fixed, mutually exclusive, and stable polar opposites, must be reconfigured in order to make sense of religion as lived experience. A new vocabulary is demanded to discuss such phenomena, a language as hybrid and tensile as the realities it seeks to describe."

In the next chapter, we survey the globalization literature in search of this new vocabulary. The analytical resources that we find there operate within the framework of a "critical postmodernism."[16] We reject the extreme relativism of naive postmodernist approaches that construe the social world as utterly decentered and devoid of any relatively stable power relations. We recognize the increasing fluidity and fragmentation of society and culture, while acknowledging the persistence, and even intensification, of forms of domination and resistance characteristic of modernity. As will become clear in the next chapter, we see postmodernism as the radicalization of modernity's stress on difference and critique. Thus, we aim to construct a self-reflexive postmodernist account of religion and society, one that is aware of its multiple points of continuity and rupture with modern theories.

2

THEORIZING GLOBALIZATION AND RELIGION

Globalization, as Bauman (1998: 1) rightly complains, "is on everybody's lips; a fad word turning into a shibboleth, a magic incantation, a passkey meant to unlock the gates to all present and future mysteries." Indeed, a recent issue of *National Geographic* declares that "today we are in the throes of a worldwide reformation of culture, a tectonic shift of habits and dreams called, in the curious argot of social scientists, 'globalization'" (Zwingle 1999: 12). As we theorize globalization, we seek to avoid mystifications of this kind. We do not claim that a globalization framework can resolve all the conundrums of religion in the Americas and thus that we must reject wholesale the methods and insights of what we have called modernist approaches. Nevertheless, a globalization framework provides powerful tools to analyze changes in the religious field in the Americas that challenge some of the core assumptions of secularization theory and the New Paradigm.

This chapter explores the theoretical implications of a globalization framework for the study of religion in the Americas. Our aim is not to offer a new theory of globalization. Nor do we seek to provide an exhaustive review of the ever-expanding literature on globalization.[1] Rather, we concentrate on those global processes that are most entangled with changes in the religious field in the Americas. We believe that a focus on the interplay between religion and globalization not only provides novel ways of studying religious phenomena but also enriches our understanding of globalization in distinctive ways, foregrounding important dynamics hitherto ignored. We argue that globalization scholars must take religion seriously, since religion in the Americas is deeply implicated in the dialectic of deterritorialization and reterritorialization that accompanies globalization. According to García Canclini (1995: 229), this dialectic entails "the loss of the 'natural' relation of culture to geographical and social territories and, at the same time, certain relative, partial territorial relocalizations of old and new symbolic productions." Religion, we believe, is one of the main protagonists in this unbinding of culture from its traditional referents and boundaries and in its reattachment in new space-time configurations. Through this interplay of delocalization and relocalization, religion gives rise to hybrid individual and collective identities that fly in the face of the methodological purity and simplicity sought by modernist sociologies of religion.

GLOBALIZATION IN A HISTORICAL CONTEXT

According to Giddens (1990: 64), globalization is the "intensification of worldwide social relations which link distant localities in such a way that local happenings are shaped by events occurring many miles away and vice versa." Defined thus, globalization is not a new phenomenon, for there have been many examples of wide-ranging translocal dynamics throughout history. Pointing to the role of Buddhism under Ashoka's empire in India (272–232 BCE) and Confucianism in China during the Han dynasty (206 BCE–220 CE), Roland Robertson (1992: 6) goes so far as to claim that "the overall processes of globalization (and sometimes deglobalization) are at least as old as the rise of the so-called world religions two thousand and more years ago." What, then, is new about the current episode of globalization? Why the sudden surge of interest in the phenomenon? To identify the distinctive features of globalization as it is experienced today, we need to contextualize it historically. Following theorist Immanuel Wallerstein (1974), we may divide previous translocal experiences into two categories: world empires and world systems. Imperial systems emerged around 1000 BCE, as advances in agriculture and transportation technology made possible the rise of centralized state apparatuses with large standing armies and relatively complex administrative bureaucracies capable of controlling extensive territories and extracting surplus through a system of taxes and levies. Despite extensive trading networks, translocal integration was weak, with limited impact over the lives of the vast majority of inhabitants in the heterogeneous cultures and societies subsumed by early world empires. Cultural and religious syncretism was limited to cosmopolitan urban centers and port towns. Integration among the various subcultural units in an empire depended heavily on military force, as states did not have the means to manage their populations in the ways that panoptical modern states exerted power at the microlevel (Foucault 1978). Using criteria defined by Held et al. (1999: 22), we can speak here of a "thin globalization in so far as the high extensity of global networks is not matched by a similar intensity, velocity or impact, for these all remain low." World empires include ancient Rome and China, Mogul India, and Ottoman Turkey.

Throughout the contraction and expansion of competing empires, Wallerstein argues (1974: 38–129), the horizon of translocal interdependence remained constant until the emergence of the modern world-system out of the fragmentation produced by the crisis of feudalism in the "long sixteenth century" (1450–1620). Technological advances, particularly in maritime transportation, facilitated the expansion of long-distance trade with Asia as well as the colonization of the Americas and the Atlantic slave trade. While physical coercion continued to play a significant role in translocal integration, the nascent world-system came to be increasingly dominated by the capitalist mode of production. As the various imperial powers competed against each other for profits, capitalism underwent rapid episodes of globalization, eventually leading in the late nineteenth century to the formation of an interstate system divided into core countries, with capital-intensive, high-wage, and high-technology economies; peripheral countries, with labor-intensive, low-wage, and low-technology economies; and semi-peripheral countries, mixing elements of both core and periphery. The result was a "thick globalization" in which "the extensive reach of global networks [was] matched by their high intensity, high velocity, and high impact propensity across all the domains and facets of social life from the economic to the cultural" (Held et al., 1999: 21). This episode of globalization, which Marx and Engels described so vividly in the *Communist Manifesto*, reached its peak in the early 1900s, before World War I.

This is a telescopic view of the emergence of the capitalist world-system.[2] Nevertheless, it offers sufficient background to identify continuities and ruptures entailed by the current episode of globalization. Thick globalization has intensified dramatically in the last three decades, producing deep and widespread processes of deterritorialization and reterritorialization. These processes have undermined the viability of the nation-state as the key analytical unit of modern social science and challenged the core–semi-periphery–periphery division of labor. More importantly, they have restructured everyday life for vast sectors of the world's population, redefining time, space, identity, and agency at the local level. The specificity of the present episode of globalization thus lies in the tight intertwining of global, transnational, and local (community and self) dynamics. Since the late 1960s, the world has experienced what Harvey (1989: 284) describes as "an intense phase of time-space compression that has had a disorienting and disruptive impact upon political-economic practices, the balance of class power, as well as upon cultural and social life." Adding specificity to Harvey's description, we can characterize the last thirty years as a period of "growing extensity, intensity and velocity of global interactions . . . associated with a deepening enmeshment of the local and global such that the impact of distant events is magnified while even the most local developments may come to have enormous global consequences. In this sense, the boundaries between domestic matters and global affairs may be blurred" (Held et al. 1999: 15).

Defining globalization as time-space compression is shorthand for a complex host of socioeconomic, political, and cultural processes. Appadurai (1996: 33–37) has characterized these processes by focusing on the overlaps and disjunctures among five global flows, which he qualifies with the suffix "-scapes" to describe the "irregular landscapes" they produce. The flows are: (1) ethnoscapes, "the landscape of persons who constitute the shifting world in which we live: tourists, immigrants, refugees, exiles, guest workers"; (2) financescapes, the movement of capital and commodities at "blinding speeds"; (3) technoscapes, global technological changes and transfers; (4) mediascapes, "the distribution of the electronic capabilities to produce and disseminate information (newspapers, magazines, television stations, and film-production studios)" and "the images of the world created by these media"; and (5) ideoscapes, discourses connected to articulation of collective (national) and individual identity.

Appadurai does not address religion directly.[3] Nevertheless, his emphasis on multiple flows and the centrality of culture is a good corrective to overly abstract and economistic readings of globalization. The notion of scapes, however, carries its own dangers: it may lead to an understanding of globalization as the product of impersonal, utterly dislocated flows.[4] Globalization is not just about flows of ideas, goods, people, and capital but also about the practices and organizational structures of territorialized actors like migrants, the state, and churches.

Globalization entails power differentials that "are embodied in specific social relations established between specific people, situated in unequivocal localities, at historically determined times" (Guarnizo and Smith 1998: 11). Taking this insight seriously, we have chosen to specify the key dimensions of globalization not as flows but as historical processes, reproduced and contested by the activities of individual and collective actors. This approach allows us to preserve the dynamism and complexity captured by Appadurai through his notion of scapes, while producing "anchored" analyses of globalization.

THE CURRENT EPISODE OF GLOBALIZATION

The Transition from Fordism to Flexible Production

To understand the current phase of globalization from an economic perspective and how it manifests specifically in the Americas, we need to begin in the early twentieth century. Following World War I, the economic dynamics of thick globalization converged around a Fordist-Keynesian regime of production and consumption. The backbone of this regime was industrial, highly centralized (assembly-line) mass production for expanding, albeit fairly homogeneous, national markets. To protect the economy against sudden crises, such as those of the late 1920s and early 1930s, the model called for heavy state intervention. Among other things, the state was charged with regulating demand by redistributing some wealth through entitlement programs. Corporate industry, for its part, sought high wages and high levels of employment, enabling an increasingly urbanized labor force not just to reproduce itself but to consume the big-ticket items produced in the economies of scale. Workers organized in influential unions entered into a concordat with the state and industry, pledging support for the model as long as their collective demands were met.

This stage of capitalism operated at an international level through a system of nation-states. While vast areas of Africa and Asia were still under colonial rule, elites in dominant centers of power articulated strong national identities, which intensified in World War II as various nations sought to carve out spheres of influence. After the war, with much of Europe and Japan in ruins, the United States emerged as the dominant national power, its industrial capacity unscathed, ready to supply the growing demand for products both domestically and internationally. With its politicoeconomic hegemony threatened only by an ascending Soviet Union, the United States advanced a global financial system based on the dollar under the 1944 Bretton Woods agreement. This system established significant controls on capital flows and fixed exchange rates, allowing national governments substantial autonomy in managing their economies. Latin American nations occupied peripheral positions within this system, either exporting raw materials and labor to the core countries or creating protected national and regional markets through import-substitution industrialization.

Pressures on the Fordist-Keynesian model began as early as the mid–1960s. By then, European and Japanese economies were fully recovered from the war. They were joined by the newly industrialized Asian countries, as well as emerging Latin American economies like Brazil and Mexico, in the search of new markets. Internally, the U.S. economy began to show signs of strain under the burden of the war in Vietnam. Added pressure came from the oil shocks of 1973 and 1975. The weakening U.S. economy, in turn, undermined the dollar, the anchor of the Bretton Woods system. This eventually led in 1973 to the adoption of a flexible exchange-rate system, which made national economies vulnerable to global currency speculation. With the collapse of Bretton Woods, the Fordist-Keynesian regime based on the coordinated interdependence and regulation of national economies could no longer maximize profits. It was too rigid, cumbersome, and energy intensive to respond to the changing economic climate. Capitalism needed release from the spatio-temporal constraints imposed by the old regime.

After a period of considerable disorder and uncertainty, the 1980s saw the gradual emergence of what experts call flexible production. Flexible production attempts to strengthen competitiveness through the strategic downsizing, dispersion, and diversification of production. Rather than centering production in the urban assembly line, flexible production relies heavily on temporary and pliable arrangements like subcontracting and outsourcing to produce small batches of goods that respond to rapidly changing demands. Since subcontracting and outsourcing often depend on cheap, unregulated labor in developing countries, they generate transnational networks of production and accumulation that challenge the state's ability to control the domestic economy. The coordination of dispersed transnational production has been facilitated by innovations in communication and transportation technology that make it possible to link distant localities almost instantaneously. In place of the Fordist-Keynesian nationally based vertical integration, we see the emergence of what Castells terms the "network society," an extensive, open-ended, transnational, and flexibly integrated system of nodes. We now may talk about global assembly lines, which link workers in Flint, Michigan, and Matamoros, Mexico, with entrepreneurs and subcontractors from Taiwan and Korea and investors and managers in global cities like New York or London.

Crisscrossed by multinucleated networks, "the global economy is deeply asymmetric. But not in the simplistic form of a center, semiperiphery, and a periphery, or following an outright opposition between North and South; because there are several 'centers' and several 'peripheries' and because both North and South are so internally diversified as to make little analytical sense in using these categories" (Castells 1996: 108). This "extraordinarily variable geometry that tends to dissolve historical, economic geography" makes the new episode of globalization distinctive. According to Castells (92), "the informational economy is global. A global economy is historically a new reality, distinct from the world economy. A world economy, that is, an economy in which capital accumulation proceeds throughout the world, has existed in the West at least since the sixteenth century, as Fernand Braudel and Immanuel Wallerstein have taught us. A global economy is something different: it is an economy with the capacity to work as a unit in real time on a planetary scale."

Castells concludes that these changes mean the "end of the third world," since inequality has been delocalized by global horizontal networks. This is an exaggerated claim. If anything, in the last decade wealth has become even more concentrated.[5] Nonetheless, we agree with Castells that we need to rethink our concepts of time and space beyond the horizons of previous episodes of globalization. The complex, polycentric connectivity informing flexible production subverts not only the notion of self-contained nation-states at the core of modernization theory, but also more sophisticated world-system approaches. The new global economic configuration is producing a "deterritorialization [that] involves the breaking down of Fordist worlds of production and related spatial divisions of labor, the long-standing political and discursive hegemony of the modern nation-state and traditional forms of nationalism and internationalism, and established patterns of real-and-imagined cultural and spatial identity at every scale from the local to the global" (Soja 2000: 212). Faced with this baffling "runaway world," as Giddens (2000) puts it, many people in the Americas draw from religious resources to recenter self and community.

Transnational Migration and the Crisis of Assimilationism

Among the most dramatic effects of the transition to flexible production in the Americas has been an increase and shift in patterns of migration. The crisis of the Fordist-Keynesian model has entailed a significant decline of the industrial sector and a rapid expansion of the service sector. The latter exhibits a wide gap between a small core of high-paying jobs in knowledge- and culture-based industries and a much larger segment of low-wage, no-benefit, and semi-skilled and unskilled labor. This segmentation has facilitated "the absorption of rising numbers of immigrants during the 1970s and 1980s—a growing Third World immigrant force in what is supposedly one of the leading post-industrial economies" (Sassen 1998: 34). Indeed, while in the 1920s 87 percent of foreign-born Americans came from Europe and only 4 percent from Latin America, today 50 percent come from Latin America and only 17 percent from Europe.

Increased immigration from Latin America and internal population growth have combined to make Latinos the largest U.S. minority. It is expected that between 1992 and 2050 the Latino population in the United States will grow almost 240 percent, from 31 to 81 million, to represent slightly more than 20 percent of the projected national population. Many of the new Latin American immigrants have settled in urban centers like New York, Miami, Los Angeles, and Chicago, with large and long-established Latino populations. However, increasing numbers are going to "nonconventional" cities such as Omaha, Iowa City, Bloomington, Las Vegas, and Raleigh. As a region, the Southeast has been particularly affected by this shift: six of the seven states with more than a 200 percent increase in Latino population between 1990 and 2000 are located there (Brewer and Suchan 2001). Moreover, in light of the decline of urban manufacturing, many recent Latin American immigrants have settled in rapidly proliferating suburbs and exurbs in cities like Atlanta and Orlando, where they serve a growing and affluent technocratic class as nannies, landscapers, house cleaners, and construction workers. All these demographic changes have begun to transform notions of citizenship and community, particularly for hitherto relatively homogeneous U.S. towns. The impact of changes in migration patterns is also felt in Latin America, as remittances from immigrants working in the United States have intensified old tensions and created new forms of stratification in small villages in Mexico and Central America (Guarnizo 1997; Goldring 1998). In many cases, villages literally become nurseries and old-folks homes because all young adults have headed to the United States in search of jobs (Matthei and Smith 1998).

In the United States, post–1965 Latin American immigrants share a great deal with their earlier European counterparts. Nonetheless, contemporary Latin American immigration is occurring in the context of vigorous challenges to the earlier discourse of assimilation. Assimilationist ideology saw immigration as a unidirectional linear movement: poor uprooted immigrants leave their land and culture behind to remake themselves, eventually becoming part of the U.S. melting pot. This ideology depended on an idea of fixed nation-states, each with a unified, homogeneous, and territorially bound culture. Within this ideology, the United States stood as the promised land of opportunity, allowing individuals to break with the past and pursue their interests while affording them democratic equality before the law. The anti-imperialist, nationalist, and civil rights movements of the late 1960s, however, delegitimized this nationalist ideology, enabling minorities to affirm particular memories. Such a reaffirmation has contributed to the legitimation of multiculturalism and other efforts to preserve ethnic, racial, and cultural identity.

For recent Latin American immigrants, the maintenance of collective (religious) identities is facilitated by the same technological changes implicated in informational networking and in the transition to flexible production. Advances in communication and transportation technologies have made it possible for Latin American immigrants to maintain close ties with their societies of origin through frequent travel, phone calls, electronic mail, and monetary remittances. Of course, earlier immigrants also sought to maintain connections with their sending countries. However, back-and-forth movements by immigrants have only recently acquired "the critical mass and complexity necessary to speak of an emergent social field. This field is composed of a growing number of persons who live dual lives: speaking two languages, having homes in two countries, and making a living through continuous regular contact across national borders" (Portes, Guarnizo, and Landolt 1999: 217). In contrast to earlier European immigrants, Latinos in the United States today have the means to carry out "systematic participation in networks that cross borders," such that the fabric of their daily lives becomes transnational. Responding to persistent discrimination and segregation, growing nativism, and a subordinate insertion in the new economy, Latinos strategically live transnationally. In other words, they "maintain and establish familial, economic, religious, political, or social relations in the state from which they moved, even as they also forge such relations in a new state in which they settle" (Glick Schiller 1999: 96).

Because transnational Latino immigrants are involved in regular, sustained, and intense relations across geographic, cultural, and political borders, they challenge not only assimilationist ideology but also the view that nation-states are the natural way of representing social space. We will argue here that religion is a key component in transnational flows and that it contributes to the formation of multiple and hybrid identities at "borderlands," sites where two or more lifeworlds meet. As McAlister (1998:154) puts it: "When national populations spread through migration to new localities, they bring their divinities with them, re-territorializing their religious practices. The supernatural world assents, and comes to bear up communities in transition."

Postcolonialism and the Relativization of the Nation-State

The emergence of transnational social fields, "unbounded terrains of interlocking networks" crisscrossing national borders, as Glick Schiller puts it, is contributing to a larger process of the relativization of the nation-state. The nation has come to be understood as an artifact that emerged out of power struggles in the nineteenth century. Deploying centralizing and bureaucratic discourses and practices, local elites were able to construct a sense of nation and attached this collective consciousness to particular territories (Anderson 1983). Nation-forming discourses and practices aimed at making the state, if not synonymous with the nation, at least the source and warrantor of its physical integrity and unified culture and language. Often religion was central in the invention of the nation. For example, Thomas Kselman (1983) shows how the Catholic Church, while attempting to counter the growing power of the secular state, participated actively in the process of nation building by promoting local miracles and Marian apparitions as national pilgrimage sites and shrines where French or Spanish Catholics could gather and come to feel part of a single Catholic France or Spain. The role of religion in nation formation, however, was far more ambivalent, for while it helped build collective identity through ritual and symbol, it was considered a bothersome anachronism, an obstacle to the emergence of the modern nation regulated by universal scientific principles. The ambivalent place of religion in the rise of the modern nation-state is evident in Durkheim's work: religion provides the cohesive energy necessary to counterbalance increasing social differentiation, but only if it becomes a generalized morality stripped of all its "irrational" elements. In other words, the nation-state simultaneously requires and disciplines religion. Thus any challenge to the nation-state has far-reaching implications for religion.

The discovery of the power-laden, "imagined" nature of the nation-state has been a long process of self-reflection inaugurated by the breakdown of the last remnants of colonial rule after World War II. This self-reflection gathered considerable intensity toward the end of the 1960s. U.S. involvement in Vietnam, student and civil rights movements worldwide, the rise of dictatorial military regimes throughout Latin America, and the Soviet repression of the Prague Spring underscored the contradictions of the nation-state in both its liberal and socialist forms. A particularly heavy blow to the legitimacy of the nation-state came with the end of the cold war. With the Soviet Union shattered in a myriad of local identities, the United States lost the external threat that had justified its national unity and dominance in the world order. As Hobsbawm puts it, the end of the cold war and the collapse of the Soviet Union "destroyed the . . . system that had stabilized international relations for some forty years . . . and revealed the precariousness of the domestic political systems that had essentially rested on that stability" (1994: 9–10).

We do not want to imply, however, that the nation and the state are "dead," as overeager analysts have declared. As Anthony Smith (1991) observes, even insurgent localisms tend to construct their alternative identities through discourses of nationalism. The state, for its part, has retooled to continue to play a central role in linking localities with global capitalism, by providing the right conditions, in the shape of free-trade zones and the disciplining of unruly working classes, to lure flighty capital. In the United States, the new "lean and mean" state has played a key role in advancing the open borders of neoliberalism, while deploying its disciplinary might to control the influx of undocumented workers and illegal drugs (Harrison 1994). Rather, the end of the cold war points to a relativization of the natural link between nation and state and between nation and an organic culture/religion, all bounded in given geographical space. The relativization of these links, in turn, is accompanied by three powerful de- and reterritorializing trends. First, at the macrolevel, global flows and actors beyond the control of nation-states gain great prominence. Second, also at the supranational level, there is a move toward regionalization, exemplified by the formation of the European Union and in the Americas by NAFTA. Finally, locality emerges, asserting its specificity against the homogenizing structures of the nation-state.

Among the "localities" that have gained greater salience are cities, as increasing sectors of the world population become urbanized. Sassen argues that while flexible accumulation has undermined the integrity of nation-states, this does not mean that capitalism is totally unbound. Rather, Sassen (1991) sees "global cities" such as London, New York, and Tokyo as the new nodes where power is concentrated. Rather than a system of nations divided according to core, semi-periphery, and periphery, we are witnessing the emergence of interlinked global urban centers offering the infrastructure and technological and human resources to coordinate and control the spatial dispersal produced by flexible accumulation.

What are the consequences of the crisis of the nation-state and the emergence of alternative spatio-temporal arrangements? In the face of globalization, the nation-state can no longer contain religion within its boundaries. Released from the disciplinary power of the modern secular nation-state, religion is free to enter the globalizing, regionalizing, and localizing dynamics described here to generate new identities and territories. In particular, as many of our case studies will show, religion regains visibility in the city, at once the secular space par excellence and "the terrain where a multiplicity of globalization processes assume concrete, localized forms" (Sassen 1998: xxv). Cities become places where those displaced by globalization—be it Latino immigrants in the United States or peasants migrating to growing metropolises in Latin America—try to make sense of their baffling world by mapping and remapping sacred landscapes through religious practices like making pilgrimages, holding festivals, and constructing altars, shrines, and temples.

Culture at Large: Links to Postmodernism

Michael Peter Smith (2001: 58–61) observes that there is a tendency among globalization scholars to privilege economic and technological explanations and to downplay "questions of agency, historicity, and the social construction of meaning." This narrow point of view misses the central role that culture and the media play in globalization. After all, commodification and mass consumption of cultural goods are part and parcel of industrial modernity. In the 1960s, Frankfurt School theorists introduced the term "culture industry" to characterize the production of standardized goods (according to logics of the Fordist-Keynesian regime) with only the "air of individuality" and the "halo of free choice." For the Frankfurt school, the rise of the culture industry ideologically reenforced the economic logic of capitalism by destroying creativity, difference, and critical thinking (Adorno 1982). Here, despite the emphasis on culture, history, and agency, the Frankfurt School simply reiterated the base-superstructure analytical duality at the core of Marxism. If religion was the dominant ideology issuing from the feudal order, the culture industry was an epiphenomenon of the capitalist mode of production.

In recent years, however, cultural production has attained a level of autonomy, intensity, and diversity that has problematized one-dimensional readings of the link between culture and power (Feather-stone 1995). The autonomization of cultural production is connected to the erosion of the industrial sector and the explosive rise of the new knowledge- and information-based economy. Not only has cultural production developed its own internal logic, with its own production technologies, institutions, specialists, modes of delivery, and audiences (youth consumer cultures among baby boomers and their children, for instance), but also it has in many cases become the main source for surplus extraction. In a world marked by fragmentation, fluidity, and borderlands, cultural production has moved away from the Fordist-Keynesian model of manufacturing standardized goods for territorially delimited and relatively homogenous markets. We can now speak of specialized and flexibly linked cultural industries involved in the production and marketing of difference, simultaneously responding to and creating the need to mark particularity and identity in a globalized context. As Roland Robertson (1995) puts it, in today's world of intense global competition, "diversity sells." The search for new markets and profitable uniqueness has, on the one hand, drastically intensified the rate of cultural production and consumption. On the other, it has led to the mining of the past (the retro look) and of other cultures for exotic cultural goods. The constant disembedding of symbolic goods from their local contexts and their reattachment to other similarly deterritorialized goods via the global media increase the mixing.

Some scholars have argued for an elective affinity between neoliberal capitalism's emphasis on consumption, short-term profit, and the hypermobility of capital and postmodernism's celebration of the free play of signifiers, fragmentation, and depthlessness (Lash and Urry 1987; Harvey 1989). In Jameson's words: "What has happened is that aesthetic production today has become integrated into commodity production generally: the frantic economic urgency of producing fresh waves of ever more novel-seeming goods (from clothing to airplanes), at even greater rates of turnover, now assigns an increasingly essential function and position to aesthetic innovation and experimentation." This has led, Jameson continues, not to the "dissolution of the autonomous sphere of culture" but to "a prodigious expansion of culture throughout the social realm, to the point at which everything in our social life—from economic value and state power to practices and to the very structure of the psyche itself—can be said to have become 'cultural' in some original and untheorized sense" (1991: 4, 48). This "cultural reductionism" bears a remarkable similarity to post-modernism's decentering of truth and identity: since all reality is "texted," constructed in local struggles over signification, there can be no appeal to an overarching, deeper, or more foundational reality.

The link between changes in the logics of cultural production and postmodernism is clear in the work of Baudrillard, who has had a major influence in the development of postmodernism. No one has gone as far as Baudrillard (1981) in declaring the "end of labour . . . production . . . political economy." Baudrillard claims that we are in the midst of a postindustrial postmodern "revolution" that has made signs the all-pervading currency. The autonomization and intensification of cultural production has created a profusion of "simulacra," a "precession" of self-referential images that constitute our perceptive and interpretive horizons. According to Baudrillard, culture works like a TV screen, bombarding audiences with endless, depthless spectacles that are more "real than the real," more intense and compelling than daily routines. Under these conditions, "referential value is annihilated, giving the structural play of value the upper hand; . . . from now on, signs are exchanged against each other rather than against the real, . . . [leading to] the emancipation of the sign" (Baudrillard 1993: 7). As referential value is obliterated, all boundaries "implode." Modernist distinctions, such as those between base and superstructure, between high and low culture, and between the real and the imagined, which the Frankfurt School held dear, no longer apply. This in turn leads Baudrillard to declare the end of history and the social, understood as durable power relations.

Baudrillard's example seems to confirm Jameson's claim that postmodernism is nothing but the "cultural logic of late capitalism." Nevertheless, the historical evidence does not support his materialist determinism. Postmodernism is not a mere reflection of recent socioeconomic changes, since its roots stretch as far back as Nietzsche's critique of Enlightenment-based philosophies and Saussure's and Wittgenstein's critique of referentiality. Rather, the relation between postmodernism and "late capitalism" is one of reciprocal determination. On the one hand, flexible accumulation, informationalism, and transnational migration produce chaos, which postmodernism helps remap. This facilitates its reception, beginning in the 1960s. On the other hand, postmodernism's delinking of the signifier from the signified helps trigger globalized capitalism's cultural overproduction. In other words, the autonomization and intensification of culture production and postmodernism's critique of metanarratives and referentiality work in tandem to liberate symbols and practices from their referents, allowing them to circulate freely throughout the globe using various media. These symbols and practices provide the raw materials for the emergence of new identities, as local and marginal voices long suppressed by grand narratives reemerge.

Liberated from the constraint of being a mere signifier of deeper structures—whether of capitalist production, social differentiation, or the libidinal economy—imposed by modern social sciences, religion moves from the margins and becomes "recentered." It becomes once again a key source of symbolic raw materials in the construction of contemporary identities and lifeworlds, often intermixing with other cultural artifacts in ways that defy dichotomies between the sacred and the profane, between the local and the global, and between the modern and the traditional. We can thus speak of a "resacralization of the profane world," with religion appearing in the least expected places, such as the window of a bank building (Vásquez and Marquardt 2000).

From Representation to Virtual Reality

The blurring of boundaries and the weakening of modernist dichotomies have arguably achieved their highest expression in the rise of computer-mediated communications (CMC), which have been both products of and conduits for the current episode of globalization. Not requiring face-to-face encounters, electronic communication produces a certain disembodiment, offering the ability to master time, space, and corporality (McLuhan 1964). Through the Internet, for example, we can instantly be in several places at the same time and build relations with people thousands of miles away whom we might never meet in "real life."

The disembodiment produced by CMC bears complex relations with religion. Traditional religious congregations based on proximity, intimacy, and authenticity find themselves challenged by the rise of deterritorialized virtual communities of faith. Moreover, as religion proliferates in the Internet, it becomes increasingly freed from the oversight of institutions and elites. Religious web sites of all kinds appear, a few presenting the official line, while a great many others represent new religious movements built by mixing and matching diverse theologies, beliefs, and rituals. The Internet also blurs distinctions between the "religious" and the "secular," as sites offering virtual pilgrimages to the Holy Land or Marian apparitions worldwide stand alongside pornographic web pages. In particular, the Internet links religion, pop culture, and business ever more tightly. It is no longer just a matter of

Catholic parishes offering their Sunday homilies on the same web pages that advertise the wares of their key benefactors. After all, parishes have been doing this for a long time in their Sunday bulletins. Now we have extensive electronic networks that sell and trade religious symbols, books, records, videos, and other "inspirational materials" as part of a large market niche focused on spiritual quest, self-improvement, and "how-to." Given all this heterogeneity, Brasher (2001) is right to conclude that the Internet marks a further stage in the disestablishment and pluralization of religion.

Beyond this, as a recent article on Yahoo! declares: "The Net has become a religious experience all its own." Indeed, the capacity that computers have to generate virtual reality—self-contained, realistic, and interactive digital landscapes—threatens to erode the distinction not just between the religious and the secular, but between reality and simulation, human and machine, and spirit and matter (Turkel 1995). In creating virtual reality, the computer itself becomes a sort of ethereal, divine machine, sending wondrous, disembodied signs throughout the social space. Like the Holy Spirit, these signs are polymorphous and work in mysterious ways. It is "no longer 'ghost-in- the machine,' but the machine-as-ghost, machine as Holy Ghost, ultimate mediator, which will translate us from our may-fly-corpses to a pleroma of Light. Virtual Reality as CyberGnosis" (Bey 1998: 4). As Paul Virilio (1991: 70) writes: "Telecommunications set in motion in civil society the properties of divinity: ubiquity (being present everywhere at every instant), instantaneousness, immediacy, omnivision, omnipresence."[6]

While work on the "metaphysics of cyberspace" is suggestive, we must be very suspicious of avowed transcendence offered by the Internet. Internet transcendence is also strongly qualified by gender, race, class, and nation-specific digital divides. Even with this caveat, it is clear that electronic media deterritorialize communication and challenge representationalism, the notion that there is a one-to-one relation between reality and image. The effect is the creation and global diffusion of alternative realities in which religion often plays a protagonist's role.

RELIGION AND GLOBALIZATION: SOME ANALYTICAL TOOLS

Having characterized the economic, political, and cultural processes at the heart of globalization, we now turn to religion's specific contributions. We are not the first to call attention to the interplay between religion and globalization. Roland Robertson (1992) argues that religion helps forge a shared consciousness of the world as a single place. On the one hand, because religions make universal claims about transcendence and the cosmos, they contribute to making the world "an imagined community" through "the global diffusion of a conception of a homogeneous, but gender-distinguished, humanity" (R. Robertson 1991: 283). Robertson calls this the emergence of "global humanization." On the other hand, dealing with personal conversion and salvation, religion also participates in a process of "global individualization: the global generalization of conceptions of the human person." In other words, religion universalizes as much as it particularizes, participating in the dialectical interplay between the global and the local. Along the same lines, Peter Beyer (1994: 3) contends that as the world becomes a single space, local cultures become relativized in the encounter among hitherto relatively segregated cultural units. This, in turn, leads to a re-affirmation of locality in the form of fundamentalist responses, which often use the tools of globalization to spread their particularistic claims beyond the local. In this "particularistic revitalization of a tradition in the face of relativization," religion plays a major role because, along with ethnicity and nationalism, it is key in the creation and maintenance of the intersubjective world where meaning, identity, and sense of place and belonging emerge (Beyer 1994: 10; R. Robertson 1992: 164–181).

There is much of value in Robertson's and Beyer's work, not least their efforts to demonstrate that religion continues "to be a determinative force in social structures and processes beyond the restricted sphere of voluntary and individual belief and practice" (Beyer 1994: 12). Robertson's and Beyer's focus on religion's role in mediating the tensions between the global and the local and between the universal and the particular is very helpful. Nevertheless, because both Robertson and Beyer work at a high level of abstraction and under the shadow of Parsonian and neo-Parsonian system models, their approaches fail to capture the multiple ways in which globalization and religion are intertwined in everyday life. As Marfleet (1998: 173) writes: "Consistent with its emphasis on larger issues, global theory strains to a higher level of generalization and 'empirical matters' are rarely a concern. The result is that global perspectives on religion strongly discourage contextual understanding. Indeed, global accounts in general evacuate beliefs, practices and institutions of their specific significance, leaving 'religion' as little more than a reference to 'the whole,' or to traditions of the supernatural, sacred, super-empirical, or transcendent—whatever definition is in use."

The issue of abstraction is connected to the problem of idealism in global theories of religion. Tiryakian (1992: 309), for instance, observes that "Robertson has neglected technology and the hard aspects of social reality in favor of more non-material, idealistic factors, such as 'the idea of the national society,' and 'conceptions of individuals and of human kind' as 'reference points' for globalization." Among the "hard aspects" of social reality, Tiryakian includes the globalization of production and capital flows. More importantly, "the communicative structures of today's high technology (fax machines, e-mail, and interactive videos, in addition to television) render national boundaries extremely porous and make it possible for the whole world to be watching and witnessing, and on occasions sharing."

Elaborating on Tiryakian's point, we argue for the need to develop "thicker," empirically richer approaches to religion and globalization that specify concrete instances where global processes intersect with local lived experience. Religion's role in globalization is at once more widespread, concrete, and vital. What interacts with globalization is lived religion—specific religious practices, discourses, and institutions which constitute the fabric of local life for large segments of the population around the world. Thus, at stake is the formulation of a "cosmopolitan ethnography" (Appadurai 1996) of religion. This ethnography calls for a careful mapping of the mobile yet always situated ways in which religion links the daily micropolitics of individual and collective identity with a dense cluster of meso- and macrosocial processes, ranging from the urban and the national to the regional and global. To achieve its task, cosmopolitan ethnography must enter into conversation with political economy, critical geography, cultural and ethnic studies, and transnational migration. In what follows we offer the nuts and bolts of our anchored approach through an analysis of five specific ways in which religion interacts with globalization. These conceptual tools will inform in varying degrees our case studies.

Deterritorialization and Reterritorialization: Religion as Map

The core of globalization's time-space compression is interplay between deterritorialization and reterritorialization, understood as the *"breaking down and reconstitution of spatial scales*, from the most intimate spaces of the body, household, and home to the metropolitan region and the territorial nation-state" (Soja 2000: 200; emphasis in original). The relativization of taken-for-granted ways of organizing space and time means that culture, which was construed as organically bound with place and nation, gains autonomy and intensity and participates in the formation of new spatio-temporal arrangements that blend local, regional, and global dynamics. In the face of these changes, Jameson (1991) stresses the need to develop new "cognitive maps," "pedagogical and political cultural tools" that would allow us to have "some new heightened sense of . . . place in the global system." Our case studies show that religion is a key cultural component in the construction of both new spatio-temporal arrangements and emerging cognitive maps through which individuals and institutions try to locate themselves in the new landscapes generated by globalization.

Concern with space, place, and maps is fairly recent in the social sciences, for, as Soja (1989) argues, modern social science always privileged time over space. Here modern social science reproduces the Enlightenment prejudice that space is merely an inert reality in and against which historical subjects exercise agency. Space was something to be dominated and overcome in the name of progress. In contrast, space, and particularly the notion of territory, has always been central to the academic study of religion. In fact, Sam Gill (1998: 301) claims that "the academic study of religion began to emerge as a distinctive enterprise with the shift from theologically based to territorially based understandings of religion." He sees this shift as part of the move away from "understanding religion as principally Christian or Western [toward] acknowledging religion as a distinct aspect of being human." Indeed, a long-standing tradition, running from Durkheim through Mircea Eliade to Jonathan Z. Smith, has focused on the ways in which religion maps and remaps space according to multiple tensions, such as those between the sacred and the profane, the this-worldly and the other-worldly, orthodoxy and heterodoxy, and elite/institutional and popular practices. Eliade, for example, argued that meaningful space and time are possible only through the appearance of foundational hierophanies, powerful expressions of the sacred in which order is created ex nihilo. "Revelation of a sacred space makes it possible to obtain a fixed point and hence to acquire orientation in the chaos of homogeneity, to 'found the world' and to live in a real sense. The profane experience, on the contrary, maintains the homogeneity and hence the relativity of space" (Eliade 1959: 23). The task of the history of religions approach, then, is to document cross-culturally hierophanies and the variety of ways in which humans seek to reenact these originative events through myth and ritual.

Clearly, in the current environment of anti-foundationalism and skepticism toward grand narratives, Eliade's ambitious comparative project of the history of religions is problematic.[7] Nevertheless, Jonathan

Smith (1978, 1987), Sam Gill (1998), and others have reformulated understandings of space and time within the discipline of religion in ways that would greatly benefit globalization scholars as they seek to "map out" global processes and to study how people and institutions are involved in "place making" amid widespread dislocation and fragmentation. For, as Smith puts it (1978: 291), religion "is the quest, within the bounds of the human, historical condition, for the power to manipulate and negotiate one's 'situation' so as to have 'space' in which to meaningfully dwell. . . . What we study when we study religion is the variety of attempts to map, construct and inhabit such positions of power [i.e., over the natural and social environment] through the use of myths, rituals and experiences of transformation."

Analysis of religion's role in the creation of space has hitherto concentrated on "primitive" and "ancient" religions—exploring the links between sacred cosmology and architecture in Mesoamerican religions or the role of mythology and ritual in mapping landscapes among Australian aborigines. However, Orsi (1999: 47) observes that dwellers in modern American cities have drawn from religious resources to appropriate "public spaces for themselves and transformed them into venues for shaping, displaying, and celebrating their inherited and emergent ways of life and understandings of the world. They have remapped the city, superimposing their own coordinates of meaning on official cartographies." Religious cartographies "disclose coordinates of alternative worlds for practitioners, re-making the meaning of ordinary places and signaling the location of extraordinary ones, establishing connections between spaces of the city and other spaces, real and imaginary, between humans and invisible sacred companions of all sorts. American cities are composed of complex topographies of interleaved, sometimes incongruous domains of experience and possibility, knowledge of which is borne in the bodies and sense of city people who move through urban worlds in their everyday lives" (54).

"Religious mappings" are particularly important to transnational migrants faced with the dislocation produced by globalization, who must draw from their religious traditions "to delineate an alternative cartography of belonging. Religious icons and sacred shrines, rather than national flags, proclaim these religious spaces. The moral and physical geographies that result may fall within national boundaries, transcend but coexist with them, or create an additional place that supercedes national borders" (Levitt 2001: 19).

Religion also enters into a hermeneutics of movement whereby migrants transform their travels across national borders into moral journeys, rites of passage, theodicies of religious conversion, rebirth, and edification (Peterson and Vásquez 2001). Confronting dislocation, liminality, and nostalgia for the homeland, many of these migrants narrativize their plight as a pilgrimage of the soul and body, producing "geographies of personal discovery" (Teather 1999). In constructing these narratives, migrants draw from religious themes like exile, diaspora and captivity, exodus and the search for the promised land, or Paul's conversion on the road to Damascus. Borrowing from cognitive psychology (Golledge 1999), we may say that religious narratives and tropes provide resources for "route learning" and "wayfinding," offering migrants moral and ritual landmarks to situate themselves amid dislocation.[8] These narratives, however, are not purely "mental" resources. They are inscribed in institutions and bodies, in local architecture, material culture, haircuts, and dress styles, as immigrants reconstruct and transpose abroad landscapes in their place of origin through the work of memory and imagination.[9] In addition, these narratives are not of one piece; they are contested and inflected by variables such as the migrant's gender, race, class, and conditions of arrival.

A focus on religion as a key variable and the use of analytical tools like religious territory and mapping can, thus, enrich our understanding of how globalization is both erasing and redrawing boundaries, and how people embedded in global processes negotiate multiple locations and identities.

Transnational Religious Networks

A genealogy of the category of religion shows that in the West religion has been tied primarily to inner mental and emotional states, to cognition and the production of meaning (Asad 1993: 40–54). Overcoming this "subjectivism," our case studies demonstrate that religion contributes to globalization not just by forming psycho-cognitive maps but also by establishing "material," organizational conduits for the flow of economic, social, and cultural capitals. As the rigid spatial centralization and temporal regulation associated with the Fordist-Keynesian regime is challenged by the geographical dispersion unleashed by flexible production, the hypermobility of capital, and new technologies of communication like the Internet, new forms of associational life emerge that are not predicated on a "metaphysics of presence and propinquity." Religious institutions, with their long experience in bridging universal claims and particularistic demands across various cultures, are well positioned to offer organizational resources for these new forms of associational life. Indeed, the breakdown of "traditional" communities—

built upon face-to-face encounters or on demographic concentration around now decaying Fordist factories—and the rise of gated communities, suburbs, and exurbs have been accompanied by the decline of mainline denominations and the rise of megachurches, small, adaptable, often interconnected storefront churches, and virtual congregations.

In other words, the new spatio-temporal arrangements generated by globalization dovetail with religious "morphologies of success," forms of religious organization and practice strategically equipped to deal with the existential predicaments generated by globalization at the level of everyday life. By changing our sense of time, space, and agency, globalization clearly affects the viability of religious congregations. The latter, however, are not mere passive subjects of more foundational economic forces. Religious congregations are also active in transmitting and shaping globalization. A case in point is Pentecostalism, which is experiencing remarkable growth in Latin America and among U.S. Latinos. On the one hand, part of Pentecostalism's success can be attributed to the fact that it offers believers resources to relocalize themselves, to renew broken selves and build tight affective communities in a world that has become increasingly baffling. On the other, Pentecostal churches can be unabashedly globalizing, combining skillfully the use of transnational webs of missionaries and storefront congregations with sophisticated global media to minister to highly mobile migrant populations. Building on Castells's work, Berryman (1999: 30) argues that, while the Catholic Church functions as a "vertical bureaucracy," Pentecostal churches appear to function under a network logic. "They are organizations built 'around process, not task; flat hierarchy; team management; measuring performance by customer satisfaction; rewards based on team performance; maximization of contact with suppliers and customers; information, training and retraining of employees at all levels.'" Thus, Pentecostal churches are not mere premodern reactions to the disenchantment of the world, as secularization theory would have it. "The network style of Pentecostal churches may indicate that, at least in their organizational form, they may be surprisingly in tune with changes taking place at this end-of-millennium moment" (Berryman 1999: 34).

Pentecostalism is just one example of how religious organizations shape transnational networks. In her work on transnational migration, Levitt (2001) has identified at least three transnational religious organizational patterns. First, there are extended transnational religious organizations like the Catholic Church, where networks of local and national churches and pastoral initiatives are "connected and directed by a single authority but enjoy a good deal of autonomy at the local level" These networks "broaden, deepen, and customize a global religious system that is already legitimate, powerful, and well organized" (11–12). The second pattern is "negotiated transnational religious organizations" where the networks are "much less hierarchical, centralized. . . . Instead, flexible ties, not subject to a set of pre-established rules must be constantly worked out" (14). In other words, "global connections are negotiated with respect to authority, organization and ritual." Many Pentecostal churches assume this pattern. Finally, there are "recreated transnational religious organizations," which "either function like franchises or chapters of their counterparts" in the sending societies. "Franchises are run primarily by migrants who periodically receive resources and guidance from sending-country leadership, while chapters are supported and supervised regularly by sending-country leaders" (16–17). Here, the example would be some Hindu and Muslim organizations in the United States.

Mahler (2001) has suggested that we expand our view beyond Levitt's patterns to include interfaith charity-based transnational ties, the activities of transnational entrepreneurial religious elites likes priests and ministers, and "religious tourism." While it is too early to provide a full account of the various facets of religious transnationalism, it is clear that religious networks serve as important conduits for transnational and global processes.

Glocalization

Transnational religious networks are particularly strong because they build bridges between universal messages of salvation and particular existential needs and between the overarching logics of translocal organizations and the discourses and practices of specific congregations. The concept of "glocalization" or "global localization" provides a helpful tool for understanding religion's capacity to build such bridges (R. Robertson 1995; Wilson and Dissanayake 1996; Swyngedouw 1997). The term originates from the Japanese practice of *dochakuka*, that is, adapting a global institution's practices to local conditions. *Dochakuka* has enabled Japanese corporations to remain globally competitive in the transition to flexible accumulation. Rather than producing for homogeneous markets under the Fordist-Keynesian economies of scale, many Japanese companies have decentralized production in ways that allow them to tailor their products to meet changing local markets. Product innovations that have been successful at the local level are fed back into the global system to augment its memory and repertoire. Under *dochakuka*, thus, global production and accumulation are not opposed to diversity and local specificity. Glocalization illustrates how globalization does not necessarily entail homogenization, the erasure of authochtonous cultures, languages, and religions, as some critics argue. Rather, glocalization sets up power-laden tensions between heterogeneity and homogeneity and between tradition and modernity, which both global institutions and dispersed consumers must negotiate.

Transposing the concept of glocalization to the production of religious goods in the Americas, we can see that for Catholicism and evangelical Protestantism glocalization is nothing new. Christian organizations have always had to craft symbolic goods that fulfilled the interests of the clerical and secular elites in maintaining orthodoxy and hierarchy while being flexible enough to respond to local worldviews and needs. These churches have been able to produce and circulate their messages across national boundaries through their dense organizational networks. This, however, never guaranteed that the religious goods would be consumed in the ways the elite producers envisioned. Despite acting under structural and institutional constraints, local actors appropriate the products in unpredictable ways, leading often to unintended consequences—like syncretism and heresy—from the point of view of the elites.

The current round of globalization has made the age-old process of religious glocalization more complex, intense, and extensive. Religious goods now enter "a giddy proliferation of communication," in Vattimo's (1992) words. But it is not simply a matter of having faster and more far-reaching means of communication and transportation that bring cultures together instantaneously. At a deeper level, the autonomization of culture and the rise of postmodernism and virtuality have led to the deterritorialization of discourses and practices, opening them to multiple appropriations and thus making them more resistant to orthodox readings. In this context, global religious institutions like the Catholic Church and evangelical Protestant churches are engaged in ever more precarious processes of glocalization. On the one hand, they have to reinforce their claims to universal authority in a world that, as Robertson argues, is increasingly felt as a single place but is also deeply skeptical of grand narratives. On the other hand, these organizations must respond to specific demands of individuals and communities who experience fragmentation and depthlessness as part of everyday life. In dealing with this tension, religious organizations often unintentionally produce more hybridity and fragmentation. Given the dynamics of the current episode of globalization, religious institutions become sources of heterogeneity and change, notwithstanding their best efforts to discipline chaos.

Hybridity and Nonexclusionary Identity

The hybridity produced by glocal or transnational religious institutions is just one aspect of the larger process of hybridization generated by the current round of globalization. This process entails the intermingling of previously territorialized cultures and the mixing or juxtaposition of temporalities, such as the premodern, modern, and postmodern (what García Canclini calls *tiempos mixtos*), in identities and cultural artifacts. In the present context, hybridization is fed by an explosion of popular culture, mass media, and electronic communications and by the subcultures of actors at the margins of society.

As in the case of glocalization, the mixing of cultures is nothing new. And here again, at least in the Americas, the discipline of religion offers conceptual elements important for understanding globalization. Terms like "syncretism," "bricolage," and "creolization" have long informed the study of religion and culture. The word "syncretism," for example, is derived from the ancient Greco-Roman world, where it was used to describe the meeting of people and cultures in the cosmopolitan cities of the Mediterranean (Stewart and Shaw 1994). In anthropology and folklore studies, Herskovits (1966) and Bastide (1978) used the term to explain the rise of mixed cultures and religions in the Americas as primarily an adaptation strategy to deal with the displacement and disorder produced by the destruction of native societies and by the slave trade. To move beyond the stress on adaptation and the functionalist view of religion and cultures as vehicles to reestablish homeostasis in the wake of social chaos, we have adopted the notion of hybridity, which has become a central concept in postcolonial studies. Homi Bhabha (1990, 1994), for instance, uses the notion of hybridity to show fractures in the sovereign, unified, and self-transparent Cartesian subject at the heart of the colonial enterprise. Empires sought to civilize those they encountered by transforming them into a homogenized and docile Other who reflected, albeit imperfectly, the colonizer's values. Bhabha argues persuasively that this enterprise failed. Instead of producing coherent and disciplined colonial subjects, it generated destabilizing mixed identities in both colony and metropole.

Extending Bhabha's thought to the field of religion in the Americas, we find in hybridity a useful conceptual device to understand multiple, fluid, and often contradictory religious identities and practices that have proliferated with globalization. Hybridity points to "how newness enters the world," and specifically how cultures become the locus for multiple contestations, for creative resistance and appropriation. The term "hybridity" refers to the politics of culture and everyday life and highlights "the intricate and complex weave of any heterodox and heteroglossic community" (Kapchan and Strong 1999). It is cross disciplinary, in contrast to discipline-bound terms such as "syncretism" (in religious studies) and "bricolage" (in structuralist anthropology).

Despite these advantages, the notion of hybridity has its own problems. The term has strong eugenic connotations: the mixing of two purebreds leading to the birth of an impure, inferior species. Even when hybridity is stripped of its pejorative connotations, as when we speak of "hybrid vigor," the term still seems caught in a biological dichotomy between purity and impurity (Stross 1999). In his foreword to García Canclini's *Hybrid Cultures*, Rosaldo (1995: xv) takes the author to task for precisely this kind of dualism: "The term hybridity, as used by García Canclini, never resolves the tension between its conceptual polarities. On the one hand, hybridity can imply a space betwixt and between two zones of purity in a manner that follows biological usage. . . . On the other hand, hybridity can be understood as the ongoing condition of all human cultures, which contain no zones of purity because they undergo continuous processes of transculturation (two-way borrowing and lending between cultures). Instead of hybridity versus purity, this view suggests that it is hybridity all the way down."

We use hybridity in the second sense suggested by Rosaldo. While hybridity has always existed, the time-space compression generated by the current episode of globalization has drastically intensified the mixing and remixing of cultural forms, placing hybridity at the center of our consciousness. Hybridity is no longer associated only with "impure," "lower" cultures at the margins struggling to adapt to modernity's inexorable homogenization and rationalization. The current round of globalization has carried hybridity to the "metropolitan" powers where the production of social scientific knowledge has been primarily located, forcing the West to come to terms with its own internal dynamics of hybridization. These dynamics, which have always simmered underneath modernity's drive to normalize difference under the straightjacket of binary oppositions, now emerge in full force (Spivak 1988; Said 1993; Bhabha 1994; Venn 1999). Hybridity is now recognized to be both local and global, part of both "traditional" and "modern" societies. Globalization makes Rosaldo's assertion that "it is hybridity all the way down" more plausible.

Recognition of the centrality of hybridity today has significant implications for the study of religion. As we saw in chapter 1, modernity and the social sciences, as products of the Enlightenment's quest for autonomy, set religion against reason in a teleological scheme. Religion would be increasingly displaced from the public arena, as each sphere of human action became self-legislating, developing its own rational rules and ground for legitimation. This was the core claim of the "old paradigm" of secularization. With the crisis of modernity and the production of *tiempos mixtos*, religion is released from modernity's teleological scheme and reenters the public sphere, becoming a key contributor to the process of hybridization. As globalization deterritorializes and reterritorializes culture, religion enters into recombination with multiple media, giving rise to hybrid cultural products that blur spatial, temporal, and conceptual distinctions at modernity's core, juxtaposing Aztec sacred buildings and liquid architecture, as in the movie *Blade Runner*, or Vedic rituals with pop music and videos, as in Madonna's "Ray of Hope."

Hybridity all the way down, however, not only challenges secularization's narrative of the decline or privatization of religion. It also aims at the heart of the New Paradigm, which presupposes that religious traditions are self-contained wholes competing against each other in a pluralistic market. As we saw in chapter 1, even the most sophisticated versions of the New Paradigm, like subcultural-identity theory, operate with an exclusionary notion of religious identity, positing a static relation between a unitary cultural or ethnic identity and a religious choice. The ever-presence of hybridity, as Bhabha argues, renders problematic binary oppositions and exclusionary difference because it constructs artifacts and identities that are "neither One nor the Other but something else beside, in between" (1994: 219). Hybridity challenges modern sociology of religion's stress on purity and full transparency, opening the way to understand phenomena such as multiple religious affiliation, cross-fertilization among religious traditions, and religious improvisation and innovation, which are at the heart of lived religion.

Lest we mistake the ever-presence of hybridity for total deterritorialization, the erasure of all distinctions or the "implosion of the social," as Baudrillard would have it, we must keep in mind that mixing also reterritorializes and reintroduces tension and power. Hybridity is not always emancipatory. The history of Latin America is full of examples of the use of notions of racial, cultural, and religious mixing to construct hegemonic ideas of nationhood (Beverley 1999). In Mexico, for example, *mestizaje* was championed by white, urban creole elites in the aftermath of the independence period as part of their nation-building projects. Such projects sought to domesticate heterogeneous populations and regions under a unified nation, which then became synonymous with the authoritarian state under the patriarchal figure of *el caudillo*. The caudillo and the new nation-state then appeared as the natural expression of the popular will, the embodiment of the (mestizo) consciousness of the masses. In Brazil the notion of *mulatez* became the key metaphor for the myth of racial democracy advanced by progressive scholars like Gilberto Freyre (1986) to attack European eugenics. This myth became part of a national discourse on race that, presenting the oversexualized body of the mulatta as the essence of Brazilianness, served the national elites to promote a romanticized image of Brazil for tourist consumption—Brazil as an exotic tropical paradise free of conflict. Further, the discourse of *mulatez* has obscured the continued exclusion and marginalization of dark-skinned Brazilians.

Friedman (1999) argues that hybridity serves as a self-justificatory construct for a "new global cultural elite." Hybridity is an ideology that satisfies the hunger for exoticism and authenticity among these cosmopolitan and "ecumenical collectors of culture." This hybridity, Friedman continues, "is quite opposed to the Balkanisation and tribalisation experienced at the bottom of the system," where poor people must form sharp defensive boundaries to protect themselves against the deleterious effects of globalization (Friedman 1997: 85). Along the same lines, Bauman (1998: 9) argues that the emphasis on mobility and deterritorialization applies only to a small cosmopolitan elite enjoying total freedom from all responsibility. In contrast, vast sectors of the population are "disempowered and disregarded residents of . . . 'fenced off,' pressed-back and relentlessly encroached-upon areas" (22). Thus, globalization "emancipates certain humans from territorial constraints and renders certain community-generating meanings extraterritorial—while denuding the territory, to which other people go on being confined, of its meaning and its identity-endowing capacity" (18).[10]

Processes of hybridization and deterritorialization are not exempt from power. We hope, however, to show that they are more widespread, more part of everyday life, than both Friedman and Bauman imagine. We agree with Neeverden Pieterse (1995) that hybridity can be deployed in multiple ways. Some deployments are hegemonic, serving to consolidate power asymmetries and advancing an integrationist agenda. Others are destabilizing, challenging exclusionary and normalizing practices and facilitating the formation of "alternative publics," to draw from Nancy Fraser (1997). But here again, we must be careful not to inscribe a new dichotomy between hegemonic and destabilizing hybridities, for

as we shall see in our case studies, all hybrid expressions are ambiguous and polyvalent. In other words, no hybridity is "pure"; all carry
both domination and resistance in varying degrees. To avoid romanti-
cizing hybridity and to show that it entails both deterritorialization and
reterritorialization, we hold hybridity in tension with border and borderlands. The notions of border and borderlands help us to "emplace"
hybridity and locate it in global processes (Mitchell 1997). They foreground the domination and resistance involved in globalization's time-
space compression.

Borders and Borderlands

In cultural studies, the notions of border and borderlands emerge from
a reflection of the contradictions of life at the U.S-Mexican *frontera*. The
U.S.-Mexican border is unique because it is simultaneously a state-
sponsored line of demarcation that produces naked difference and exclusion and a zone of contact and cultural creativity. On the one hand,
the border is the epitome of environmental degradation, economic exploitation in *maquilas*, and sharp militarization by both the INS and
global drug syndicates. (*Maquiladoras,* labor-intensive industrial operations normally supported by multinational corporations in cooperation
with local capital or management, have been connected to labor and
environmental abuses.) On the other, it is a liminal place, a landscape
of transculturality, "one of the biggest laboratories of post-modernity,"
in García Canclini's words. The border is a place where Spanglish is the
lingua franca and where age-old Catholic shrines stand side-by-side with
maquilas, the monuments of neoliberal capitalism, where *el dia de los
muertos* and mariachis meet the *electrónicas*. Chicana writer Gloria
Anzaldúa expresses this ambivalence well: "The U.S.-Mexican border es
una herida abierta where the Third World grates against the first and
bleeds. And before the scab forms it hemorrhages again, the lifeblood
of the two worlds merging to form a third country—a border culture"
(1987: 3).

Cultural and Latino studies scholars like Rouse (1991), Kearney
(1991), Gómez-Peña (1996), and Saldívar (1997) have used the ambivalence of border life to capture the dilemmas posed by the time-space
compression associated with the present round of globalization. For example, without denying the specificity of the U.S.-Mexican border,
Anzaldúa (1987: v) affirms that "psychological borderlands . . . sexual
borderlands and . . . spiritual borderlands are not particular to the Southwest. In fact, the borderlands are physically present wherever two or

more cultures edge each other, where people of different races occupy the same territory, where under, lower, middle and upper classes touch, where the space between two individuals shrinks with intimacy." By deterritorializing culture and bringing together in ever new ways a plurality of lifeworlds, globalization and postmodernism have led to a proliferation of borderlands. Now, as Rosaldo (1989: 206) puts it, "our everyday lives are crisscrossed by border zones, pockets and eruptions of all kinds."

The notions of border and borderlands help us make sense of how religion operates in a global setting. Like borders and borderlands, religion marks both encounter and separation, both intermixing and alterity. On the one hand, religion generates hybridity, opening, in the same ways borderlands do, liminal spaces of transcultural creativity and innovation. For no matter how rigid they might be and how hard the nation-state and elites work to maintain them, borders are always permeable. On the other hand, religion, like borders, signals difference and even violent physical exclusion.

More than anything, the ambiguities within and between the notions of border and borderlands define religion's involvement in globalization. These ambiguities capture better than even the most sophisticated modernist approaches the complex and often contradictory roles religion plays in the Americas today. The New Paradigm has undoubtedly advanced the sociology of religion beyond the secularization paradigm by demonstrating that social differentiation is not opposed to religious vitality. Religion is after all key to marking identity in an increasingly pluralistic world. Nevertheless, in focusing so narrowly on religious competition in unregulated markets, the NP can only tell us about the "border-making" aspects of religion without explaining the accompanying processes of "border crossing" and "border blurring." This is because the NP continues to operate with a static notion of border and a functionalist understanding of culture and religion, out of sync with deterritorializing aspects of globalization.

It is undeniable that religion marks antagonistic difference, perhaps even more so amid the turbulence created by globalization. Demerath (2001), for example, sees religion deeply involved in a "tribalistic culturalism," whereby ethnic and linguistic groups build claims to nationhood on the basis of invented myths of origin and traditions. Often this tribal culturalism is accompanied by violent and xenophobic attachment to homeland. Yet this militant affirmation of the "spaces of belonging" (Morley 2000) is also often supported by transnational networks and diasporic populations, as Kurien (1998, 2000) has shown in the case of Hindu fundamentalists outside India. These fundamentalists eagerly "take their place at the multicultural table" in the United States, while simultaneously supporting the BJP's politics of Hindu nationalism and religious purity in their country of origin. Such apparent contradiction illustrates that the production of territorialized, exclusionary difference does not exhaust the multiple roles religion plays in the Americas.

3

MIRACLES AT THE BORDER
A Genealogy of
Religious Globalization

Each year, hundreds of thousands of people from throughout the Americas travel to the Lower Rio Grande Valley of Texas to visit the Basilica of Our Lady of San Juan del Valle National Shrine, on the border between the United States and Mexico. Some come as tourists to view the elaborate sanctuary, others come as worshipers to attend daily masses. Some arrive at the shrine simply to get their morning exercise in the form of a brisk walk around the mile-long stations of the cross, but the vast majority come to this place to make or pay a *promesa*. For these pilgrims, two activities are absolutely crucial. First, they kneel at the altar below the Virgin of San Juan to light a candle, offering petitions or prayers of thanksgiving to *la Virgen* for answering their earlier requests. Then they visit the Miracle Room, a small space tucked into the back corner of the sanctuary. Here pilgrims take their time to wander around and gaze at the thousands of photographs left there over the years, inscribing their own petitions in a large open book, and generally immersing themselves in the testimonies of the miracles performed by the Virgin of San Juan. Many pause to read handwritten notes on scraps of paper attached to the *quinceañera* bouquets, baby shirts, and hospital bracelets piled on tables next to a large cylindrical container filled with small bronze body parts (*milagritos*). They gaze at the walls, where crutches, cowboy hats, baseball caps, work shirts, and graduation gowns hang alongside dresses from weddings, baptisms, and *quinceañeras*, and numerous plastic baggies filled with *trenzas*—long,

FIGURE 3.1. This painting of the Holy Trinity is one of many objects that have been placed by pilgrims in the miracle room in the Basilica of Our Lady of San Juan del Valle. Typical items left by pilgrims surround the painting, including graduation gowns, wedding bouquets, and plastic baggies filled with *trenzas*.

dark ponytails of women's hair that have been offered in thanksgiving to the Virgen. They bear such messages as this one: "Thank you Virgencita de San Juan for all the miracles that you have done for me and my entire family. I am bringing you my *trensa* [*sic*], that I promised to you when my husband was in jail and I was pregnant."

Thousands of people come through this room daily who are themselves border people—people on the margins of society by virtue of their age, their health, their economic status, or their migratory status. They converge on a place that might be understood as a site of double liminality, a place "betwixt and between," in the words of anthropologists Victor Turner and Edith Turner, by virtue of both its status as a popular, unorthodox pilgrimage destination and its location in the borderlands. Although Turner and Turner (1978: 35) identify pilgrimage as not fully "liminal," since it is "voluntary, not an obligatory social mechanism," they acknowledge that pilgrimage shares many of the attributes of liminal phenomena: "release from mundane structure; homogenization of status; simplicity of dress and behavior; communitas . . . healing, and renewal; ordeal . . . ; movement from a mundane center to a sacred periphery which suddenly, transiently, becomes central for the individual" (252–253).

This Turnerian approach to pilgrimage certainly helps explain the multivocality of symbols and practices at San Juan del Valle, especially those connected with healing and the sacredness and spontaneous comradeship experienced by pilgrims. However, as Bowman (1985: 3) argues, the Turnerian approach fails to give sufficient account of the historical and social contexts in which pilgrimage occurs, presenting the latter as a "transhistorical and omnipresent archetypal form." In this chapter, we resist the temptation to simplify the pilgrimage destination as the bearer of certain universally recognizable characteristics. Rather, we see it as "an arena for competing religious and secular discourses, for both official co-optation and non-official recovery of religious meanings, for conflict between orthodoxies, sects, and confessional groups, for drives towards consensus and communitas, *and* for counter-movements towards separateness and division" (Eade and Sallnow 2000: 2). Furthermore, we argue that those "competing secular and religious discourses" we observe at the Shrine of Our Lady of San Juan del Valle emerge, in large part, from the shrine's embeddedness in long historical processes of globalization. At the San Juan shrine, the act of pilgrimage has served as "a mediator between macro-levels of globalisation and micro-levels of involvement" (Eade 2000: xxii).

This chapter recounts the history of Our Lady of San Juan del Valle National Shrine for a very specific purpose: to show how this "betwixt and between" place has been at the center of historical and contemporary processes of globalization, de- and reterritorialization, transnational network formation, glocalization, and hybridization. In other words, the chapter argues that at a Marian shrine in the Lower Rio Grande Valley, in one of the poorest counties in the United States and the "center of the periphery" (Saldívar 1997: 19), we find a historical testing ground for those processes of globalization and transnationalism on which so much popular and theoretical attention has focused in recent years.[1]

GLOBAL CATHOLIC MISSIONS AND THE FORMATION OF TWO SAN JUANS

The Virgin of San Juan del Valle is an exact replica of Our Lady of San Juan de los Lagos, who has resided in Jalisco, Mexico, since the sixteenth century. In 1542, that image of the Virgin Mary was brought to the town of San Juan de Los Lagos by a Spanish priest, Fr. Miguel de Bologna, as a small image of the Virgin of the Immaculate Conception. She did not assume her identity as Our Lady of San Juan until after 1623, when a miraculous healing was attributed to her (Durand and Massey 1995: 60). While a family of traveling acrobats prepared to perform in San Juan de los Lagos, their young daughter incurred a fatal injury while practicing her act. In response to the "plea of a local Indian woman," the acrobats placed the image of the Virgin over her body and the girl was miraculously brought back to life (Oblate Fathers 1980). As news of the miracle spread, so did devotions to the Virgin who resided in San Juan. After an official investigation by the local diocese and ecclesial authorities, the miracle was deemed authentic and the Virgen officially changed her identity from the universally recognized Virgin of the Immaculate Conception to the particular, locally identified Virgen de San Juan.

In the mid–sixteenth century, Catholic missions in another part of the Americas were setting the stage for the creation of the Shrine of San Juan del Valle near the northern banks of the Rio Grande. Around the same time Fr. Miguel de Bologna arrived in San Juan de los Lagos with a small statue of the Virgin of the Immaculate Conception, a group of Franciscan missionaries accompanied Spanish conquistadors across the Rio Grande in search of legendary cities of gold. They did not settle in the Lower Rio Grande Valley of Texas, however, until after 1746, when the king commissioned José de Escandón to colonize the area. By 1808, at least six Franciscan missionaries along the Rio Grande had been joined by seven secular priests from the diocese of Nuevo León, headquartered in Monterrey (Wright 1996; Moore 1992). Many of these diocesan priests were "native sons" of the region (Wright 1996) who traveled from the burgeoning settlements south of the Rio Grande to its northern side to provide religious services. It was not until the Compromise of 1850 that this region north of the river became the Lower Rio Grande Valley of Texas. A year earlier, Jean Marie Odin, a native of France and the first bishop of Texas after it became part of the United

States, had entrusted what are now the eight southernmost counties of Texas to the care of members of a French religious order, the Oblates of Mary Immaculate.

Thus began a second wave of global Catholic missions in the Lower Rio Grande Valley. As the U.S. Catholic Church gradually assumed control of the border area, residents of the valley continued to receive pastoral services from Mexican clergy and also became acquainted with the French oblates. By 1875, the process of transition was complete, as the U.S. Catholic Church had created the vicariate apostolic of Brownsville to include the region between the Rio Grande and the Nueces River. The new vicar, Bishop Dominic Mauncy, was entrusted with the care of approximately forty-two thousand Catholics, forty thousand of whom were of Hispanic descent (Moore 1992: 184). Mauncy, who bore a "disdain for most of the laity, engendered by ethnic and racial prejudice" (Moore 1992: 187), wrote to a friend of the news of his appointment: "I consider this appointment as Vicar Apostolic of Brownsville the worst sentence that could have been given me for any crime. The Catholic population is composed almost exclusively of Mexican greasers—cattle drovers and thieves. No money can be got out of these people, not even to bury their fathers" (Sandoval 1991: 32). Mauncy was also jealous of the Oblates, who were by this time an established presence in the region and the owners of church property in the area. He soon decided to move his residence to Corpus Christi, leaving the Lower Rio Grande Valley largely in the care of the Oblates. The Oblates' superior, Fr. Florente Vandenberghe, could not be expected to change the sentiments of Mauncy, since he shared most of them (Moore 1992: 188). Nevertheless, by 1888 seven dedicated Oblate Fathers were traveling a circuit 150 miles long and 40 miles wide, offering masses in homes at more than two hundred ranches (Moore 1992: 195). The Oblates also built small chapels on the property of private ranches, one of which was the San Juan Plantation, where in 1908 they dedicated a chapel to St. John the Baptist on the banks of the Rio Grande. Soon after, when the railroad arrived, the town of San Juan, Texas, was established.

In the years that followed, two events converged to increase and transform the population in the Lower Rio Grande Valley. First, a series of canals was built to irrigate the semi-arid valley, bringing farmers from other parts of the United States into the valley in search of fertile soil. Second, the Mexican Revolution (1910–1919) and Cristero Revolt (1926–1929) sent many families in flight across the Rio Grande in search of safe haven. Pablo Villescas, whose grandparents played a key role in the establishment of the Shrine of San Juan de Valle, explained: "My grandparents came here from Mexico because there was a war in Mexico. They said, either get killed in Mexico or leave to come here. So they came and decided to start a new life here." The Villescas family, like most new immigrants to the valley during this time and throughout subsequent decades, earned a living as farm workers. Arriving in San Juan in the early twentieth century, the Villescas family would have encountered a deeply segregated place.

An anonymous history of the San Juan shrine written in the early 1970s recalls the region during this time: "The city of San Juan, unlike most other cities in the Valley, followed a very slow and conservative development both materially and religiously. But, like most towns, the Anglos formed the formal part of town on one side of the tracks, while a cluster of families of Mexican origin, utterly poor and migrant and almost unanimously of the catholic [sic] faith formed a mexiquito-type colony on the other side of the tracks without enjoying any benefits and commodities of modernizing cities." Mexiquitos (little Mexicos) were residential areas that developed because of legal restrictions in the form of property covenants that banned Mexicans from buying or renting property in the "formal part of town." Hinojosa describes them during this era:

> Mexiquitos served as camps for agricultural laborers. Every morning, save Sunday, troqueros, crew leaders who were lent trucks by the farm owners, picked up the laborers—men, women, and children—and transported them to the fields, where they worked until sundown. In the towns the workers lived in paper-thin wood frame houses built around a central courtyard. . . . The developers often cut expenses by providing water lines only to the center of the block, where two or three spigots were placed. Sometimes drainage lines were extended to the central courtyard for the common toilets; more rarely even some common bathing rooms were built. . . . Barrio lots and homes were often flooded and drainage lines—culverts in the Anglo American side, but open canals in the Mexican town—carried sewage to lakes just beyond the barrio. . . . Mexiquitos could not boast any paved streets. . . . There was no street lighting. (Hinojosa 1994: 35)

While these "little Mexicos" were clear signs of the devastating results of institutionalized segregation, they also served as buffers against the discrimination, exploitation, and violence that characterized the region during this period. As Velez-Ibanez reports: "From 1836 to 1925 and beyond, 'the killing of Mexicans without provocation [was] so common as to pass almost unnoticed'" (1996: 94). The police could not be expected to stop such violence, since they often participated in it, and the courts were unlikely to offer a fair trial, since they were notorious for discriminating against Mexicanos (Hinojosa 1994: 38).

Father Pat, a diocesan priest in San Juan who came to Texas from Ireland in the late 1950s (illustrating, once more, the Church's reliance on a global cadre of priests to minister to the valley), described the region upon his arrival: "Well, the region at that time, there was a lot of . . . segregation because in almost every town in the valley, there were two churches: one for the Spanish-speaking and one for the English-speaking. In fact, we were told when we arrived that we [diocesan priests] would be working more with the English-speaking because the Oblate Fathers were here for years and years and they were working with the Spanish-speaking people."

Although in some parts of Texas, secular (diocesan) priests did work among Catholics of Mexican origin, in the valley, as in other parts of the United States (Orsi 1996), religious clergy (order priests) were expected to minister among Mexicans, while the secular priests of the local diocese devoted their attention entirely to Anglo Americans. By the time Father Pat arrived in the region, the Oblate Fathers were solidly dedicated to ministry among Spanish speakers in the valley, and most Mexican Americans in the region shared their enthusiasm. Although many statewide centennial events of the Catholic Church, such as the creation of the first Texas diocese, went unnoticed in the Lower Rio Grande Valley, the Spanish-speaking parishes in the valley organized a massive parade and field mass to commemorate the centennial of the Oblates' arrival (Hinojosa 1994: 100). Though they had come to the valley one hundred years before as part of the globalization of Catholicism, the Oblates were now committed to helping Mexican Americans in the valley construct a specific regional identity. As we will see, consistent with broader trends in the U.S. Catholic Church during this period, they did this by embracing long-standing popular devotions to a particular form of the Virgin Mary. By choosing the Virgin of San Juan, they would also assist the valley's Mexican Americans in creating strong transnational ties between San Juan, Texas, and the region of Mexico from which their parents and grandparents had migrated.

TRANSNATIONAL RELIGION AND THE TRAVELS OF THE VIRGIN OF SAN JUAN

In the early 1940s, residents of Mexican descent in the Lower Rio Grande Valley faced a new crisis that was at once unique to them and broadly experienced across the United States: their sons went off to war. Young Mexican American men volunteered for the war effort in record numbers, seizing the opportunity to prove their "Americanness" by their willingness to make the ultimate patriotic sacrifice, their lives. While the young men were flocking to the war, their parents were making *promesas* to *la Virgencita* that if their sons returned from the war in safety they would make a long and costly pilgrimage to her shrine in thanksgiving. Mexicans in the valley who faced the crisis of World War II thus found themselves also facing what Karen McCarthy Brown (1999) calls the "cosmologistical problem": how to practice a religion that is tied to place when one is no longer in that place and when travel to that place can be difficult or prohibitively expensive.

In the Lower Rio Grande Valley of Texas, as is often the case, the Catholic Church was slow to respond to this "cosmologistical problem." So Mrs. Saenz, a local *curandera*, took matters into her own hands. While working in the fields near her home, she found a small shard of pottery bearing a likeness of Our Lady of Guadalupe. She built a small shrine for the image in her bedroom, immediately transforming her home into a sacred space and the broken mosaic into an object of devotion. In the 1950s, an observer described the shrine:

> Over the years, the shrine has grown. New pictures have been added. Vigil lights have been lit. Candles have been set about the room. Tinsel and decorations have accumulated. Little altars have been placed around the central figure. So many gifts have been showered upon the Virgin that the original little mosaic is almost lost among them. . . . In the war years local citizens called to the [armed] service[s] brought offerings and parents came to pray for the safe return of sons. Veterans returned to give thanks and left their uniforms as gifts to the Virgin. Today the room is always crowded with humble worshipers and [is] truly the center of the village. (Hinojosa 1994: 93)

Concerned about the popularity of this unofficial shrine and "certain that it could be misinterpreted" (Oblate Fathers 1980), Fr. Juan Aspiazu, an Oblate who was pastor of the parish in Pharr and responsible for the tiny mission church in San Juan, sought a way to bring the community a "Church-approved Marian devotion" (St. Johns Parish 1999).

The "Brief History of San Juan Shrine," a carefully typed and hand-corrected document written for the shrine sometime in the early 1970s by an unknown author, evocatively describes how the cosmologistical problem and Mrs. Saenz's unorthodox solution precipitated Father Aspiazu's founding of the Shrine of San Juan del Valle:

> The [Second World] war was getting into its full blast: their sons were being inducted into the military service and the families hurried in pilgrimages to the Shrine of San Juan de los Lagos in Jalisco, Mexico. At

the same time a certain lady living just outside of San Juan [Texas] at the Check Point of the big canal found in her yard a cut flint stone in which she pretended to see the physical form of the blessed Virgin Mary. She lost no time in communicating this to her friends as a milagro, installed the flint stone on a little altar in her house, and in no time hundreds and literally thousands of people from near and far hurried in curiosity by herds to her house. The room was soon filled with milagritos and even crutches. The supposed likeness of the Blessed Virgin became known as "la Virgen de los tres cheques" and many people understood it literally in the monetary sense, and the lady of the house delighted in it: gifts and offerings were left on the little altar in visible abundance. Priests not only all over the valley but far beyond it were quite concerned and preaching against it was commonplace. So, Father Aspiazu, anxiously wanting to satisfy the demands for the devotion to the Virgen de San Juan not only of his own parishioners but also of the great portion of the Mexican diaspera [sic] in the United States, especially the poorer struggling portion that was making pilgrimages at great risks and expense to la Virgen de San Juan de los Lagos, Jalisco, and also wanting to counteract the deceit of the pretensions of the woman of the Virgen de los tres cheques, ordered an exact image of la Virgen de San Juan de los Lagos to be made in Guadalajara.

Centuries before, at the urging of a "local Indian woman" (Oblate Fathers 1980), the Church had created the Virgin of San Juan in Jalisco, Mexico. Now the unorthodox practices of a curandera were driving the Church to establish a shrine in her honor in San Juan, Texas.

Father Aspiazu installed a "common, ordinary picture" of the Virgin of San Juan in the small chapel and began to make plans to convert it from a mission into a parish church.[2] He presented the diocese with a $15,000 plan for a new parish, and, to raise funds for the project and to support and develop devotions to Our Lady of San Juan throughout the valley, he installed a sound system outside the tiny mission and began a radio program. The program proved popular, in large part because of the participation of soldiers and their family members, and he soon returned to the diocese with a building plan for $35,000. This was during World War II, so building materials were difficult to find and permits were hard to obtain. The plan stalled until after the war, but devotions to Our Lady of San Juan continued to flourish in the valley.

The Virgin of San Juan was a logical choice, both because there was a local town by that name and because many residents of the valley had come from Jalisco or Guanajuato, near San Juan de los Lagos, and brought a devotion to her with them. Bernardina Villescas explained in a 1991 interview why it was important for her to have the Virgen de San Juan in Texas: "Seeing that this town was lost, and that my husband wanted to work here, well, I thought of having the Virgin [of San Juan] here so that my children could grow up well" (Durand and Massey 1995: 64). This would prove to be an extremely popular, church-approved solution to the "cosmologistical problem." It would reterritorialize the Virgin north of the Rio Grande and create in San Juan, Texas, a new sacred terrain tightly linked to San Juan de los Lagos. As Monsignor Nicolau, the rector of the current Shrine of San Juan del Valle, explained: "Most people here are devoted to Our Lady of San Juan de los Lagos. So many people, instead of going over there, they come here. If they're from the States, they don't have to go to San Juan de los Lagos and the saint is the same. It's the same. Many people, they don't have to spit out the money to go there. They can stay here."

The tight connection between the shrines of San Juan is evidenced in part by the way in which the history of the Shrine of San Juan del Valle replicates that of San Juan de Los Lagos, placing its origins in a story of the Virgin's ability to save lives. When Father Aspiazu returned to Guadalajara to retrieve the replica of the Virgen de San Juan de los Lagos that he commissioned with the help of Bernardino and Bernardina Villescas, he was accompanied by two young parishioners. The car in which they were traveling ran off the road in the mountains of San Luis Potosi. Pablo Villescas recounts the legendary story: "So they went on that trip, and there's a mountain that you have to go through. It happened at night. The person who was driving fell asleep. They went over a cliff, but the car they were driving was held up by something, they really didn't know what. So the story goes that the next day they went to a little tiny town. Someone from there helped them that night and brought them into the town, and the next morning they went back and saw that the car was being held up barely. It's a miracle they weren't killed. So Father Aspiazu said, 'This is a sign that I should start devotions to Our Lady of San Juan.'"

On December 5, 1948, the replica of the Virgin of San Juan was blessed and placed in the San Juan Chapel. Soon thereafter, on August 24, 1949, the mission was named a parish. People came to the little church not only from Texas, but also from throughout the United States and northern Mexico. Meanwhile, Father Aspiazu expanded his radio program to places as far away as Oregon, California, and Wisconsin. The program targeted many of the places to which farm workers from the valley annually traveled, again deterritorializing the Virgin and developing a powerful devotion to Our Lady of San Juan among migrant farm workers that remains to this day.

Bridgit Vela, who typed the transcripts of the radio program for Father Aspiazu, described the program:

> They would start the program with some reading, like the reading of the day, and he would give, not a sermon, but a little explanation, and then, every week, they would read some of the letters that would come in. Most of the letters were from people who had asked the Blessed Mother for a favor and it had been granted. . . . Most of the people wrote about loved ones who were soldiers. . . . It was mostly people who had somebody in the army, and they would light candles for them if they escaped. Most of them were fighting men. Not all of the letters were because of that. Some were for healing, some were because of restored marriages, and some were for people who found jobs. They were coming from all over the United States.

So many letters and donations came in that Father Aspiazu returned to the diocese in 1950 with a plan to build a $200,000 shrine instead of the $35,000 structure he had earlier proposed. Witnessing the outstanding success of Father Aspiazu's project, some local clergy began to express concern. They wrote letters to the Oblate provincial, the bishop, and even Rome, "accusing him of heresy, superstition, monopoly, etc." After a thorough examination by the local bishop and Oblate theologians, who "found nothing heretical," the building plan was allowed to move forward. Construction began on a shrine that would seat eight hundred people.

On May 2, 1954, Bishop Mariano Garriga dedicated the Shrine of Our Lady of San Juan in the presence of sixty thousand people from across the United States and northern Mexico, many of whom, as Bridgit Vela recalls, were soldiers dressed in uniform who had served either in World War II or the Korean War. The shrine was designed to elicit comparisons with the most renowned cathedrals throughout Europe and the Americas. Although not directly modeled on the basilica in San Juan de Los Lagos, it shared the basilica's ornate façade, its imposing structure crowned by a bell tower, and its lavish interior. The altar of the Virgin, like that in the San Juan de los Lagos Basilica, was designed in Renaissance style: she sat in an alcove surrounded by tall ionic-style columns trimmed in gold. The Virgen de San Juan had been installed initially in a small side chapel, but, as the shrine's anonymous history recounts, "words and notes of protest were many and loud, so Bishop

Garriga consented to transferring the statue to a beautiful throne over the main altar."

Clearly, by moving the Virgin of San Juan to the Lower Rio Grande Valley, Father Aspiazu had solved the cosmologistical problem for many thousands of Mexican immigrants and Mexican Americans. He had also embraced a pastoral strategy extremely popular in the U.S. Catholic Church in the 1940s and 1950s, the heyday of Catholic devotionalism and the "great age of Catholic monumentalism" (O'Toole in Orsi 1996: 15). This was an era in which many pastors measured their success by the size of their physical plants, and the popular devotions they fostered also provided a dependable source of revenue for their projects (Orsi 1996: 16). This brick-and-mortar sensibility drove the next decade of the shrine's history, during which offerings from the faithful supported the construction of a rectory, convent, school, pilgrim house, cafeteria, nursing home, and many other structures on the grounds of the shrine. In this intensely nationalistic postwar phase of U.S. history, the U.S. Catholic Church strove to establish its own sacred sites and practices so that its members' devotions would be not only Catholic, but also distinctly and proudly "American" (Dolan 1985). Shrines mushroomed across the United States, as did devotional radio programs and newspapers (Orsi 1996: 29–31).

In 1965, as the Second Vatican Council was coming to a close, the Diocese of Brownsville was established and the San Juan Shrine came under its authority. Over the next few years, the new bishop undertook two tasks that would greatly affect the future of the shrine. First, Bishop Medeiros took over the shrine's savings to bring an end to the construction boom and establish an endowment fund for the diocese. The change marked a shift in the attitude of the U.S. Catholic Church and the local Catholic diocese toward popular devotional practices. By moving the economic focus of the diocese away from the shrine, the actions of Bishop Medeiros conformed to the broadly held view that "the liturgical reforms inspired by the Second Vatican Council . . . brought an end to the great era of popular piety" (Orsi 1996: 32). Guided by the principles of the Second Vatican Council, the "modern" Catholic Church in many parts of the United States and Latin America strove to replace popular devotions with "moral exhortation," and the tangible, material elements of Catholicism were either downplayed or resignified as outward symbols of an inward faith (Orsi 1996).

Second, the bishop officially put an end to the long-standing segregated parish structure. The diocese redrew parish lines according to geographic boundaries, offering Spanish masses in the parishes that required them but making English masses standard. These changes signaled the beginning of a new era not only in the Church, but also in the Lower Rio Grande Valley. In this era, the boundaries that segregated the region's Anglo residents from its Mexican American residents would gradually weaken, allowing Mexican Americans to assume positions of authority in local society that they had been denied in the earlier part of the century. However, as the future of the Shrine of Our Lady of San Juan del Valle would reveal, the borderlands of the Lower Rio Grande Valley would continue to be sites of both thriving popular devotions and the sometimes violent imposition of boundaries.

CONFRONTING THE "COSMOLOGISTICAL PROBLEM" . . . AGAIN

On the morning of October 23, 1970, while fifty priests concelebrated mass in the sanctuary and more than one hundred school children ate lunch in the cafeteria next door, a small plane slammed into the roof of the Shrine of Our Lady of San Juan del Valle and exploded into flames. Though the plane remained lodged in the roof of the sanctuary, burning gasoline rapidly set fire to the entire structure, including the altar. While the priests and children quickly evacuated the shrine, Fr. Patricio Dominguez climbed onto the altar to rescue the Virgin of San Juan from the inferno. The shrine burned to the ground, but no one was injured and only the plane's pilot, Francis B. Alexander, was killed.

The plane crash was not an accident. Alexander, a fifty-two-year-old evangelical preacher, had called local air traffic controllers earlier that morning, warning that they should evacuate all Catholic and Methodist churches in the Lower Rio Grande Valley. He did not explain why, nor did he offer any motivation for his suicide mission. What is known about Alexander is that he had failed in an attempt to establish a church called the San Juan Center for Christian Culture seven blocks from the shrine, and most of the valley's residents assumed his motivation was jealousy. At the time, a friend of Alexander's explained that the act was "a symbolic gesture aimed at all organized religion. He was very opposed to the materialism of organized religion" (King 1970). According to this argument, he chose the shrine simply because it was the largest church in the valley.

As Pablo Villescas explained, those at the shrine attributed to Alexander a somewhat different motive: "One of the motivations was that he was a pastor. . . . You know, there's always been the misconception that people go [to this shrine] to pray to the Virgen de San Juan statue. But you don't pray to the statue. You pray to God. This is a Marian shrine: we use Mary to get to God. So when somebody who is another religion thinks we're going to visit this little statue, and he sees the amount of people—he was just jealous of what was happening."

The actions of Francis Alexander on that day served as a reminder that, in border zones, different ways of life are brought into "vivid, often violent juxtaposition" (Rouse 1991: 18). Although the valley was slowly moving away from the explicit forms of segregation that characterized its early years, it continued to be "*una herida abierta*," an open wound where "the third world grates against the first" (Anzaldúa 1987) and the world of Mexican popular Catholic devotions rubs raw the aspirations of an Anglo evangelical would-be pastor.

Whatever his motivations, the preacher had achieved his goal: the shrine was destroyed and the Diocese of Brownsville was faced with the question of what to do next. The statue of the Virgen de San Juan was placed on a makeshift altar in the large dining room adjacent to the leveled sanctuary, and, as devotees continued to arrive daily to the temporary chapel, the bishop weighed his options. Pablo Villescas explained: "After that, the bishop didn't want to make another shrine because he said that the people were so poor, and why would you burden them with building another. But the amount of letters and the amount of people who wanted this built were what convinced him to continue." By the time the San Juan shrine was destroyed by flames, the era of Catholic monumentalism had passed and the Catholic Church in the Americas had entered a new phase. In a new, post–Vatican II milieu, encouraging poor migrant farm workers to devote their hard-earned money to the construction of an elaborate Marian shrine would seem to many in the Church hierarchy inappropriate, at best.

However, the changes initiated by the Second Vatican Council could not erase the need of everyday Catholics to deal with crisis and dislocation through the reaffirmation of locality and tradition. During this period of uncertainty about the fate of the shrine, the anonymous author concluded her account: "Since the tragedy, the veneration of la Virgen de San Juan has persevered without a letdown in the provisional chapel. The devotees from all over the States have been generous with donations for the restoration of the shrine, but for the last number of months they are inquisitive and rather puzzled why nothing has been started for the restoration of the shrine. . . . many are returning back to the shrine in Jalisco to satisfy their own characteristic faith, confidence, gratitude, and love for the Virgen de San Juan" [ellipses in original]. Rita Gamez was one of those for whom the problem persisted. Her eight-year-old daughter, Maria Cecilia, had been eating lunch in the cafeteria when Francis Alexander slammed his plane into the roof of the shrine. Gamez joined a group of pilgrims who traveled 525 miles from the Shrine of San Juan de los Lagos carrying a silver rose to the Shrine of San Juan del Valle. On April 25, 1971, Gamez presented the Virgen of San Juan del Valle with the sixteen-inch-stemmed rose, a replica of the one pictured on the front of the Virgin's gown. Such an act signifies both the enduring connection between the San Juan shrines and the degree to which the Virgin of San Juan's devotees require a sacred place, a physical and material locale, as the destination of pilgrimage and as the site of fulfillment of *promesas* earnestly made to the Virgen.

It was not until nine years later that the cosmologistical problem was once again solved for those like Rita Gamez who shared a devotion to the Virgen de San Juan. On April 9, 1980, in the presence of fifty thousand devotees, hundreds of priests, and dozens of members of the local and national press, Fr. Patricio Dominguez again climbed high above an altar, this time to return the statue of the Virgen de San Juan to her rightful place, towering over an elaborate shrine built in her honor. In his dedication, Cardinal Humberto Medeiros explained that the $5 million structure was "paid chiefly with the painful toil, sweat, blood, and tears of the poor, in particular the poor migrant farmworkers, who came and come here in vast numbers" (Oblate Fathers 1980). He explained: "This is important to the Mexican-Americans, the poor of the valley. It is a testimony to the richness of their faith" (Raub 1980).

The shrine is indeed a testimony to richness. Unlike the original shrine built to resemble traditional European cathedrals, the new shrine is a modern structure modeled after the new Basilica of Our Lady of Guadalupe in Mexico City, dedicated just four years earlier in 1976. As in that basilica, hidden behind the main altar on which mass is celebrated is a walkway and altar on which to place candles. Such a design permits pilgrims to visit the Virgin and light a candle without disrupting masses or other events occurring in the main part of the sanctuary. The seating in the sanctuary, laid out in the shape of a fan, gives the shrine a peculiar and significant shape: when viewed from above, it replicates the conelike shape of the Virgin of San Juan herself. However, like the original shrine, this structure boasts elements designed

FIGURE 3.2. The bell tower of the contemporary Shrine of Our Lady of San Juan del Valle, dedicated in April of 1980, behind a long line of tour busses bringing pilgrims to weekend mass.

by famous artisans from throughout Europe and the United States such as hammered-brass doors and faceted-glass windows. The most striking of these is the relief sculpture surrounding the alcove that houses the Virgin of San Juan. A brochure available at the entrance to the sanctuary describes this feature:

> In the interior of the shrine, the most prominent feature is the small image of Our Lady of San Juan set like a jewel at the center of a series of concentric circles. . . . The outer circle contains life-sized figures that represent the people that look to *la Virgen* as their mother and model: the sick, the farmworker, the elderly, the migrant family. Among the figures are also included a priest, a nun, and a bishop, reminding the pilgrims of those who have answered Our Lord's invitation to give up everything for the sake of the Kingdom of God. The figure of a bishop is representative of the authority of the Church, which has so strongly encouraged the renewal of devotion to the Mother of God in recent years. In this way, the interior artwork of the shrine represents graphically those who will come here in praise, thanksgiving, supplication, and reparation, while it raises their minds to those eternal truths which the shrine represents. (Basilica 1999)

Indeed, these material elements of the shrine make tangible, both representing and giving form to, the processes that occur daily at the

Shrine of San Juan del Valle. And, just as the bishop hovers over the other figures in the sculpture, the Catholic institution presides over the shrine, using it as a means to make orthodox the heterodox popular religion practiced by many who visit this place. As it has since Father Aspiazu established devotions to the Virgen de San Juan, the contemporary shrine embraces popular religiosity while also striving to purify it.

REFRAMING ORTHODOXY: BORDER AS CENTER
IN CONTEMPORARY RELIGIOUS PRACTICE

It is almost noon on a warm Sunday morning in November, and the Shrine of Our Lady of San Juan del Valle is gearing up for its fourth mass of the day. Under a clear blue sky, acres of parking lots fill rapidly with cars and trucks bearing license plates from throughout the United States, Canada, and northern Mexico. Pilgrims make their way toward the sanctuary, pausing to buy a candle or exchange greetings with the ushers. Inside the sanctuary, the pews have long been full and people mill around searching for a comfortable place to stand, while a long line of penitents stretches toward the confessional. A few minutes before mass is to begin, the mariachis emerge from a back room, dressed in gala suits: green pants with gold studs and white capes bearing the image of the Virgin of San Juan. The group of more than a dozen paid musicians comes each weekend from Monterrey, Mexico, to perform during the masses at the shrine. As they begin to play, a long traditional procession makes its way down the aisle, led by incense bearers, a cross, a Bible, and the gold, jewel-encrusted image of the Virgen that marks this shrine's status as a Vatican-recognized minor basilica.

The somewhat odd juxtaposition of incense and mariachi becomes even more striking when the rector, Monsignor Nicolau, begins to welcome pilgrims and the mariachis strike up the national anthem, state song, or some other ballad honoring the city, state, or country from which they have come, including among traditional Mexican ballads and Texas state songs such tunes as "O, Canada" and "New York, New York." The rector then proclaims: "Welcome to all of Mexico in the name of San Juan de los Lagos and San Juan del Valle!" as two altar boys bring the Mexican and U.S. flags to the center of the altar and cross them over each other below the statue of the Virgin. The language of the mass is the language of the valley, a smooth back-and-forth between Spanish and English, favoring Spanish. Even the mariachis employ this language, as the band plays popular Spanish *canciones* like "Vienen con Alegría," bilingual songs such as "Pan de Vida/Bread of

FIGURE 3.3. "Praise and Worship" time at the Shrine of Our Lady of San Juan del Valle, when the mariachi join the shrine's rector in front of the altar to lead a series of songs. Behind the altar rises a large relief-sculpture surrounding the Virgin of San Juan, with the bishop poised above her right side.

Life," and English words set to traditional mariachi tunes for elements of the liturgy like the Lord's Prayer. In his short homily, the rector reminds the pilgrims gathered, as he always does, of the transformative power of pilgrimage to this sacred space: "We cannot leave this place, the sacred place of the Virgen, the same way that we came in. The Virgin Mary can . . . change your life." As the liturgy proceeds, some visitors to the shrine who seem uninterested in attending mass make their way through crowds of people to the altar of the Virgin, where they offer prayers, light candles, and visit the crowded *milagro* room.

After celebrating the Eucharist, Father Nicolau initiates a "praise and worship" time: the mariachis strike up a medley of Spanish-language praise songs and file onto the stage while the rector and young altar servers engage in a choreographed and sometimes comic routine of clapping, arm waving, and boisterous dancing, encouraging the thousands of pilgrims gathered in the sanctuary do the same. For the next quarter hour, the performance that many at the shrine call "Father Nicolau's show" continues. While most of those in the pews seem to enjoy the "show" thoroughly as they sing along, sway, and clap, a few stare incredulously at the stage or simply walk out wearing an exasperated grimace. As the "show" winds down, the mariachi, altar servers, and priests turn their backs to the congregation, face the Virgen de San Juan who hovers overhead, and sing "Adios mi Virgencita. . . . Vaya con Dios mi Madre."

This Sunday mass gives voice to the multiple discourses and expression to the multiple practices that intersect and sometimes clash at the contemporary Shrine of Our Lady of San Juan del Valle. While the mass gathers together pilgrims from throughout the Americas, it exhibits a particularly tight linkage between the United States and Mexico through such practices as invoking the Virgin of San Juan de los Lagos, bringing mariachi from Monterrey, and crossing the U.S. and Mexican flags to honor the Virgen. It also embraces popular devotions to the Virgen by including such traditional songs as "Adios mi Virgencita," but it inserts these into a hybrid "praise-and-worship time" in which the mariachi plays not only traditional devotional songs, but also new praise songs used more commonly in evangelical Protestant worship services.

The mission statement of the Basilica of Our Lady of San Juan del Valle offers a starting point for making sense of this complexity: "To give emphasis in this basilica, in communion and participation, to the new evangelization, keeping Christ as our only option so that we can build one Church alive and dynamic in order to make present the kingdom of God in our culture following the example of Mary, star of Evangelization." Historically, Mary was able to assume the role of "star of Evangelization" because she was the means by which universal Catholic doctrine became particularized and made accessible to people in locales far from the center of Catholicism. What the church failed to foresee was the broad range of ways in which the image of Mary and the other symbolic elements of Catholicism would be appropriated in the varieties of "popular Catholicism," some of which the Church found unacceptable. The Church also could not predict the degree to which evangelical and Pentecostal forms of Christianity would appeal to its members as the twentieth century came to a close. The New Evangelization aims to address both of these contemporary challenges to Catholic orthodoxy. As we discuss extensively in many of the chapters that follow, the New Evangelization is a cornerstone of the contemporary Catholic Church's pastoral strategy in the Americas and a clear exemplar of "glocalization." Five hundred years after the Catholic Church particularized the universal by establishing local Marian devotions, it now strives to universalize the particular by ensuring that those devotions are orthodox.

Pastoral workers at the shrine often express concern about "ignorance of the faith" or "superstition." Father Mario explained that the "legacy" of the "syncretism between the Spanish and indigenous cultures that we as Mexican Americans are part of" is "people who are steeped in superstition." He understands his responsibility in the face of this "superstition" to be "the evangelization of the people." Father Mario described the New Evangelization as a process in which the Church aims to "rescue what's good in the culture." To do this, however, the New Evangelization must cast aside what is not "good," striving to purify "syncretic" practices:

> My ministry here at the shrine is not to criticize people who are steeped in superstition, but to try to reach through that because they are hurting. . . . Here in the valley we have a big problem with curanderas, which is like a witch healer, a faith healer mixing religion with witchcraft. A lot of curanderas in the area tell people, "Go to the shrine and light a candle." It's not just a religious candle. Usually it's a witchcraft candle with hair embedded into the wax, with chili peppers in the wax. And they usually do some ritual with the candle as they sign themselves on their bodies with the candle, and it's very disturbing because we are a Christian place and I see the superstition.

The shrine has attempted to curb the practice of lighting candles prepared by curanderas by allowing only candles purchased at the gift shop to be brought into the sanctuary. If any nonofficial candles are left on the altar, a volunteer immediately removes them.

The standardization of candle use at the shrine is one of many ways in which those at this pilgrimage destination recenter popular religious practice on the universal principles of the Catholic Church. For instance, pilgrims who come to the shrine often ask priests to bless their cars. Although pastoral workers in the past fulfilled this request, they have recently changed their policy. Instead of going to the parking lot to bless cars, they ask people to enter the shrine and participate in the mass. At the end of mass, those who want their cars blessed are invited to come forward with their keys to receive a blessing. A lay person at the shrine explained of this shift: "So they kind of educated us, saying, 'We don't bless the cars. We bless you.'" Pastoral workers also remove novenas from the Miracle Room and preach against their use in homilies, calling them "superstition" performed to "keep the Lord from punishing you."[3] In one homily, Father Mario decried this practice as "religion from afar." He begged those who engaged in it to follow the biblical example of the tax collector Zaccheus and "come down from the tree" to have a "powerful encounter with the risen Lord Jesus."

Father Mario's impassioned call to radical conversion suggests that, as they attempt to purify the hybrid religious forms that have developed through the long history of universal Catholicism's particularization, priests at the shrine create their own hybrid religious forms that draw not from the indigenization of local religious devotions but from the evangelical influences pervading the valley. On both sides of the Rio Grande, evangelical and Pentecostal groups have grown rapidly. Father Pat, who spent five years working on the Mexico side of the border, explained of those among whom he ministered:

> They did fine until the evangelistic Protestant churches went in there. Up until then, they were doing okay. They said the rosary every night and they had their devotion, and they had their annual fiesta of the patron saint and they were very much Catholic. They did go into the main church for the sacraments and so on. But an awful lot of damage has been done to the Catholic Church there in these little towns. In many places almost half the population is not Catholic. Here in the valley, I think that we don't realize, because the population has grown so much, we don't realize how many people have left the Catholic Church. One day we will wake up and we will be surprised to see that 40 percent of baptized Catholics are no longer Catholics.

Father Pat understands the evangelical influence as a threat to the health of Catholicism in the valley, but another priest at the shrine, Father

Mario, understands it to be—in some ways—a resource. At thirty, Father Mario, the youngest priest at the shrine, is also the only "native vocation," or priest who is himself a product of the valley. In his words: "I was born across the border, but it's basically the same." As someone who was reared in what borderlands theorist Gómez-Peña calls the "crack between two worlds," Father Mario, like many residents of the borderlands, seems to share a "view of culture that is more experimental, that is, multifocal and tolerant" (in García Canclini 1995, 238–239). He displays much more comfort than does Father Pat (reared in the highly orthodox, exclusively Catholic setting of early-twentieth-century Ireland) with the mixing and blending of liturgical styles.

When Father Mario preaches a homily, he gets excited. He wanders out of the pulpit, pacing back and forth, gesticulating and sometimes even jumping up and down. In a style more typically associated with traditional African American pastors than with Catholic priests, he repeats one or two phrases as a refrain, increasing his animation and volume until the homily reaches a crescendo and falls off. Father Mario explained his novel preaching style:

> I was reared Catholic, but in the charismatic movement, and also I have a lot of good Protestant friends. . . . The Bible says test everything and keep what is good, and if [Protestants] have anything good that we can use, why not? They're praising God, too. I'll be honest with you, I watch EWTN [a Catholic television station] and I watch TBN [an evangelical station]. I watch EWTN for the good documentaries and for some of the people they have there, and I watch TBN for their style of preaching. I don't get their content because sometimes it's a little bit heretical in my eyes, but I see their enthusiasm. I see what works.

In a sense, Father Mario takes seriously the New Evangelization's call to "rescue what's good" in a cultural setting pervaded not only by unruly popular Catholicism, but also by "heretical" evangelical Protestantism. In striving to purify popular Catholicism of its "superstitions," he infuses it with a new set of practices, pairing orthodoxy with heteropractice, that is, using hybrid practice to convey a "pure" message.

All of the priests at the shrine have been influenced heavily by the Catholic charismatic renewal movement, and all are committed to evangelization. Father Pat is the diocesan expert on "Life in the Spirit" seminars. The rector, Father Nicolau, is renowned for his monthly healing night, when the shrine turns into a "clinic of the Spirit" and its pews fill with more than five thousand people who are "sick, spiritually and emotionally, especially." As Father Nicolau explained, they "come with hate, jealousy, lack of forgiveness," and "many of them are leaving this place healed." The shrine also has a renewal center in which it offers a series of retreats and classes, such as Cursillo (a short course in Christianity) and "Life in the Spirit," that encourage Catholics to study the Bible and share testimonials—practices historically associated with Evangelicals. These charismatic practices are not peripheral to the everyday life of the shrine but enter into even its most widely attended event, the weekend mass.

Father Mario explained the rector's rationale for adding the praise-and-worship time to the traditional mass: "In our Catholic liturgy . . . mass itself is our worship and our praise; sometimes it can be very dry if you don't celebrate it well. So we are lacking in what Protestants have as praise and worship, where you sing and clap. We are people with emotions and we have to . . . use our emotions as well as other senses. And the liturgy does that, but I think sometimes people are left wanting a bit more." When Father Mario presides over a weekend mass, he adds an interesting twist to the praise-and-worship time. He, too, dances across the stage with the young altar servers, clapping and calling out "Alleluia!" and "Praise God!" However, rather than sing traditional Spanish songs accompanied by the mariachi, he has the band play Hebrew praise songs. As he boldly proclaimed in an interview: "I can guarantee you that they are the only mariachi in the whole world who sing in Hebrew!" As the chapters that follow should make clear, he may very well be wrong. In the current phase of globalization, an increasingly wide array of imaginative possibilities exists for worship practice, as well as for other cultural and organizational compositions. As actors like Father Mario choose between these, forms are separated from practices and recombine in new forms and practices in a process of hybridization (Nederveen Pieterse 1995).

THE LONG HISTORY OF GLOBAL AND TRANSNATIONAL RELIGION

At the Shrine of Our Lady of San Juan del Valle, such hybrid practices as praise-and-worship time exist alongside traditional popular devotions and transnational worship practices that tightly link two places across national boundaries. All of these take place under the roof of a shrine that was on March 24, 1998, declared a national shrine by the U.S. Conference of Catholic Bishops and a year later made a minor basilica by the Vatican's Congregation for Divine Worship and the Discipline of the Sacraments. Such designations suggest that, rather than a peripheral space of double liminality in the Turnerian sense, the Basilica of the National Shrine of San Juan del Valle, with its surprising juxtapositions and novel hybrid forms, is situated at the center of contemporary global Catholicism. This centrality does not mean, of course, that the San Juan shrine is typical either of Catholicism as practiced in the valley or of global Catholicism. The specific forms of the shrine's long history of globalization and transnationalism, its recently developed hybrid religious practice, and the range of discourses and practices it holds in tension are certainly unique, rarely seen in either Marian shrines or other Catholic parishes of the Lower Rio Grande Valley. However, as the shrine's recognition by both the U.S. Conference of Catholic Bishops and the Vatican confirms, creation of hybrid worship forms, management of tension and contradiction, and embeddedness in global historical processes are not marginal or peripheral to the life of the Church, but instead constitute it.

Thus the history of the Basilica of Our Lady of San Juan del Valle National Shrine offers a unique perspective on the centuries-long trajectory of religious globalization in the Americas. Hervieu-Leger (2002: 102) rightly warns us not to "set up an unimaginative contrast between the supposed territorial stability of religious societies in the past and the deterritorialization that, in modernity, is said to accompany the dislocation of so-called natural communities, the affirmation of individual forms of autonomy and the general trend towards mobility. These tensions, in reality, have coexisted with the history of Christianity since its beginnings, and they are also characteristic, in specific forms, of the Jewish and Muslim traditions." And within Christianity, "the transnational character of Catholicism can almost be taken for granted, but historically the nature and manifestations of that transnationalism have changed radically along with changes in the worldly regimes in which Catholicism has been embedded" (Casanova 1997: 121).

The origins of the Virgin of San Juan, the founding of the Shrine of San Juan del Valle, and the contemporary practices at the shrine offer insight into the specific ways in which the Catholic Church entered, and in some cases initiated, global and transnational dynamics during three distinct phases of history. The Virgin of San Juan came into existence during the seventeenth century, in what Roland Robertson calls the "germinal phase" of globalization. During this phase, the Catholic Church was a primary actor in the "compression of the world" as it undertook global missions that bolstered the emergent world-system of capitalism by particularizing universal doctrines and devotional practices (1992: 58). The creation of a Virgin of San Juan comprised part of a large-scale strategy employed by the Church to both encourage conversions to Catholicism in areas of missionary activity and unite disparate peoples throughout the world as members of a universal Catholic Church. Generalized images of Mary like the Virgin of the Immaculate Conception assumed very particular identities, such as that of the Virgin of San Juan. Thus, they became closely associated with certain localities, helping to reterritorialize global Catholicism.

By the time the Virgen de San Juan de los Lagos migrated with her devotees to the U.S. side of the border in the early twentieth century, a new phase of globalization had begun, which Robertson calls the "takeoff phase" (R. Robertson 1992: 59). During this era, it was not the Catholic Church that universalized particularism, but rather a modern political system of nation-states created to undergird new forms of capitalism. This system globalized a political form, the nation-state, whose content was universally expected to be particular and unique. In other words, it developed a close association between a national territory (e.g., "the United States") a people ("Americans") and a culture ("U.S. culture") (Gupta and Ferguson 1992). After World War II, the vision of the world as a "terrain of independent nation-states" triumphed, meaning that scholars, political leaders, and even sometimes transmigrants themselves no longer paid attention to transnational networks (Glick Schiller 1999: 114). By building the Shrine of Our Lady of San Juan del Valle during this postwar period, Father Aspiazu assisted migrants to the Lower Rio Grande Valley and their children to develop distinctly Mexican American identities. Through their religious devotions, they became patriotic citizens of the United States while also remaining fully Mexican during an intensely nationalistic phase of U.S. history, when those identities were seen in broader U.S. culture as antithetical. As the Virgin of San Juan in their midst solved the "cosmologistical problem" (Brown 1999), she also tightly linked the sacred space of San Juan, Texas, to that of San Juan, Jalisco, maintaining the transnational ties that made possible this dual identity.

When the Shrine of Our Lady of San Juan del Valle burst into flames in 1970, globalization, like the shrine itself, was entering an "uncertainty phase" marked by a constant back-and-forth between the universal and the particular. A rise in globewide social movements (including those affiliated with the post–Vatican II Catholic Church) occurred simultaneous with, and was undergirded by, the formation of increasingly complex identities, multiculturality, polyethnicity, and the ascendance of concerns for civil rights (R. Robertson 1992: 59). As the world entered this contemporary phase of globalization, often described as the "proliferation of border zones" (Rouse 1991: 16), the U.S.-Mexico borderlands were poised to move from the periphery of everyday life to its center. Suddenly, border zones like the Lower Rio Grande Valley were no longer "marginal zones, thin slivers of land between stable places," but instead were touted as increasingly familiar social landscapes and, indeed, the "normal locale" of people living in the contemporary world (Gupta and Ferguson 1992: 18). As Garcia Canclini (1995: 261) proclaims: "Today all cultures are border cultures."

These affirmations should not lead us to "overvalue mobility and hybridity" (Pratt 1999: 153). Nor should they lead us to forget that the U.S.-Mexican border is a particular place, with a long history of violent segregation and racist imperialism. Nevertheless, that transnationalism and transculturality are at the heart of one of the starkest assertions of difference and nationhood demonstrates the need to move away from reified notions of borders. For all their power to divide, borders are porous; they involve cultural exchange. Such exchange does not always result in synthesis. Rather, it more likely sets a tension between "dwelling and traveling" (Clifford 1997), between juxtaposition and hybridity. The contemporary Shrine of Our Lady of San Juan del Valle offers plentiful evidence that "border zones are sites of creative cultural creolization, places where criss-crossed identities are forged out of the debris of corroded, formerly (would be) homogenous identities, zones where residents often refuse the geopolitical univocality of the lines" (Lavie and Swedenburg 1996: 15). Perhaps the most striking image of these multiple boundary blurrings at the San Juan Shrine is the Mexican mariachi band that performs evangelical praise-and-worship songs set to traditional Hebrew melodies in a Vatican-approved minor basilica. Yet, the Shrine of San Juan also reminds us of the processes of border making in "minefields, mobile territories of constant clashes with the . . . imposition of cultural fixity . . . zones of loss, alienation, pain, death" (Lavie and Swedenburg 1996: 15). Of course, in the history of the San Juan shrine, the most striking image of "clashes" across borders is the sanctuary burning to the ground at the hands of an Anglo evangelical pastor, but more subtle examples of the imposition of "fixity" abound, such as the removal of unsanctioned candles from the altar of the Virgin and photocopied novenas from the Miracle Room.

The history of the San Juan shrine also makes clear that in the long history of religious globalization in the Americas, there has been complex and creative interaction between hierarchical (and seemingly hegemonic) global institutions and those locals who often stand on the margins of institutional life. This interaction repeatedly emerged at key turning points in the history of the Shrine of our Lady of San Juan del

Valle: the plea of an "Indian woman" resulted in the creation of the Virgin of San Juan, and the actions of a local curandera drove Father Aspiazu to establish the Shrine of San Juan. Such actions remind us that—as they interact with powerful institutions—locals, women, "Indians," and practitioners of unorthodox "superstitious" religion are key actors in the formation of global and transnational religious regimes.

4

CROSSING THE
ELECTRONIC FRONTIER
Religious Congregations and the Internet

The Maha Kumbh Mela is an ancient six-week religious festival in which Hindus travel to the Ganges River to seek absolution for their misdeeds. According to a report by ABC News, last year seventy million Hindus made the pilgrimage, creating an enormous logistical problem for the government of Uttar Pradesh, the Indian state where the festival takes place (Blakemore 2001). More surprising perhaps than the sheer quantity of those in attendance were the practices of those unable to attend the events in person.

> Hindus unable to make it to the Ganges River for the festival can be absolved in a more modern way: via the web. Hindus can log on to the web site *www.webdunia.com/kumbhuinfo*, which is written in Hindi and run by the government of the Indian state of Uttar Pradesh. The visitor must then fill out a questionnaire which asks for his caste, gender, color, body type (slim or portly), and choice of auspicious days to be virtually cleansed. The user must also attach a passport-size photo. Once the information is submitted and the photo received, the profile is considered for the date selected. On that date, participants will be able to go to the web site to see virtual representations of themselves (their photo superimposed on a body chosen to match what they described in the questionnaire) being cleansed in an animated image of the Ganges River. The webmasters say they also dip a photo of the supplicant in the actual river.

It is difficult to assess the number of people who took part in this virtual pilgrimage, as we were unable to access the web site for several days. However, ABC News reported that the site was literally mobbed during the festival. Examples such as the virtual Kumbh Mela appear to lend support to the claim that, by obliterating distance, dispensing with physical presence, and tinkering with identities, computer-mediated communications (CMCs) are opening new frontiers of human action. According to Castells (1996: 375), through the Internet "localities become disembodied from their cultural, historical, geographic meaning, and reintegrated into functional networks, or into image collages, inducing a space of flows that substitutes for the space of places. Time is erased in the new communication system when past, present, and future can be programmed to interact with each other in the same message. The space of flows and timeless time are the material foundations for a new culture, that transcends and includes the diversity of historically transmitted systems of representation: the culture of real virtuality where make-believe is belief in the making."

The virtual Kumbh Mela also shows that religion is playing a major role in this transformation. Indeed, religion is a ubiquitous presence on the Internet. Every month, twenty-five million adults visit more than a million religious sites on the Net (Kaiser 2001). Matching this enormous public interest, since the mid–1990s there has been a veritable explosion of academic studies of the Internet, cyberspace, and virtual reality. These works range from highly theoretical analyses of the way in which electronic media are redefining metaphysics, transforming the relation between spirit and matter, to ethnographies of on-line communities and studies of the social profile and psychology of Internet users.[1]

In keeping with our aim of anchoring the study of the interplay between religion and globalization and our methodology of looking at "in-between" places, in this chapter we explore the impact of the Internet and other cyber-realities on localities, more specifically on religious congregations.[2] While we need to be cautious about generalizing from the results of our study, especially given the limited sample, certain interesting patterns emerge that suggest how traditional congregations are negotiating the challenges of the Internet. First, most congregations do not see the Internet as an unequivocal harbinger of new, more egalitarian and participatory communities. Nor do they see it as an utterly oppressive force eroding self and social solidarity and disenchanting the world with a flood of commercialism. Second, the impact of the Internet on the relation between spirit and matter, between the sacred and the profane, and between the real and the virtual is more subtle than some theorists of cyberspirituality have presumed. Crossing the electronic frontier does not spell the end of all physical frontiers. Rather, for most of our congregations, the Internet is, despite its dangers, above all a tool to extend the local. In the words of a Presbyterian pastor, the Internet is primarily a "glorified phone line" that beckons us toward the "real," the sacred as it is experienced in the life of physical communities.

THEORIZING CYBERSPACE: THE ISSUES AT STAKE

A good place to start is by defining terms like the Internet, the World Wide Web, cyberspace, and virtual reality, which are often used interchangeably. The Internet comprises the emerging morphology of CMCs, that is, the myriad of interconnected, interactive, and decentered networks through which electronic data flow. The World Wide Web is a heavily trodden component of this network of networks. The WWW permits the integration of multimedia—text, image, and sound—in a single system that can be accessed from multiple points. The first use of the term "cyberspace" is commonly attributed to science-fiction writer William Gibson (1984), who used it to characterize the "consensual hallucination" produced by the worldwide exchange of electronic data. Building on Gibson, we use the term "cyberspace" to refer to the shifting public spheres and subcultures, the cognitive and social digital "matrix," generated by the Internet. Finally, "virtual reality" (VR) or "virtuality" denotes the metaphysical effects of cyberspace, that is, the ways in which our conceptions of reality, space, time, and selfhood are redefined by the use of electronic media. Obviously, given the fluidity of these media, these definitions are closely linked and can only be heuristic. Nevertheless, they allow us to identify some of the most important issues at stake as congregations negotiate the use of electronic media. Since cyberspace and virtual reality deal most directly with the question of individual and collective identity, they have been the main focus in cultural studies. They are thus a privileged point of entry into our theoretical discussion.

Let us take cyberspace first. Some scholars have argued that the morphology of the Internet has led to the creation of a cyberspace that dispenses with "the metaphysics of presence." As Derrida (1974) has argued, Western thought has operated with heavily visual—and to a lesser degree, aural—metaphors that have equated truth with full presence. This assumption privileges the spoken over the written word, as texts are open to multiple misreadings in the absence of the author. In the same way, authenticity in communication has traditionally been construed as directly correlated with the proximity of those involved; all forms of exchange are measured against the yardstick of face-to-face interactions. The dominance of presence and proximity has not been challenged by any new communication technology thus far. Even the telephone, which, unlike television, disembodies the interlocutors, relies on the notion that there is a real human being on the other end of the line whose authentic identity can be retrieved through his or her voice. Enter CMCs. According to Poster (2001: 16): "The Internet transgresses the limits of the print and broadcast models by (1) enabling many-to-many communication; (2) enabling the simultaneous reception, alteration, and redistribution of cultural objects; (3) dislocating communicative action from the posts of the nation, from the territorialized spatial relations of modernity; (4) providing instantaneous global contact; and (5) inserting the modern/late modern subject into an information machine apparatus that is networked." In other words, the asynchronous, anonymous, and text-intensive nature of computer-mediated communication allows a level of dematerialization and disembodiment hitherto unseen, generating identities and forms of sociability quite distinct from those built on face-to-face exchanges.

If CMCs have indeed superseded the metaphysics of presence, then there are serious implications for religious congregations, based as they are on communal life built and sustained by webs of localized relations and face-to-face encounters. In place of traditional communities, often centered around the *axis mundi* of sacred architecture, there could be a myriad of fluid "virtual" or "on-line" communities built on common interests and lifestyles. Or as Howard Rheingold (2000: 51) puts it, cyberspace produces deterritorialized imagined communities because it is "a cognitive and social [place], not a geographic [one]." These imagined communities are veritable new forms of "social habitation," "homesteads" in an opening "electronic frontier." Along the same lines, Brasher (2001: 25) argues that cyberspace represents the "ultimate diaspora," which by "materializing a perpetual present . . . offers the ideal public space for a people without history."

Theorists of cyberspace have proposed two scenarios in this transition from traditional to virtual community. The first one is positively dystopian. Echoing the Frankfurt School's critique of capitalism and consumer culture, Margaret Morse (1998: 3–35) sees CMCs as vehicles that compensate for the increasing objectification and instrumentalization of human relations and everyday life by generating intimacy and pleasure in the abstract realm of digital data. "The paradox of the development of the media generally in this century is that as impersonal

relations with machines and/or physically removed strangers characterize ever-larger areas of work and private life, more and more personal
and subjective means of expression and ways of virtually interacting
with machines and/or distant strangers are elaborated." In this context,
intersubjectivity, "the mutual recognition, communication, and reflection of subjects that are the foundation of sociality and civility," gives
way to interactivity, purely operational and instrumental data feedback
under the economic imperatives of the informational society. The result is an "impoverished" sociality, where the "apparatuses which forge
the bonds of affinity and link disparate groups into a well-functioning
society are loosening."

Morse's scenario dovetails with the current concern for the deterioration of community life, especially of social connectedness and civic
engagement, in the United States. Robert Putnam (1993) has documented the decline of "social capital," resources such as "networks,
norms, and social trust that facilitate coordination and cooperation for
mutual benefit." Among these tools, Putnam underscores the importance of public trust in sustaining associational life. While acknowledging the dangers of predicting the long-term effects of an ever-changing
medium, Putnam (2000: 176–177) points to the fact that "the poverty
of social cues in computer-mediated communication inhibits interper-
sonal collaboration and trust, especially when the interaction is anonymous and not nested in a wider social context." Whereas "face-to-face
networks tend to be dense and bounded, . . . computer-mediated communication networks tend to be sparse and unbounded. Anonymity and
fluidity in the virtual world encourage 'easy in, easy out,' drive-by relationships. That very casualness is the appeal of computer mediated
communication for some denizens of cyberspace, but it discourages the
creation of social capital. If entry and exit are too easy, commitment,
trustworthiness, and reciprocity will not develop." As we shall see in
our interviews with religious leaders, the effect of CMCs on social capital, on trust, commitment, and solidarity, is a key point of contention
within congregations.

In the second scenario of the transition from traditional to virtual
communities, cyberspace, with its inherent resistance to centralization
and under conditions of maximal access, would become an emancipatory arena, the source and site for a new "electronic democracy." As
Rheingold (2000: xxx) puts it: "The vision of a citizen-designed, citizen-
controlled worldwide communications network is a version of the 'electronic agora.' In the original democracy, Athens, the agora was the
marketplace, and more—it was where citizens met to talk, gossip, argue,

size each other up, find the weak spots in political ideas by debating about them." Rheingold is aware of the danger of the Net becoming a more insidious form of Jeremy Bentham's panopticon. Nevertheless, he argues that the anonymity and multiple connectivity of the Net allows for broad participation and frank discussion, serving as a powerful antidote to the often rigid, hierarchical, and exclusionary character of traditional communities. "Because we cannot see one another in cyberspace, gender, age, national origin, and physical appearance are not apparent unless a person wants to make such characteristics public. People whose physical handicaps make it difficult to form new friendships find that virtual communities treat them as they always wanted to be treated—as thinkers and transmitters of ideas and feeling beings, not carnal vessels with a certain appearance and way of walking and talking (or not walking and not talking)" (11).[3] Extending this argument to religion, Brasher (2001: 6) sees in on-line religion the potential "to make a unique contribution to global fellowship in the frequently volatile area of interreligious understanding. Fueling the trend that widespread mobility began, cyberspace diminishes the relevance of location for religious identity. As it widens the social foundation of religious life, cyberspace erodes the basis from which religion contributes to the destructive dynamics of xenophobia. In the process it lessens potential interreligious hatred." We hear echoes of this view among our interviewees below, particularly among the Bahá'ís.

Rheingold and Putnam, like most advocates and critics of the Internet, are cautious not to overplay the avowed transition between traditional and virtual communities. Rheingold (2000: xxv), for example, talks about "virtualization community" where activities in "real life" mix with life on the screen. "Not only do I inhabit my virtual communities; to the degree that I carry around their conversations in my head and begin to mix it up with them in real life, my virtual communities also inhabit my life. I've been colonized; my sense of family at the most fundamental level has been virtualized." Putnam (2000: 179), for his part, argues that it is a "fundamental mistake to suppose that the question before us is computer-mediated communication versus face-to-face interaction. Both the story of the telephone and the early evidence on Internet usage strongly suggest that computer-mediated communication will turn out to complement, not replace face-to-face communities." As we shall see later on, our case studies support Putnam's critique of the artificial dichotomy between traditional and virtual communities, at the same time they problematize the idea that computer-mediated communication simply complements face-to-face interaction. Our case studies demonstrate that the impact of the Internet on local religious life is highly differentiated. The Internet produces neither the demise of locality and the "real," nor the creation of new egalitarian and fluid forms of religiosity standing against rigid and hierarchical traditional forms of organization. Rather, what we have is the simultaneous reaffirmation/extension of traditional forms of sociability and the emergence of alternative identities.

IS THE INTERNET ALL IT'S CRACKED UP TO BE?

Our first-case congregation, a Presbyterian/Disciples of Christ student center in the college town, has a simple web page that provides basic information about the center's weekly calendar of activities, mission, physical location, and affiliation with other churches. According to Pastor Don, the center "wanted a very functional page, one that would put out the essential information about us without all the bells and whistles, all the floating icons and data-intensive pictures. Basically, we wanted people to find us, to know quickly what we are doing. I wanted a visually compact web page, easily and quickly downloadable, with all the information in one screen. It had to be easy to update."

The student center's pragmatic view of the Internet is also reflected in its understanding of the role of electronic communication in fulfilling its mission. The web page describes this mission as two-pronged: to offer "an alternative to the library or dorm room to study; a place to hang out between classes and make new friends" and "to participate in creating a better world through the love and teachings of Jesus." In Pastor Don's eyes, CMCs definitely help to carry out the center's mission.

> On a large campus like this, with more than forty thousand students, we seek to provide a community, a family that people can feel loyal to, real friends, in other words. E-mail is a means to keep in contact. It facilitates networking with people. It helps us to keep them informed, especially our board council members, who are in the loop week by week rather than getting outdated reports every six months. E-mail also allows you to avoid burnout, to handle size more efficiently. There is almost a moral responsibility, an expectation that one has to respond to e-mails. When they see me, students often tell me: "Did you get my e-mail? Why didn't you respond in twenty-four hours?"

Nevertheless, for Pastor Don, the Internet is an ambivalent tool, "a poor second or third to meeting someone in person."

> I always worry about the Net taking over or serving as an excuse for not doing what we should be doing. Take social justice, which is one of

our key missions. We serve as a homeless shelter, for example. Hospitality is affected by distance. It is as important to meet persons face-to-face, to regard them as real persons, as it is to simply provide a roof over their heads. So the Internet can only enable the building of community but it cannot in and of itself create community. Only face-to-face interaction can create community. I just don't buy this whole hype about virtual communities. People may have ongoing conversations on-line but it tends to be with people they already know. In our case, less than five new students have come to us through the Internet; they have e-mailed us. They were all referrals or they were already from the same denomination. In other words, electronic communication for us serves people who are already connected, who know there is a Presbyterian and Disciples of Christ center on campus. The Internet is nothing but a glorified phone line. We don't have to make so many phone calls and we also save on postage.

Pastor Don's pragmatic approach toward CMCs was shared by several other congregations that we studied. For Rabbi Ari at the college town's Hillel, "electronic media is a tool, not a substitute for getting together. A web site is like a fax machine, a way to communicate fast when people cannot come together." Hillel's web page is more elaborate than the student center's, offering not only a calendar of activities and a mailing list, but also opportunities to donate on-line and to link with other Hillels throughout the state. Interestingly, at the time we conducted our interview with Rabbi Ari, the web site did not contain a statement of Hillel's mission, which is to "maximize the number of Jewish college students doing Jewish [activities] in a compelling environment to join them to the world-wide Jewish family." According to Rabbi Ari, Hillel seeks to involve as many as possible of the six thousand Jewish students on campus. "We try to keep the human touch within the multitude. We invite four hundred or five hundred students to 'do Jewish,' defined broadly as activities that Jewish people do worldwide. It is a way to establish connection with Jews around the world while giving intimacy to our contact. We bring together people who might not under normal circumstances come together."

Like Pastor Don, Rabbi Ari recognizes the benefits of the Internet in terms of efficiency and connectivity. "The Internet makes information available at our fingertips and allows us smoother communication with our regional offices and parents of prospective students, who would like to know what Jewish life is like here. The Internet also allows us to be an international Hillel. Students and staff can keep abreast of what's going on in Israel and the global Jewish community, which is essential in 'doing Jewish.' And all of this is good because I can spend more of my time being a rabbi, and being a rabbi is all about face-to-face contact and building local community." In other words, Rabbi Ari sees the Internet not as a harbinger of deterritorialized virtual communities but as a support tool for his primary mission: to build and sustain locality. He goes even further:

> I wonder about all this talk about virtual communities and the end of traditional congregations. True, the Internet may challenge some rigid religious organizations, but for us Jewish people, the Internet is not that revolutionary. It will not bring radical changes to the ancient ways of Judaism. We are a people who know about transferring information. The Talmud is a hypertext, a bunch of running commentaries and conversations; the Talmud is intertextuality on steroids. Electronic media make it easier, helping scholars systematize the information and allowing common Jewish folk to have access to study sources. But the character of interpretation, the method of approaching texts is the same. The same can be said about the vaunted global outreach of the Internet. We have always been a global people, perfectly outfitted for globalization: we speak many languages, we live in many countries and cultures. It is something that is in our own backyard. So, for us, the global outreach of the Internet is not as transformative as it may be for other religious traditions.

Rabbi Ari's comments are echoed by Rosen (2000: 8–10), who thinks that, like the Talmud, the Internet is a vast "divine library." Rosen observes that a "page of the Talmud . . . bears an uncanny resemblance to a home page on the Internet, where nothing is whole in itself but where icons and text boxes are doorways through which visitors pass into an infinity of cross-referenced texts and conversations." He continues: "When I look at a page of Talmud and see all those texts tucked intimately onto the same page, like immigrant children sharing a single bed, I do think of the interrupting, jumbled culture of the Internet. For hundreds of years, responsa, questions on virtually every aspect of Jewish life, winged back and forth between scattered Jews and various centers of Talmudic life." Like the Talmud, the Internet is an ongoing plethora of conversations that makes all those who enter coeval and coterritorial, that bridges different times and spaces. Or as Rosen puts it, everyone in the Talmud, from sages who died several centuries ago to a rabbi in a U.S. college town or in Jerusalem, is alive. This leads Rosen (2000: 14) to conclude that both the Talmud and the Internet are profoundly diasporic.

> The Talmud offered a virtual home for an uprooted culture, and grew out of the Jewish need to pack civilization into words and wander out

into the world. When the Jewish people lost their home (the land of Israel) and God lost His (the Temple), then a new way of being was devised and Jews became the people of the book and not the people of the Temple or the land. They became the people of the book because they had no place else to live. The Internet, which we are continually told binds us all together, . . . engenders in me a similar sense of Diaspora, a feeling of being everywhere and nowhere. Where else but in the middle of Diaspora do you *need* a home page?

Both Rosen and Rabbi Ari, then, agree that the Internet does not represent a radical break with the past, one that ushers in a new historical phase. Rather it is the intensification of ancient processes of deterritorialization and reterritorialization. It deepens and widens age-old experiences of homelessness and openness of interpretation. Where Rabbi Ari and Rosen part company is on the question of embodiment and ritual. According to Rosen (2000: 15), Judaism has gone from "being a religion of embodiment to being a religion of the mind and of the book. Jews died as a people of the body, of the land, of the Temple service of fire and blood, and, in one of the greatest acts of translation in human history, they were reborn as the people of the book." In its challenge to the metaphysics of presence, the Internet might be operating a similar kind of disembodiment, moving us to a religion of the virtual. In contrast, when we asked Rabbi Ari whether he would be comfortable conducting virtual rituals on the Internet, he responded by separating scholarly interpretation of the Talmud from ritual life. Whereas the former can be performed in absence of the local community, the latter must involve real, physical presence to be effective.

My reading of rabbinic sources tells me that prayers are powerful only in community, only when you have at least ten people present in order to have a quorum. You need to be physically present to fulfill obligations through prayers. You can ask someone else to pray for you and this lets you get a feel for the event, but you cannot be counted as present. That we are a people of the book does not mean that we are merely about symbols. In fact, we need the physical book in our hands when we are praying, when we are all as a group reciting the text. Not having the book makes us nervous. Judaism is a religion of the concrete. A virtual menorah is not the same thing as an actual menorah, which has to be physically burning to mark the physical victory of the weak over the strong.

Here Rabbi Ari is articulating a Durkheimian notion of religion: the core of religion is the collective conscience and effervescence generated when the group as a whole encounters the sacred. This encounter needs to be embodied, enacted periodically in collective ritual practices around the totem or totemic principle, in order to be able to recharge the group and integrate the individual effectively. Because virtual rituals on the Internet are only second-order representations of mana, the raw sacred power generated by the social intercourse in physical ritual, they can offer only a "thin religion." It is thin because the symbols and rituals involved will be far less successful at fulfilling what Durkheim saw as the primary function of religion: to unite all adherents into "one moral community called a church."

O'Leary (1996) takes issue with approaches that conceive "ritual strictly in terms of situated action, as a drama involving chant, gesture, and props such as chalices, bread, wine, incense, etc." In O'Leary's eyes, the effectiveness of virtual rituals on the Internet comes from the illocutionary force of the texts involved. Virtual rituals are complex performative speech acts which fuse signifier and signified, transforming word and image into the "real" object they represent. Virtual rituals are thus no different from the Catholic doctrine of transubstantiation, where the declarative force of the word, uttered under the right conditions, transforms reality. "From the perspective of the social science of religion, Technopagan rituals [on the Internet] are no different in principle, and no less worthy of study, than the belief system that underlies the daily utterance of the ancient, fateful, and endlessly contested words 'This is My body,' in churches throughout the world" (O'Leary 1996: 800). The fact that new Net technology, such as webcam and streaming video, now allows the exchange of not just texts but also live images and sounds only dramatizes the power of symbols to simulate reality. Thus, for O'Leary, it is not "too far-fetched to think of cyber-communication as coming to play a major role in the spiritual sustenance of postmodern humans. The possibilities are endless. On-line confessions? Eucharist rituals, more weddings, seders, witches' sabbats? There will be many experiments" (805).

Bourdieu (1991) argues that the power of a speech act does not come from its internal structure. Rather it emerges from the context and the audience, which recognizes it as legitimate and effective. If this is the case, then the power of virtual ritual resides in the affective and social involvement of on-line participants. O'Leary recognizes that this poses a special challenge to virtual rituals. "Rooted in textuality, ritual action in cyberspace is constantly faced with the evidence of its own quality as constructed, as arbitrary, and as artificial, a game played with no material stakes or consequences; but the efficacy of the ritual is affirmed, time and again, even in the face of a full, self-conscious awareness of its artificiality." This affirmation, however, is predicated on the durable commitment of on-line participants to sustain the "consensual hallucination."

To Pastor Lenny of a midsized Christian Congregational church in the college town, the fragility of commitment is precisely the Achilles heel of cyber-religion. The Congregational church serves many graduate students and professors at the university, who are attracted to the congregation's inclusiveness and progressive politics. Prominent in this church's web page are its goals: "We join as a spiritual community in this compact: to worship God, however known, to welcome into our church those of differing understanding and theological opinion, to follow, even imperfectly, the way of Jesus in personal involvement with each other, and, strengthened by the bond, to act in Christian concern for the welfare of all people." In other words, the Congregational church brings together the kind of people—well educated and cosmopolitan—who would be receptive to, or at least comfortable with, CMCs. Indeed Pastor Lenny sees CMCs as a useful vehicle to bring together people with similar spiritual and social concerns: "Since we are not strongly linked to our denomination, new people run electronic searches and find us because of the sub-issues that are our focus. We are an open and affirming church, welcoming and supporting gays and lesbians, for example. So, many times when people who share this worldview come into town, they already have found us, our web site, as part of a national network of churches and organizations working on progressive causes."

Nevertheless, Pastor Lenny is concerned with the Internet's libertarian individualism, with the ephemerality and shallowness of on-line interactions. Echoing Rabbi Ari, Pastor Lenny thinks that the Internet can certainly form community at the level of ideas, bringing people with common intellectual and social interests together. It may even bring people together at the level of emotion by providing support from afar. However, there are still significant differences between face-to-face and electronic communities.

> My worry is about the anonymous nature of the Internet communication, particularly the lack of personal accountability. If you look at chat rooms, for example, people drop off whenever they want. They can almost say anything they want and there is no promise to treat each other well, to look out for the concerns of the other, as we say in our mission statement. I know chat rooms have ways of policing electronic abuse, but this is much more difficult when the participants are not really invested personally in the community. I worry about

pseudocommunities of opinion substituting for communities based on covenant. It takes more than lifestyle or opinion to form a community; it takes commitment, compacts made in public and reinforced in daily life, in working together to feed and clothe each other. This is not to say that on-line communities are not valuable and valid. But they are different from face-to-face communities and cannot replace them. I would say that a good face-to-face community can use electronic communication to bring out the benefits of a virtual community. The reverse is far more difficult.

Pastor Lenny's reference to covenant and commitment brings us back to Putnam's contention that trust is central to the building of social connectedness and civic engagement. As we have seen, Putnam (2000: 176–177) argues that CMCs are useful in "sharing information, gathering opinions, debating alternatives, but building trust and goodwill is not easy in cyberspace." This is because CMCs are "sparse and unbounded. Anonymity and fluidity in the virtual world encourage 'easy in, easy out,' 'drive-by' relationships." Thus Putnam hypothesizes that the extensive use of CMCs may actually require more face-to-face interaction. "In other words, social capital may turn out to be a *prerequisite for*, rather than a *consequence of*, effective computer-mediated communication." Dawson (2001: 7) argues along the same lines—she finds Internet communication excessively "one-dimensional and self-referential." In her view, "while the Internet may augment the creation and spread of new religions by overcoming some of the constraints imposed by space, time, and the criteria of social stratification, in the process it may be working against the development of the bonds of true group identity." This is because the Internet is "saturated with an implicit ideology of romantic individualism. This ideology is not conducive to the ethos of self-sacrifice and submission to the will of the group that is characteristic of many religious movements."[4]

When we asked Pastor Lenny about virtual rituals, his answer dovetailed with Rabbi Ari's.

A sacrament is the outward sign of inner grace. Although images and texts are central in the sacrament, you cannot stay at that level. The word has to become flesh, it has to be lived by the community. That's why the Eucharist is all about coming together, in our human bodies. Now, you can enhance this sacrament: add nice sacred music, lighting, . . . but these exterior things are not a substitute for being together. My concern is that virtual reality with its sleek presentation may exacerbate a tendency in our society toward passive and addictive consumption of entertainment, toward isolation from even one's family.

Here Pastor Lenny's comments echo Morse's point that the Internet displaces intimacy and desire to the realm of digital data in response to the increasing disenchantment of everyday life.

Pastor Lenny's last comment brings into sharp relief the concerns some religious leaders have about CMCs. While these leaders recognize that the Internet plays valuable roles for their congregations, they refuse to celebrate its radical newness and revolutionary character. CMC is a powerful tool to enhance face-to-face interactions, to make them faster and more efficient, but it can never be a substitute for them.

LINKING THE LOCAL AND THE GLOBAL

A second cluster of the churches we studied does not set as sharp a contradiction as do the preceding congregations between the bounded nature of local community and the unboundedness of the Internet. Typical of this second cluster is a relatively new Catholic parish in the college town. Founded in 1987, this parish is located in the rapidly expanding west side of town and serves about thirteen hundred families, mostly upper middle class, professional, and white. Since 1994, the parish has grown at a quickening pace, adding an average of two hundred families per year. To minister to this expanding population, the parish recently dedicated a $7 million sanctuary that can comfortably seat fifteen hundred people. When asked about the Catholic parish's structure and the place of CMCs within it, Mary, a laywoman who oversees the web page and the stewardship committee, told us:

> We have a concentric model of church anchored in our wonderful new temple, which is where we all come together to worship as one. But community is not the building; the building is just a sign and a space where we come together. The church is not a building, however beautiful. It is the people who are involved in multiple things, from choir to our twelve Renew communities throughout the parish and to our academy, which now has pre-K to second grade. The Internet helps us to make sure that all these people stay connected. They can be with us wherever they are. The fact that you have a demanding job does not mean that you cannot be involved. You don't have to go to church as a physical space every single day to be active, to undertake your stewardship. Your can be a witness for God everywhere. We see it as a journey of discipleship.

Mary sees a direct correlation between the journey of discipleship and the parish's concentric model. As members deepen their faith and grow in their commitment to God's work, they move toward the center of concentric circles, increasing their physical and financial involvement in the life of the parish. Here the example of stewardship is particularly illustrative. According to Mary, this church's central goal, reiterated in its mission statement, is to become a full-stewardship church, where all members pledge their "time, talent, and treasure."

> The Internet is a good outreach tool. An average of four families a week register on-line. Many of them are busy; they are the movers and shakers in the larger community, and the Internet allows us to plug them into our parish. The Internet serves as the first, the outside, circle of our community, because they not only register but we ask them to sign an electronic commitment card, where they pledge what they are willing to do in terms of time, talent, or treasure for the community. In other words, this commitment card brings you into deeper concentric circles. I know some people say that the Internet destroys communities. I don't think so. I think it gives you the opportunity to extend community. As soon as people get in touch with us through e-mail, there is a door opened to evangelize, to draw them into our church. E-mail helps us reach people we couldn't reach with our limited staff.

Mary thus articulates a more positive view of CMCs than did our previous informants. Nevertheless, like other pastoral agents, she continues to privilege the local, physical community over virtuality.

> Catholicism is all about community. You cannot have a mass of one, in your isolated cubicle. And it is not enough to witness mass on TV or through streaming video. Unless you are too old or sick, you have to be with your fellow others. That's what Jesus meant when he said: "When two or more are gathered in my name, I will be there with you." Not only that, but you can't receive the body of Christ, which we Catholics believe is in the substance of the consecrated Host, over the computer. So, I don't know about virtual rituals. But the Internet is key to extending our work within and beyond the parish boundaries, to have a presence in people's daily lives.

Like our preceding informants, Mary sees the Internet as a tool rather than a new way of life. However, she has a less ambivalent view toward it. It is not a threat to locality or intimacy, but a way to extend the congregation beyond its physical limits, to project its mission and outreach globally. This "unbounding" of the local has paradoxical effects: rather than eroding face-to-face interactions, it makes them possible by serving as the key medium to collect the donations that went into the construction of the new temple and schools that have become the new anchors for parish life.

The fluid interplay between the local and the global, between deterritorialization and reterritorialization, is also central to the mission of the Bahá'í Center in the college town. McMullen (2000: 12) has described Bahá'ís as "reflexive situated universalists. They are universalists in that both their ideology and their ecclesiastical structures orient their perspective toward the world-as-a-whole, promoting 'unity in diversity,' the 'oneness of humanity,' and the 'oneness of religion.' Bahá'ís are conscious that what they are doing in Atlanta [the site McMullen researched] is similar to what Bahá'ís are doing throughout the world: erecting the Kingdom of God." Bahá'ís are also situated, because this universalist worldview is directed toward and enacted in the local community, which, like the Catholic parish, is geographically determined. In McMullen's words: "The daily practices of the Bahá'ís to institutionalize their vision of the world order begins in the local community. Bahá'í evangelization efforts are 'universalized' to all humanity. But the concern for the oneness of humanity leads them back to their local community as the crucible in which this universality is 'particularized'."

From the perspective of their congregation in the college town, senior members Robert and Sarah see the ultimate goal of the Bahá'í as "unifying the world, making it a gigantic family. But for this we need to serve humanity. For us work is worship. We promote social justice, the equality of men and women, of the races. We fight prejudice through peace education. And this is where the Internet is very helpful. It is a vehicle to make information available, to allow for the free exchange of ideas, to allow each of us to encounter the diversity and unity of humanity." In other words, the Internet is a tool that allows the college town's Bahá'ís to be situated universalists. On the one hand, as Robert puts it: "Our web page allows us to offer our community as a model, albeit not a perfect one, to humanity. We feel we have something wonderful here that we want to share. We want to reflect who we are, in our daily commitments, to reflect our community and connection with our larger, global family." On the other hand, the Internet allows local Bahá'ís to link with other Bahá'í on-line communities in the United States—in Atlanta, Chicago, or Washington, D.C. Through *www.bahai.org* they can also have access to material published by House of Justice, the international governing body. According to Robert:

> Connecting with a family beyond your own community, our Bahá'í family spread throughout the world, is very empowering. The Internet allows us to remain engaged in our global efforts. We can pose questions about Bahá'í scriptures and other specific issues in our locality to the governing body. You e-mail the questions and you get a quick response

from the research department. Also, if you don't have money, you can undertake a virtual pilgrimage to our holy sites. The Universal House of Justice has not ruled on whether these pilgrimages are sufficient, though.

The dialectical relation between the local and the global at the heart of the Bahá'í faith explains the favorable reception of the Internet among Bahá'ís we studied. Sarah goes as far as finding the rise of the Internet foretold in the writings of the founders of the faith. She quotes Shoghi Effendi, head of the Bahá'í from 1921 to 1957: "A mechanism of world inter-communication will be devised, embracing the whole planet, freed from national hindrances and restrictions, and functioning with marvelous swiftness and perfect regularity" (Effendi 1938: 203). Nevertheless, despite this positive view of the Internet, Robert and Sarah do not see the electronic community as a substitute for the local community. In Sarah's words: "If our goal is to teach justice, tolerance, and peace, we need the local community. Socialization is important for us. That is where you learn these values, because that is where we see each other as human beings, where we meet face to face. How can I learn to love and respect others, if I don't see their eyes, if I don't see what's in their heart? Only when I meet people in person can I know about their needs and their desires and then I can offer help, whether it be mowing their lawn, baby-sitting for them."

What we see in the Bahá'í and the Catholic parish is a simultaneous affirmation of the globalizing power of the Internet and the power and authenticity of locality. Local community does not stand in stark contradiction to the deterritorialization and disembodiment brought by the Internet, as Castells theorizes. Rather, the Internet becomes a vehicle to strengthen the local by "unbounding" it, that is, by extending it and reinscribing it in a global context. Rather than "substituting the space of flows for the space of places," the Internet globalizes the local and localizes the global.

SACRALIZING THE PROFANE

One common concern about the Internet is its rampant commercialism, which threatens to desacralize religion by making it just another commodity sold in the global market for mass culture. For instance, Dawson (2001: 6) notes a tendency on the World Wide Web to trivialize all content, including religion, as users become "disappointed with the endless barrage of advertising and insidious links to nested commercial sites masquerading as sources of public information." From the standpoint of some congregations we studied, particularly those that can be characterized as megachurches, reality is considerably more complex and ambiguous.

Like the Catholic parish we studied, the first megachurch we studied is located in the college town's rapidly expanding western suburbs. It describes itself as nondenominational, but it has a strong Pentecostal flavor. Tom, senior team pastor and administrator, characterizes his congregation as a young church. "We were founded in 1987, when Pastor Garry came from Texas after having graduated from the Christ for the Nations Bible Institute and having served in the Florida Panhandle. We serve about six hundred families, most young families. Adults tend to be between thirty-five to forty years of age." This megachurch's web site is far more sophisticated than any of those reviewed so far, with flashing letters, upbeat music, and a video clip offering a message from Pastor Garry. The site also provides a library of streaming videos of previous services. When asked about why the congregation created a web site, Pastor Tom responded:

> Other churches back away from technology and the arts. They are in the Dark Ages. So Christians are forced to be schizophrenic. Our society is highly technological, but on Sunday we seem to step back in time. We wanted to break with this. We wanted to be fresh, to look at every possibility to promote the word of God. After all, nothing is evil in itself. God created everything and the devil nothing. We are created in God's image and we are using all the gifts at our disposal. So we do arts, drama, dance, ranging from progressive to traditional, like ballet. And we embrace technology to promote the kingdom of God. For us the Internet is advertisement. We present our church as a church that truly rocks. When people check our web site, we want them to say, "Wow, this looks pretty cool." In fact, our first motto was "You never knew church could be like this."

For Pastor Tom, thus, there is no contradiction between making religion entertaining, presenting it as an appealing product in the Internet, and Jesus' core message.

> It is all about the great commission, about going out into the highways and byways of life, about touching people in their everyday life. To change people, to teach Jesus' message, and make them God's sons and daughters you have to reach them where they are at. And today, that means reaching through the popular culture they consume. That's why we place advertisements in movie theaters, for example. I have heard of a web site with an address something like girlsgirlsgirls.com, and when men go there expecting to find pornography they find instead the word of Jesus. I would love to come up with an idea like that

because, you see, it is all part of God's salvation plan for that person who was hooked by the web-site name.

Because of their understanding of the great commission, Pastor Tom and his assistant are planning to move the web page to the "next level," making it more interactive. "In 1996 we started with a rough site, two or three flat pages with the time of our services and our calendar. We now want to enhance our site with all the latest media technology, to have good video and sound, and make it that you can almost touch people one-on-one. We are thinking about creating a 3-D game of salvation that folks can play from their homes and workplaces."

Despite the congregation's willingness to be at the cutting edge of CMC technology, the church continues to stress the importance of physical presence, intimacy, and commitment. The first images that flash across the screen as one enters its web site are the questions: "What is family? Are you in covenant? Do you know what home is?" Moreover, Pastor Tom balks at the possibility of his congregation ever becoming an e-church.

> I don't see it in the future. We want to save the real person. It is hard to duplicate the spirit that you find in this church when you walk in on Sunday. Besides, we see our church as a spiritual family, led by a strong father. Like any family, our family reproduces, we birth sons and daughters inside and outside. The Internet is the tool to birth offspring outside, to make our family an extended one. But the core, the immediate family, is there anchoring this extended family. You see, it is like Thanksgiving: it is best to be with your folks, to eat the feast they have prepared, to hug them, watch football with them. If you can't be with the family, you can call and that is fine, but it is not the same.

The interpenetration of the sacred and the profane is more profound in the other megachurch where we undertook research. This nondenominational African American megachurch and televangelism center, located in the suburbs of a major southern city, was founded in 1986 by eight people and has grown to more than twenty thousand members. The church is part of a larger international corporation that produces books, tapes, records, and television programs. The church also conducts special events, "Changing the World Conventions," organized and supported through the efforts of more than 150,000 partners, both individuals and congregations, around the world. The church also runs Project Change, which brings together more than fifty ministries, addressing issues ranging from health and fitness to drug addiction to marital conflict. Project Change also offers food and shelter to the poor in the city's metropolitan area.

John, the director of communications, articulates his church's philosophy thus:

> We think globally. Our founder got the name of our church from an inspiration he received from the Holy Spirit, who said, "I see you reaching people all over the world." Our founder always tells us not to buy things on a short-time basis. We believe that there is a harvest coming in these next few years of people to the kingdom based on many factors, and we want to be prepared to service millions of people as they make the decision to become believers. Our goal is to bring the message from Elizabethan English into everyday layman's terms. And that's why the church is so big, because the pastor teaches a lot of the practical perspective, of the how-to, how to bring the power of Christ into your life. Instead of saying "Enhance your life," he'll be telling you exactly how to pray, the things to say, confessions you ought to make as part of your routine.

In light of this global perspective, John sees his congregation's use of the latest CMC technologies as a mark of the ministry's quest for excellence and a way to give the ministry a leading edge in "building a big basket to catch souls when they decide to come into the kingdom."

> The technology is simply to support the ministry mission. We don't want to be bound by what our machines can't or can do. You want to use the technology to facilitate things. If the world can build all these things, fabulous sports arenas, civic centers, halls of justice, why can't the people of God have excellent stuff? So we have no qualms about having marble in certain strategic places, whether it'd be columns or the floor. The technology enhances; it is part of that excellence. It allows us to do more in a given amount of time and to communicate with the world. Technology saves us money. It makes us speedier when we respond. It used to take us the standard four to six weeks to send a product, books and tapes, you know. We can now outsource some of that to a specialized high-tech company that can have the product in the customer's hands in two to four days. So now it is almost like going to the mall—sometimes you get the product tomorrow versus what used to be a month or six weeks.

This urban megachurch thus does not see a contradiction between the things of God and the things of the world. Like the Pentecostal megachurch in the college town, it is proactively involved in modern technologies as a way to globalize its message of salvation, to bring it to the "highways and byways of life." This urban megachurch is more explicit in tying economic success with evangelical and pastoral success. As John puts it:

We are not just a ministry. Just like any other organization or business we offer services, we offer products. So we need to make things
scalable for growth, but yet efficient for a speed market. Because everything is now driven by speed. We want to make it easier for the
people who call us to get a response. On our web site there is a place
that says contact us or send us your prayer request. If we see the
word 'prayer' next to a request anywhere in that message, we can fire
an e-mail response that says "Thank you so much for your prayer request and it will be forwarded to the right person." On a daily basis an
average of two hundred e-mails come in. Once they come in, we can
scan the e-mail. Is it a prayer request? Is it about divorce? A death in
the family? The idea is to build triggers that would generate automated
responses. Right now we have about six to eight people handling mail
on a daily basis. Right after September 11, we got flooded with messages and we had to organize a phone tree to get people talking. We
got to be ready to weather the storm. When something like that happens, everybody wants to pray, everybody wants to turn to God.

We now are partnering with a firm working with artificial intelli-
gence. We are trying to develop smart software other than e-com-
merce, which the IBMs of the world are doing, software that will help
you find the optimal way of launching in a particular town or geographic area, or country, or whatever. So, we are trying to create
software that would allow us to make decisions in a predictive way,
rather than saying that we are going to try something off the wall and
see how it works. The software will take into account demographics,
geography, and average income, and other indicators that allow us to
know who people are and where people are and try to figure out
where our typical member or partner is so that we can get the message to him or her.

Such massive efforts to disseminate its message might lead one to
suppose that this urban megachurch is homogenizing Christianity, linking it to the exploding on-line mass market for religious products. However, this church deploys a glocal strategy, tailoring its products to
particular contexts, as John makes clear.

About 600,000 homes worldwide have access to our products. But
we also have our conventions in Dallas, Philadelphia, Minneapolis, in
which the local congregations work on the logistics, the transportation, the catering, the hospitality. Local volunteers who serve as ushers, for example. One of the things that we are careful [about] is not
stepping on the toes of other churches, because we don't do market
recruiting. We believe in sharing the word of God with people and in
encouraging people to give their lives to Jesus and to join a church.
But we don't have them join our church five hundred miles away. And
we try to schedule accordingly. Sundays and Wednesdays are normally

when churches have services, so we always try to avoid scheduling events on those days in other cities. And when during our meetings people come to the altar to accept Christ, the message is to plug into local churches. There are always local churches [represented] there.

We see once again that even for a megachurch that "thinks globally" and is not afraid of using marketing techniques common among transnational corporations, the local continues to play a central role. CMCs become not only a way to extend the reach of this particular congregation worldwide, but also a vehicle to seed and strengthen other local congregations in partnership in the global enterprise of capturing souls for Jesus.

NEW SELVES, OLD SELVES

Compared to the congregations cited so far, the third Pentecostal group we studied is fairly new and small. Founded in the summer of 2000 with ten people, it now has fifty members, drawn from the growing gay and lesbian population in this large southern city. Among the most interesting aspects of this congregation are the blend of traditional and transgressive beliefs and practices and the tension between anonymity and authenticity, in which CMCs play a major role. Pastor Robby characterizes his congregation thus:

> We are doctrinally conservative. We believe very firmly that Jesus Christ is the only way, the truth. A lot of what's happening today in the gay and lesbian community is because of liberal theologies that have let go of that universal message. So we are mainline, old-school conservatives. We believe in holiness and monogamy. The only form of a successful relationship is marriage. And even though we can't be married, we can still be in the eyes of God. So we perform ceremonies. Just last month I performed three. We also do monthly prayer walks. We go out in the community and do nothing but pray. We pray in the spirit quietly, over clubs, restaurants, and adult bookstores frequented by gays and lesbians, walking or riding by them. We pray for the salvation of these people, and there is a lot of spiritual warfare because they are in bondage, in the bondage of lust or drugs, which are rampant in our community. You see, the devil has a particular plan for the gay and lesbian community. He has done a lot to destroy it. That's why you see a lot of unhealthy behaviors. But God is raising the standard of holiness and our prayer walks help by changing the spiritual atmosphere in those places.

When we asked Pastor Robby how he reconciles his reliance on conservative evangelical theologies with homophobic attitudes common among evangelical Christians, he responded by affirming the power of individuals to challenge prejudice and create new, more open forms of collective identity. "We believe in the core of the Christian message among Evangelicals, but not in the ideas that we are going straight to hell just because of who we are. I always tell my congregation, 'When you go to a grocery store you don't buy everything, but buy only what you need to use at home.' I hate to use the buffet mentality here, but when you are dealing with a group of people that have been marginalized, you need to break with some old patterns. I wouldn't, for example, take literally Paul's injunction for women to be silent." This gay and lesbian congregation thus demonstrates the innovative character of religion at the grassroots, mixing and juxtaposing the "old" and the "new" in new hybrid configurations. The Internet contributes another layer to this process of hybridization, adding the tensions between anonymity and authenticity and between reality and virtuality.

> Gay and lesbian people are very electronically savvy because we have been so ostracized from the mainstream that the only places we had to meet were clubs and bars. But when we saw that this was not working, we went on-line. In fact, we have several couples here in the church that originally met on-line, where they e-mailed each other. The Internet is a safe place because you don't have to drive your car anywhere. You don't have to be seen anywhere. Lots of times, even within this church, we have had people come in who have sat in the back, who parked their cars many blocks away not to be seen. They tried to hide, to give false names. Only later did we learn [their real names]. So, because of its anonymity, the Internet is a safe outlet. Most of our growth has come from either word of mouth or our web page. We have married men struggling with their homosexuality who have seen the site and e-mailed me. By pretending to be someone else, they can seek dialogue and encouraging words. Anonymity helps people to come forth.

Pastor Robby's comments about the value of anonymity on the Internet for the growth of his congregation appear to support Rheingold's argument about the democratizing and transgressive consequences of disembodiment and dematerialization in CMCs. The fact that identities on-line are protean, not subject to the tyranny of the gaze, thwarts any efforts to regiment them and opens the possibility for experimentation. However, for Pastor Robby, anonymity is a double-edged sword. "The Internet is also a place for cruising, in the chat rooms where those destructive casual relations and promiscuity begin. In the Internet you can tell people anything, be anyone, look like anything. How can you build a life of holiness and integrity in this setting?" To address

the "negative aspects" of anonymity, Pastor Robby is planning to create "Covenant Keepers, a sort of gay man's version of Promise Keepers."

> We would have accountability partners that people can reach when
> they are struggling with the lust of the flesh. They can pray together,
> talk for a few minutes, to help in the case of a spiritual emergency.
> And here the Internet is a valuable asset, because phone calls are ex-
> pensive, letter writing takes too long. With chat rooms you can be
> there in seconds. So I would like to have Covenant Keepers chat
> rooms. They would of course be monitored very carefully so impropri-
> eties do not seep in. Anonymity helps as a first step for people who
> want to shield their identity, but the ultimate goal is to turn people's
> hearts to God rather than towards the lust of the flesh. We want the
> medium to help people to be real, to be held accountable one-on-one
> with their partners. The idea is not to be anonymous but honest with
> one another.

Thus, despite recognizing the importance of anonymity, this small
gay and lesbian congregation sees CMCs ultimately as vehicles to
rematerialize identities, to stabilize them according to a very traditional
confessional mode, where subjects seek and tell the truth about themselves (Foucault 1980).[5] Just as in the other congregations we studied,
the leadership of this small Pentecostal church rejects the more extreme
claims that CMCs are totally deterritorializing. While celebrating the
power of the Internet to create new identities and practices, Pastor
Robby is skeptical of the Internet's capacity to transcend the metaphysics of presence.

> I really believe it in my heart that the Internet is going to be the fulfill-
> ment of the prophecy that the Gospel shall go to all the corners of the
> earth. Yet I wouldn't try to start an on-line church. The Internet can
> help us reach people by allowing them to expose themselves to the de-
> gree that they are comfortable. But we move them from there, little by
> little, to get them to eventually open themselves fully. Because Chris-
> tian fellowship needs to be face-to-face. Jesus laid hands on the sick;
> he literally touched people. And you see the example of the woman
> who had the issue of blood touch the hem of Jesus' garment. So there
> is a tangibility to Christian fellowship that transcends everything. That's
> why Jesus celebrated the communion. "Taste and see that the Lord is
> good," that's what the word says.

BETWEEN REALITY AND VIRTUALITY

What then can we discern from the ways the congregations we studied use CMCs? Dawson and Hennebry (1999: 30–31) observed that "web

meisters" for new religious movements "seemed to approach the Internet simply as a tool and showed little or no appreciation for the potential downside of their efforts." While the congregations we studied approach the Internet instrumentally, they are not monolithic in their response to CMCs. These congregations respond to computer-mediated communications in diverse ways, ranging from deep skepticism of their transformative potential to nuanced acceptance of their great outreach capabilities. To the extent that we can generalize and discern patterns from our limited data, they suggest that reception of CMCs among congregations appears to be mediated by factors such as the tradition, religious doctrine, size, type of audience, and style of leadership. Mainline Protestant churches appear to approach the Internet and other electronic means of communication with more caution than do others. They see CMCs primarily as appendages to the congregation's core activities, which are centered on traditional liturgies and face-to-face interactions. For these churches, electronic communications are above all tools for efficient administration—"glorified telephone lines" that reduce the need to send out mass mailings or establish telephone trees for communication. The Internet allows these congregations to direct like-minded newcomers to the physical congregation and to keep members informed about the calendar of activities.

Religious groups that either have more experience of global and transnational missions or have a long history of living in diaspora, such as the Catholic church and Hillel, tend to have a more sanguine view of CMCs. They see the Internet as the most recent medium to enhance practices, like interpreting the Talmud or engaging in lay stewardship, that already have been taking place worldwide. Pentecostal, especially neo-Pentecostal, and charismatic churches show the greatest willingness to embrace electronic media. In fact, while mainline congregations tend to take a reactive stance vis-à-vis CMCs, seeking to adapt in order not to fall behind, Pentecostal and charismatic churches are more likely to want to be at the forefront of electronic communication. This is particularly the case for megachurches, which often use CMCs to coordinate a myriad of ministries that extend beyond the confines of their headquarters. As we saw in the case of the African American megachurch, the heavy reliance on the Internet also dovetails with the congregation's evangelical stance. Churches that make proselytism their central goal see CMCs as key to spreading a deterritorialized, universal message of salvation. These churches are more likely to see global electronic media as an essential ingredient in their mission—the great commission—which is to announce to the world the power of a personal relationship with Jesus. In this mission, self, locality, and globality intersect. This evangelical approach stands in contrast to that of congregations which have a more sacramental focus and give primacy to face-to-face encounters around ritual life.

However, it is not just proselytizing evangelical megachurches that use the Internet simultaneously to globalize and localize their religious eschatologies. The Bahá'ís, who do not advocate a sectarian message, also embrace CMCs as tools that can bring greater understanding among cultures. This perspective is rooted in the Bahá'ís' mission to achieve "unity in diversity" and to "think globally and act locally." The small congregation serving gays and lesbians offers yet another model of outreach through the Internet. The anonymous character of electronic exchanges allows a small nascent church to serve a well-educated professional community that has been marginalized because of its sexual orientation.

A final variable influencing the reception of CMCs among our congregations was leadership. Here the case of the African American megachurch is again instructive. In congregations in which material and spiritual success are closely intertwined—in a gospel of health and wealth, for example—with the head pastor as the paragon of excellence, one is more likely to see an openness to CMCs, because such media are among the most important "secular" marks of progress and power. Pastors who embody material and spiritual success are more likely to bring their congregations into the secular world of the CMCs. This move commodifies religion as much as it sacralizes the technology.

Despite these differences, all the congregations we studied shared a nondualistic view of CMCs. Rather than setting electronic communications as totally deterritorialized media against a static, homogeneous, and territorial locality, our congregations saw the Net as in dynamic interplay with their physical communities. *Pace* Castells, not all territories are washed away by the onslaught of electronic data.[6] Rather there is a complex superimposition of old and new identities and an intersection of electronic and nonelectronic maps that often result in reinforced physical locality, community, and self. Even in the case of Kumbh Mela, with which we started this chapter, disembodiment and identity shift are accompanied by a reaffirmation of presence and the real over against the virtual. Even in this extreme case of virtualization, the virtual pilgrims' photos must be dipped into the actual river to guarantee the ritual's authenticity and to ensure the power of its electronic reenactment.[7]

For the congregations we studied, the Internet is not primarily or essentially about the "virtualization of the real," erasing the distinction between virtuality and reality, which some theorists see as the fulfillment of postmodernity (M. Taylor 1999). The Internet represents a space where the faithful can reinscribe the local, where the intimacy and immediacy of the physical congregation can be stretched, beamed globally to and experienced vicariously in diaspora. For these congregations, crossing the electronic frontier is about beckoning back to the face-to-face community, about reinventing narratives of family, covenant, authenticity, and home, not about the end of the metaphysics of presence. This does not mean that congregations remain unchallenged. Networked individualism and anonymity, in particular, stand in tension with the narratives of belonging that congregations circulate through CMCs. Moreover, the emergence of multiple digitally mediated territorialities and identities crisscrossing congregations "unsettles" approaches that see the latter as bounded "local cultures," often centered around physical structures like temples, synagogues, and mosques (Ammerman 1997a; Warner and Wittner 1998; Becker 1999). In allowing congregations to make their boundaries more flexible and permeable, CMCs turn them into border zones where the global and the local, the sacred and the profane, and face-to-face and virtual networks meet. CMCs highlight how congregations are best understood as borderlands where processes of glocalization and the dialectic of deterritorialization and reterritorialization play themselves out.

CMCs are undeniably having an impact on religion. Nevertheless, like the processes of globalization with which they are closely intertwined, computer-mediated communications have a heterogeneous impact on religion. Rather than deriving sweeping generalizations and utopian or dystopian predictions from the capabilities and "metaphysical" properties of emerging technologies, as the early literature on CMCs tended to do, we need to examine the contexts in which these technologies are deployed (DiMaggio et al. 2001). In the case of religious groups, context extends beyond the religious variables of doctrine, leadership, and denomination that we highlighted. Configurations of gender, race, class, sexuality, and nation-specific digital divides also shape the deployment of CMCs. After all, digital networks are "embedded in societal structures and power dynamics," notwithstanding claims about information technology's "hypermobility and neutralization of distance" (Sassen 2000: 28). From the anchored points of view of congregations negotiating the challenges posed by the emerging communication and transportation technologies, the impact of CMCs is more heterogeneous, uncertain, and modest than the grand theorists have imagined.

5

SAVING SOULS TRANSNATIONALLY
Pentecostalism and Youth Gangs in El Salvador and the United States

Bodies and . . . environments are transversed by very different
speeds of deterritorialization, by differential speeds, whose
complementarities form continuums of intensity, but also give rise
to processes of reterritorialization.

—Gilles Deleuze

According to Erik Erickson (1968), adolescence is a perilous liminal period involving the simultaneous articulation of a strong, autonomous
self and the formation of stable social ties that ensure successful integration into community life. In the case of adolescents in postwar El
Salvador, this period is further complicated by global and national processes that generate poverty, violence, disintegration of community life,
and anomie. In this chapter, we compare and contrast the ways in
which gangs and Pentecostal churches help young Salvadorans respond
to dislocation resulting from war, migration, and economic change.[1]
According to Marcela Smutt and Jenny Miranda (1998: 11), who conducted a study sponsored by UNICEF, youth gangs (maras, as they are
known in El Salvador) are the "most important and complex cultural-
generational problem in the country in the decade of the '90s. The high
number of young people involved in this form of youth organization
and socialization and the presence [of gangs] throughout the national
territory have made this phenomenon, and its accompanying forms of
violence, an integral part of quotidian life among Salvadorans."

In our reading, gangs offer disenfranchised and dislocated Salvadoran youths discourses, practices, and forms of organization that allow them to reterritorialize their lives, that is, to reassert locality against
global forces that have torn asunder their communities and families.
Gangs also provide a context where the self can be recentered in an
intimate setting, where loyalty and collective identity are central. We

argue, however, that the localizing and reordering resources provided by gangs are themselves shot through with conflict and implicated in some of the same global processes they seek to address.

In light of these contradictions, evangelical Protestantism has emerged as an alternative space where the synthesis between self and community that Erickson saw as key to the successful negotiation of adolescence can take place. Although Pentecostals are often locked with gangs in a battle for young souls, the two groups share striking similarities in terms of their practices and the unintended consequences of their actions. Both Pentecostal churches and gangs operate through transnational networks leading to a reinscription of locality through the creation of tight-knit community and a strong sense of individual identity. Moreover, both groups, perhaps unintentionally, are implicated in reproduction and expansion of larger hegemonic dynamics, such as global crime syndicates and authoritarian regimes.

EL SALVADOR AND SALVADORAN YOUTH IN THE POSTWAR PERIOD

From 1981 to 1992, El Salvador experienced a full-scale civil war that claimed the lives of at least eighty thousand people.[2] While the conflict had local roots, traceable to centuries of sociopolitical marginalization of the vast sectors of Salvadoran society by a recalcitrant elite, it became a flash point in the geopolitical struggles that preceded the collapse of the Berlin Wall and the Soviet Union. With neighboring Nicaragua in the hands of the socialist-nationalist Sandinistas, the Reagan administration made Central America, particularly El Salvador, the linchpin in a hemispheric counterinsurgency campaign. More concretely, the United States poured upward of $4 billion to prop up a notoriously repressive and corrupt Salvadoran army in its fight against leftist guerrillas supported by the international solidarity movement in countries like Nicaragua, Cuba, Mexico, and France.

This globalized conflict had profound local effects. In addition to the large number of civilian casualties, the conflict brought widespread dislocation, uprooting about one-fifth of the country's population. Particularly in areas where the army followed a scorched-earth strategy, as in the eastern and northern parts of the country where guerrillas operated, entire villages were literally wiped off the map. This radical deterritorialization was exemplified perhaps most dramatically by the massacre at El Mozote (Danner 1994), where close to a thousand people were executed by the army, leaving just one survivor. The massacres and aerial war sent masses of people fleeing to precarious refugee camps in San Salvador and in neighboring countries like Guatemala and Honduras. Others fled to the United States, Canada, and as far away as Australia. For many Salvadorans, especially young people, the end result of all these upheavals was the dismantling of the local webs that constituted family and community life, the terrain where their daily interactions were sustained. Often men were the first to flee the conflict, leaving behind female-headed households struggling to survive. A whole generation has grown up in broken families, surrounded not by tight-knit nurturing communities but by uncertainty, violence, and death.

Agustín, a former gang member from Morazán and now a theology student in the Assemblies of God, is typical.

> I began my life in the maras when I was twelve. I was looking for something that would fill the void left in my heart; . . . you see, I come from a family that has experienced a lot of hardship. My father died when I was seven years old, when the war started. He was a soldier in the army and was killed, just like one of my older brothers. Then there was a void in my life and, knowing that my father could not fill it, I tried to look for friends. I began to drink with them, to do drugs, and to look for the money I needed to satisfy my cravings.

In this context, youth gang violence can be seen as the reproduction of antisocial and violent patterns internalized during the civil war. These patterns are now deterritorialized, displaced from the combat zones to every street and neighborhood in the country, serving as the only vehicles to resolve conflict. The pervasiveness of a culture of violence helps us understand why El Salvador has the highest annual per capita rate of homicide in the Americas (150 per 100,000), exceeding even those of Colombia and Haiti. DeCesare (1998: 23) observes that violence in El Salvador is now greater "than during the 1980s, when the civil war grabbed international headlines and hundreds of thousands of peasant refugees escaping mayhem and economic collapse sought sanctuary in the crowded slums of Los Angeles."

On the surface, by putting an end to the armed conflict and creating the conditions for reconciliation and reconstruction, the 1992 peace accords between the Salvadoran government and the guerrillas would seem to address the problem of violence. Indeed, central to the accords is the demilitarization of Salvadoran society, with a drastic reduction in the size of the army, the disarming and incorporation of the guerrillas into a competitive electoral system, and the creation of an independent civilian police. Moreover, following investigations by special commissions, the military has been "cleansed" of those in leadership positions who committed egregious human rights violations. Other important provisions of the accords include measures like the transfer of land to ensure the productive reinsertion of ex-combatants.

Despite significant advances, the impact of the peace accords in creating a peaceful and democratic El Salvador has been limited, first by endless delays in the implementation of land transfer provisions, and second by the failure of the accords to deal with the underlying causes of the conflict, the concentration of economic power in the hands of few. In fact, in the 1990s wealth has become more concentrated in El Salvador as a result of neoliberal reforms introduced by ARENA, the rightist party in power since 1989. As in other Latin American economies that have become globalized, the brunt of the "social cost" of economic restructuring has been borne by poor families, particularly by women and children. While the Salvadoran economy has continued to expand, aided by the $1.2 billion pumped into it by Salvadorans abroad, wealth has not trickled down to the masses. For one thing, the Salvadoran economy is not generating enough jobs to employ a growing young population (44 percent of the population is under seventeen). Further, new jobs tend to be in the service and construction sectors, which are characterized by low wages and instability. *Maquiladoras*, which have been one of the government's key strategies to link the Salvadoran economy to the global market, also employ many Salvadorans in similar harsh conditions. Many *maquiladoras* and export-trade zones are located in areas like San Marcos, Soyapango, Apopa, and San Martin, where the gang problem is particularly acute. The scarcity of secure well-paying jobs with full benefits has dovetailed with a drastic downsizing of the welfare state, leaving many poor families in precarious circumstances.

Like families, young people face economic insecurity. A 1997 survey of 1,025 gang members by the IUDOP (the Public Opinion Institute at the Central American University) in the greater metropolitan area of San Salvador found that 75 percent of the respondents were unemployed. Of those employed only 52 percent had stable jobs, with women more likely than men to have stable employment. Only 41 percent of those employed held "specialized occupations" as shoemakers, bakers, mechanics, and seamstresses. The rest worked as errand boys, house cleaners, drivers, and street vendors, all unskilled jobs with relatively low pay. And while gang members had an average of 8.4 years of schooling (as opposed to 4 years for the entire nation), only 32.5 percent finished high school. About 76 percent of those surveyed had dropped out of school.

In addition to the landscape of broken families and communities, drastic economic change, and educational crisis, other factors shape the lifeworld of young Salvadorans. Among them are the availability of weapons left behind by the war; a still weak civil police and judicial system; the formation of shadowy crime syndicates by ex-military men turned businessmen; and the presence of another global dimension, transnational youth gangs founded by Salvadoran immigrants in the United States, which are now operating not only in the capital but also in cities in the interior, such as San Francisco Gotera, where we conducted our fieldwork.

SALVADORAN YOUTH IN THE UNITED STATES

For many Salvadorans migration to the United States has not resulted in the fulfillment of the American dream. Mahler's (1995) study of Salvadorans in Long Island is full of poignant stories of undocumented Salvadoran migrants caught in "niches of low-paying jobs," with little security and hope for mobility—a sort of "parallel world" of disillusionment and alienation at the margins of mainstream society. What Mahler finds confirms our discussion in Chapter 2 on the subordinate insertion of Latino immigrants into the growing service sector. Some Salvadorans have been able to bring their families to the United States after saving money by working two or more jobs and rooming with several other immigrants in small apartments. However, even they have experienced considerable turmoil in the form of family and intergenerational conflicts. In addition to parental absence due to the demands of the labor market, many immigrant men became involved with women in the United States and formed new families. This set the stage for transnational conflicts, as families vied for limited resources.[3] In many cases, men abandoned their families in El Salvador or brought only the children to live in their new U.S. households, generating conflict among half-brothers and half-sisters and between children and their new stepparents.

The story of David, a Salvadoran gang member in Los Angeles who came to the United States when he was seven years old, serves to illustrate these points.

> David was initially excited about coming to the United States. He remembered thinking that "Everyone in the United States had a big car, fancy house, and lots of money." But when he arrived in Los Angeles, he and his mother lived in a tiny apartment in a small building that itself was incredibly overcrowded, with 10 to 15 people sometimes living in one apartment. His neighborhood, in the middle of Los Angeles, was teeming with other recent Salvadoran immigrants. Despite

the presence of other Salvadorans, however, he felt incredibly home-sick, as he was separated from his extended family and even from his mother. To support their new life in the United States, she cleaned houses 7 days a week, 10 to 14 hours a day. His mother remarried, and David transferred all his anger and disappointment with his biologi-cal father to his stepfather. Consequently, David refused to obey his stepfather, and his mother who was often absent. (Vigil and Yun 1996: 150–151)

Add to this complex set of problems the general crisis in urban pub-lic schools and conflicting views on parenting. According to Carmen Sosa, a counselor at Comité Hispano de Virginia, which conducts so-cial work among Hispanics in Fairfax, an area with a high concentra-tion of Salvadorans:

One of the main problems in the Latino community is how to discipline kids. The parents usually are first-generation immigrants, the majority coming from the countryside, where they are used to clearly defined roles and authority structures. The kids, on the other hand, either came to the U.S. very young or were born here. They are more used to American mores. However, their parents want them to be like they were when they grew up in El Salvador or Colombia, and this leads to conflict. Parents don't know how to deal with all the freedoms and op-tions their kids have here. They often resort to violence to discipline their kids, which in my view leads to violence at home and in the streets. Or they ignore what's going on because they really don't un-derstand this society or because they don't have the time to be there with their kids. I also have cases where parents are afraid to physically punish their kids for fear that they will report the case to the police and possibly face deportation.

Salvadoran youth thus suffer "multiple marginality," a complex host of economic, social, cultural, and ecological (spatial segregation in barrios) factors that place them at the margins of society, that push them to find alternatives sources of "attachment, commitment, involve-ment, and belief" (Vigil 1988: 11). For Salvadoran youth, multiple mar-ginality occurs transnationally: they do not find conventional vehicles for identity construction and empowerment in El Salvador or in the United States. The fact that they straddle two cultures, that they are sent back and forth from parents to grandparents or aunts and uncles across national borders, adds to the fragmentation and dislocation they feel. Trapped in a transnational cycle of marginalization, young Salva-dorans, like some other minority youths, develop their own unconven-tional subculture, social structures, and localities. This represents an attempt to reterritorialize their lives, that is, to cut social problems down to size and to deal with the structural and systemic forces that have wreaked havoc with their families and lives. Before we explore in more detail what gangs do for youths in El Salvador and the United States, we need to provide more information on the history of Salvadoran gangs as well as on their configuration and modus operandi.

TRANSNATIONAL SALVADORAN YOUTH GANGS

Maras are not a new phenomenon in El Salvador. According to Smutt and Miranda (1998: 30), the origins of Salvadoran youth gangs can be traced to the late 1950s, among students in elite high schools in San Salvador: "These students taunted and confronted each other in the streets during and after basketball games played by their high schools. These rivalries, however, did not go beyond sporadic street fights without consequences." As Salvadoran society began to slide into chaos and civil war in the 1970s, maras became more violent and organized, establishing bases in various city neighborhoods. Although it is difficult to pin down precise dates, organized Salvadoran gangs like *Mara Salvatrucha* (MS) and *Los de la 18* (the Eighteenth Street Gang, or the Eighteenth) emerged in full force in the late 1970s. As a result of the civil war, large numbers of Salvadorans and other Central Americans migrated to cities like Los Angeles, Houston, and Washington, D.C., settling in poor neighborhoods previously occupied by older, more established Latino groups such as Mexican Americans and Puerto Ricans. Particularly in Los Angeles, young Salvadoran immigrants felt the need to carve out their own space at school and in the streets vis-à-vis Chicano gangs, active in the city since the 1920s (Mazón 1985). This led to the creation of "self-defense" groups structured around national identity. Because Salvadoran youths have built a subculture in the context of a dominant Chicano culture, they have adopted a lifestyle, speech, and dress similar to that of *cholos* and *cholas* (gang members). Vigil characterizes the "choloization" of first- and second-generation Latino youth as the process of developing a hybrid culture that blends elements of both the sending and receiving societies: "Although cholos are Americanized, either by accident or by design, they refuse or are unable to be totally assimilated" (1988: 7). An example of this hybrid culture is mara language, which combines Salvadoran Spanish, Chicano Spanish, and African American English to include such words as *"pijiada"* (a beating), *"raza"* (neighborhood, gang, or Latino ancestry), and "homeboys."

Smutt and Miranda (1998: 35) estimate that the MS has thirty-five hundred members in Los Angeles County alone, with possibly as many as eight thousand in California. The Eighteenth Street Gang, on the other hand, is considered the largest gang in Los Angeles, with more than ten thousand members. In contrast to the MS, the Eighteenth has a reputation for being panethnic. It has moved from its Chicano origins in the Pico Union District of Los Angeles and is now dominated by Salvadorans. Nevertheless, the gang has members of other Latin American nationalities and even includes Asian Americans and some African Americans. Both the MS and the Eighteenth have established chapters virtually everywhere there are Salvadorans, especially in Long Island; Fairfax and Alexandria, Virginia; and Langley Park, Maryland.

The formation in 1992 of a special antigang unit at the INS, together with changes in immigration laws that have made it easier to deport aliens who have committed crimes, has added a transnational dimension to Salvadoran gangs. In 1993, seventy gang members were deported back to El Salvador. A year later, six hundred Salvadorans with criminal records, including gang activity, were sent back, and of the more than twelve hundred Salvadorans deported by 1996, more than half were connected to gangs. Because of their hybrid *cholo* identity, many of the deported find themselves alienated from Salvadoran culture. In a context of high unemployment, social breakdown, and violence, deported gang members have been able to form Salvadoran chapters of their gangs quickly. In the metropolitan area of San Salvador alone, the National Civilian Police has identified fifty-four *clicas* (cliques) connected with the largest Salvadoran maras in the United States.[4] Smutt and Miranda (1998: 38) have found that the connection between Salvadoran and U.S. groups is so tight that local actions, like the peace accords between the MS and the Eighteenth in San Martín and El Congo, small western towns, are not considered valid without approval from Los Angeles. In the IUDOP survey of gang members in San Salvador, close to 20 percent of those interviewed indicated they had entered the gangs in the United States. The great majority (99 out of 111) had joined gangs in Los Angeles.

Despite the close links between U.S.- and Salvadoran-based gangs, DeCesare has shown that transnational relations are not without conflict. On the one hand, maras in El Salvador respect those who have been gang members in the United States. They are considered older brothers, wiser and closer to the originative gang experience. Nevertheless, many gang leaders in Los Angeles and Washington, D.C., criticize those in El Salvador for being "wild," "reckless," interested only in "*el vacil*" " (the fun and games associated with gang life) and not concerned about *la raza* and the neighborhood. This critique has filtered down to El Salvador through the transnational networks. Smutt and Miranda (1998: 38) quote Julio, a gang member in El Salvador:

> There are many *vatos* [guys, gang members] from Los Angeles who don't like what goes on here [*el rollo aquí*]. When they return to Los Angeles they say that here [in El Salvador] we rape, kill children, and that is not approved of. There [the United States] they respect children, being Salvadoran, you respect your partner [*compa*]. So the styles are different, because those who come to form *clicas* of the MS in El Salvador are those who have had problems there [Los Angeles] with the *vatos* in the *mara*. They are kind of mercenaries, they kill for enjoyment and because of that the MS doesn't want to see them. And because they can't find refuge there they come here.

Julio's declaration provides clear evidence of transnationalism among Salvadoran gang members. To borrow from Basch, Glick Schiller, and Szanton Blanc (1994: 7), gang members "forge and sustain multi-stranded social relations that link together their societies of origin and settlement." Gang members, like other transmigrants, "take actions, make decisions, and develop subjectivities and identities embedded in networks of relationships that connect them simultaneously to two or more nation-states."

YOUTH GANGS, LOCALITY, AND THE NETWORK SOCIETY

Now that we have enough elements to understand the history, composition, and field of activity of Salvadoran gangs, we can ask why Salvadoran youths join these groups. As Jankowski (1991: 313) reminds us: "It is a gross oversimplification to attribute all gang members' reason for joining a gang to any one motive, such as the lack of a father figure, the desire to have fun, or submission to intimidation. Gangs are composed of individuals who join for a wide variety of reasons." Nevertheless, we can discern some patterns among Salvadorans. For example, Larry Carrasco, a twenty-year-old leader in Barrios Unidos, a group of former gang members that works to promote social awareness, explains the appeal of youth gangs in the following terms:

> There ain't nothing here for us young Latinos. No jobs, no rec places, you know, like places to play *futbol* [soccer] or basketball. The schools stink and the police is racist. Our parents ain't there or just want us to be like them. But you have your homies *que te alivianan* [who help and take care of you]. You have your barrio where you live *la vida loca con tu raza* [a crazy life with your race—your people/gang]. And *la vida*

loca vale [crazy life is worth it], you know, because you're saying that you're somebody to be respected. It is a way of telling your parents, teachers, the police to go to hell. [Interview conducted in English]

Along the same lines, Dimas, an eighteen-year-old Salvadoran who recently left the MS, reflects on his experience: "Gang life is crazy but it has some good things about it. If you live by the rules you're somebody, somebody for your brothers. They respect you and are loyal to you. You belong to some place, your barrio, with your homeboys, which you defend from outsiders, even if they are just other Latinos."

Larry and Dimas demonstrate that gangs contribute to the simultaneous reaffirmation of self, family (as an extended community), and place. Gangs allow young Salvadorans to respond to dislocation and multiple marginalities by reasserting territory in the most radical way. Through initiation beatings and turf battles centered on the neighborhood, gangs reconstruct local geographies in response to the deterritorializing processes they confront. These geographies not only resignify the space where gang members have been segregated, revalorizing these "ecologically inferior" spaces (Vigil 2002), but also introduce "territories of the subject" (Pile and Thrift 1995). Scars and mara tattoos inscribe identity and belonging on the bodies of gang members, making the self part of the constructed landscape. Just as graffiti marks the territory the gang controls, tattoos map a way of life and a sense of belonging and group control on the body of the gangbanger. As Appadurai (1996: 179) reminds us: "A great deal of what has been termed *rites of passage* is concerned with the production of what we might call *local subjects*, actors who properly belong to a situated community of kin, neighbors, friends, and enemies. Ceremonies of naming and tonsure, scarification and segregation, circumcision and deprivation are complex social techniques for the inscription of locality onto bodies. Looked at slightly differently, they are ways to embody locality as well as to locate bodies in socially and spatially defined communities." In other words, *la vida loca* is a gang's creative way of "being in the world," a way to rearticulate selfhood, locality, and community at the margins of national and global processes. In the Washington, D.C., area, many Salvadorans have tended to concentrate in geographic enclaves that correspond to the towns from which they migrated. There is, for example, the now famous area of Chirilandria in Alexandria, Virginia, made up of Salvadorans from the town of Chirilagua.

To understand the full localizing thrust behind youth gangs, we can draw from Manuel Castells's discussion of the network society and informational capitalism that characterize contemporary society. According to Castells (1996: 469), because of recent changes in information technology, "networks constitute the new social morphology of our society." In this "society of the Net," social actors organized as flexible, decentralized, and open-ended interconnected networks of local nodes thrive, while traditional corporate actors such as unions and political parties suffer. Working under the shape of global capitalism, the Net creates "a sharp divide between valuable and non-valuable people and locales. Globalization proceeds selectively, including and excluding segments of economies and societies in and out of the networks of information, wealth, and power, that characterize the new dominant system" (1998: 161–162). Castells calls those social segments excluded by the new economy "the black holes of informational capitalism," which together form a Fourth World of often territorially confined and "systemically worthless populations, disconnected from networks of valuable functions and people." People in these black holes, in turn, form "defensive" identities, "trenches of resistance and survival on the basis of principles different from, or opposed to those permeating the institutions of society" (1997: 8).

People in these trenches seek to find value in identities denigrated by the system and in localities shut off by globalization. They operate according to the principle of "the exclusion of the excluders by the excluded. That is, the building of defensive identity in the terms of dominant institutions/ideologies, reversing the value judgement while reinforcing the boundary" (Castells 1997: 9). Facing a condition of multiple recalcitrant exclusion, young Salvadorans in El Salvador and the United States "may then refuse to accept the rules of the democratic game, or accept them only partially. Their response may then become social *violence*. The economically excluded do not become individual or collective subjects in the newly emerging public and political sphere: They may resist and protest, living under different rules, the rules of violence. Their (limited) energies and resources are not geared to integration, 'acting out' instead of participating; at times, this is manifest in forms of communitarian resistance" (Jelin 1998: 408).

The foregoing discussion would seem to imply that gangs provide transnational spaces for the articulation of subaltern oppositional practices. While this carries an element of truth, Castells's and Jelin's assertions indicate that reality is more contradictory: gangs may oppose the systems that have marginalized them, but they do so by recognizing and reproducing the exclusion, by failing to produce subjects empowered to participate in the system in order to transform it. This reality challenges scholars who see transnationalism "as something to celebrate, an expression of a subversive popular resistance 'from below'" (Guarnizo and Smith 1998: 5). In these romantic portraits, "cultural hybridity, multi-positional identities, border-crossing by marginal 'others,' and transnational business practices by migrant entrepreneurs are depicted as conscious and successful efforts by ordinary people to escape control and domination 'from above' by the capital and the state."

The experiences of Salvadoran gangs reveal that transnationalism does not always result in the formation of transgressive, counter-hegemonic subjects. Building further on Castells's work, we might even say that the construction of a rebellious identity through *la vida loca* is "a twisted mirror of informational culture" defined by a "culture of urgency, . . . a culture of the end of life, not of its negation, but of its celebration. Thus everything has to be tried, felt, experimented, accomplished, before it's too late, since there is no tomorrow" (Castells 1997: 64). Gang identity would be a type of "communal hyper-individualism," or as Jankowski (1991: 28) puts it, "organized defiant individualism." Such individualism combines a radical Hobbesian emphasis on the self and the immediate gratification of its needs—be it respect, catharsis, or the latest brand of sneakers—with a reactive defense of immediate networks and localities. Indeed, in the IUDOP survey of gang members in San Salvador, 46 percent of the respondents affirmed that they joined gangs for "*el vacil*" (the gang's carefree life-style). This percentage is substantially higher than those for "problems with parents" (12.3), "lack of understanding" (10.3), and "searching for protection" (5.8), the other significant responses offered. In addition, slightly more than 60 percent indicated that what they liked the most about gang life was "el vacil" and "*llevarse bien con los homeboys*" (getting along well with fellow gang members), demonstrating again the simultaneous affirmation of self, family, and locality enshrined in "communal hyper-individualism." A further example of this tense affirmation is provided by an untitled poem by Nika, who is involved in the Washington chapter of Barrios Unidos.

> It's hard to think straight when you lose somebody you love.
> You look for the easiest way to escape tu pasado y tu dolor homes.
> La botella de whiskey and the funny cigarettes que make you laugh
>   becomes your family
> And the trigger of a .45 becomes part of you,
> They beat at the same beat that your heart does.
> They all embrace you in a circle of bittersweet memories.
> The feelings que te dan cuando te hacen volar compadre,

Te llevan a tocar las clouds, they play a sweet melody that you don't
want it to stop.
It's love, it's friendship, it's sadness, it's triumph, it's sorrow, it's
darkness, it's light.
Oh, who gives a fuck homes, nobody man, nobody.
It's only us now young'n, it's only us . . . Drink me! Inhale me! Smell my
sweet aroma.
Take me higher, don't ever let me go.
Take me sweet Mary, indulge me sweet Jane, soy tuyo Baby.
Has de mí lo que tú quieras. I'm yours, take me 'cause I don't give a
fuck no more.

While Castells is right in seeing gangs as local, highly territorialized cultures of urgency that are "the reverse expression of global time-
lessness," we would like to take his argument further and propose that
gangs are not just defensive reactions to contemporary social change,
particularly globalization as expressed by transnational migration. Gangs
not only oppose globalization (in ways that reproduce its exclusionary
effects) but also may participate actively in global processes. In other
words, gangs deterritorialize as much as they reterritorialize.

Journalists have uncovered the way organized crime, including the
Colombian drug cartels, the Mexican Mafia, and other U.S. gangs, has
taken advantage of the neoliberal push to open markets to set up
"branches in countries such as El Salvador and [recruit] new foot soldiers from among the poor and veterans of the region's recently ended
civil wars" (Farah and Robberson 1995; see also Alder 1994; O'Connor
1994; Wallace 2000). Transnational gangs like the MS and the Eighteenth are now becoming part of a "growing array of organized crime
rings that specialize in cross-border trafficking and have turned Central America and Mexico into a hemispheric clearinghouse for drugs,
contraband and stolen property." A particularly flourishing transnational business for Salvadoran gangs has been indiscriminate kidnapping
and smuggling stolen vehicles and car parts, some of which have been
traced to Belize, Colombia, and Jamaica.[5]

Castells himself discusses how transnationalism allows for the formation of networks in the informal economy (particularly that sector
connected to criminal activities) that mimic the modus operandi of global capitalism. According to Castells (1998: 179): "The key to the success and expansion of global crime in the 1990s is the flexibility and
versatility of their organization. Networking is their form of operation,
both internally, in each criminal organization, . . . and in relation to

other criminal organizations. Distribution networks operate on the basis of autonomous local gangs, to which they supply goods and services, and from which they receive cash." Castells elaborates: "It is this combination of flexible networking between local turfs, rooted in tradition and identity, in a favorable institutional environment, and the global reach provided by strategic alliances, that explains the organizational strength of global crime" (180). In this sense, youth gangs such as the MS and the Eighteenth are part of a "perverse connection" in which crime takes advantage of "desperate attempts" to affirm identity, community, and place to "foster the development of a global criminal economy" (337).

If young gangs betray the desires of their members for self-recognition and for solidarity and intimacy in the face of globalization by reinscribing global processes at the heart of *la vida loca*, what options are left?

SAVING PABLO

To illustrate how churches provide alternative ways for young Salvadorans to negotiate dislocation and multiple marginality, we focus on the testimony of Pablo, a twenty-four-year-old former mara member who is now a minister in training in the Assemblies of God in San Francisco Gotera, Morazán. Pablo got involved in the maras in El Salvador when he was fourteen, recruited during his frequent visits to San Miguel, the most populous city in the area, as he sought to escape "the boredom of Gotera." After years of petty criminal activity in high school, he left for Langley Park, Maryland, to join his mother and "to get away from it all." There he entered a drug gang and eventually became the leader of 144 youths. Pablo characterizes his life as a gang member before his religious conversion:

> My life was real garbage because I lived in the streets. When I worked, I used the money to buy drugs. I felt strong; I felt that I was on top of the world, that I was handsome, and a superman. And yet, quite the contrary, I was getting thinner and thinner. People would tell me that in the U.S. you are supposed to get strong because of the food. "Why don't you get vitamins?" I would respond yes, but in my mind I was thinking of buying marijuana, that will make me strong. Eventually I didn't just buy the drug, I also sold it with my gang. I also started ingesting drugs. I snorted coke, drank alcohol, and smoked crack.

One day, some of his friends disappeared. After asking around, he learned that a mysterious van, which he thought was associated with the INS, had taken them. Later he found out his friends had been taken to a church for rehabilitation.

> And from then on I also wanted to look for God, so I started to search for the address of the church, calling numbers in the phone directory. I told all the pastors: "I want to change my life. I don't want to be what I am anymore. I am trapped by drugs and alcohol. I need somebody to help me." But I couldn't find the right phone number, because the church had just set up the house, a home especially for young people trying to get away from the drug. Finally, the van arrived again. I saw some policemen get down from the van; for a moment, I thought that they were immigration agents because they were wearing suits and ties; their hair was short and prim; they had shaved and were wearing nice shoes. I didn't recognize them. But then I looked at them more closely and they were my friends. And they told me, "Hey, *Flaco*, get up and let's go. We are taking you to the church." And I went. It was a wonderful experience to arrive at my new home. In two days I received the fullness of the Holy Spirit and I began to pray for my family, my family who were the guys in my new home.

For all its intensity, the conversion proved short-lived. Within a week of his conversion Pablo returned to the streets and drug addiction. The police arrested him, took him to jail, and eventually transferred him to an INS detention center.

> Then I humbled myself before God. I asked Him for forgiveness for everything I had done. I told him I wanted to be a clean person. I told him that if he got me out of jail that I would never turn my back on him. And God helped me grow spiritually in jail. In jail I taught the Bible, prayers, and hymns to young people. One day American *hermanos* [missionaries from the Assemblies] came to preach and I accepted God again. I didn't care that they spoke English. God was building up my soul. My heart was joyous; I didn't feel sad or frustrated because I was in jail. Then I was sent back here [El Salvador]. And I came directly to this church [the Assemblies of God in Gotera, Morazán]. You see, the *hermanos* here knew about me, they prayed every day for me. They came looking for me once they knew I had arrived in Morazán after eight months in the INS detention center in the U.S.

After joining the church in Morazán, Pablo started working with the youth ministry. "I'm the commander of the Explorers of the Kingdom," he states with great pride. The Explorers, who include former gang members, are youths training to stay away from the contaminating power of street vices. These young men, many recently returned from the United States, "are learning how to control themselves. They are taking control of their lives not through drugs but through the spirit of God. You see, a Christian person must live in brotherhood. That is what I preach to young people; they must walk in brotherly love. Just as Christ loved us, so we must walk. A Christian home must persevere in love. Today when we get home, we behave more like wolves."

PENTECOSTALISM'S MULTIPLE TERRITORIALITIES

Pablo's case raises several important points in relation to the roles Pentecostalism plays vis-à-vis transnational Salvadoran gangs. First, Pentecostal churches operate transnationally due to a mixture of theological and sociological variables. In Pentecostalism, conversion marks a radical transformation, an experience of being born again in Jesus Christ. It follows then that the greater the sin, the greater the glory to God, who has redeemed an utterly depraved sinner. Gang members, who have rejected all societal conventions to live a life of crime and drug addiction, are among the greatest sinners. This logic, in effect, turns conversions of gang members into symbols of status, signs that the churches which achieve them are filled with the spirit and thus should be taken seriously in the fierce competition for souls that now characterizes the Salvadoran religious field. Since gangs are transnational, churches must follow their potential converts, tracking them, as in the case of Pablo, across national borders. This is not difficult for a global organization like the Assemblies of God, which can mobilize its network of local congregations to deal with the challenges posed by transnational migration. Pablo, who has experienced a transnational conversion, now becomes the anchor for local efforts in local prisons to convert other transnational gang members. Working with other transnational youth ministers he has been able to bring "about fifteen" former gang members to the church. Several of these gang members have been deported from the Washington, D.C., area.

Pablo's case supports Berryman's (1999) contention that Pentecostalism has grown rapidly throughout the Americas largely because Pentecostal churches function as Castells's network society, that is, as decentralized, flexible yet integrated networks providing customized services and goods to individuals and communities. Pentecostalism succeeds because it combines deterritorialization (the operation of transnational webs) with reterritorialization (recentering of self and community). As Droogers (2001) observes, the notions of space and territory have always been central to evangelical Christianity, since it takes seriously Jesus' great commission: "Go therefore and make disciples of all nations, baptizing them in the name of the Father and of the Son and of the Holy Spirit" (Matt. 28:16–20). Indeed, "while on the one hand Pentecostalism preaches the rejection of the outside world, on the other hand the world is transformed into the most intense battleground. In the battle against Satan it is necessary to invade his territory, to spread the testimony of conversion to the very heart of unbelief and sin" (Waldo 2001: 32). Recently, a genre of evangelical Christian literature called "spiritual warfare" has exploded onto the scene. According to this literature, missionary work among urban groups like gangs involves first of all a "spiritual mapping," "the discipline of diagnosing the obstacles to revival in a given community. Through fervent prayer and diligent research, practitioners are able to measure the landscape of the spiritual dimension and discern moral gateways between it and the material world" (Otis 1999: 256). Spiritual mapping is followed by "strategic-level spiritual warfare," which involves "power encounters" against spirits that "have authority over places and territories, such as buildings, cities, and temples. Additionally, they appear to have authority over social organizations and groups, and influence sinful behavior such as homosexuality, drug addiction, lust, incest, rape, and murder" (Kraft 1992: 19). In the struggle to break down demonic strongholds, profane territory must be sacralized through "prayer walks," "pilgrimages of repentance," and other "street-level intercessions" in the targeted neighborhoods (Wagner 1992, 1993).

For Pablo, this reterritorialization is marked by his identification of the church with his "new home," his "new family." The solidarity and intimacy Pablo found in the gang gives way to new intense and close ties within the safe environment of the congregation, where he can learn to control himself through the spirit of God. The rearticulation of family and a place called home is accompanied by the emergence of a new, cleansed self. While the physical scars of his involvement with the mara remain, Pablo now inscribes a new locality onto his body by wearing the signs that mark his "community of the elect"—his neatly cut hair, his carefully ironed shirts and pants, his deliberate yet soft voice.[6] The testimony of Juan José, an eighteen-year-old former gang member in Morazán, mirrors Pablo's experience:

> There have been times this month that I have felt tortured [atormentado], but because the power of Jesus is great I have been able to contain them [the members in his gang] no matter how hard they have tried. I base my life on Jesus because by myself the gang would be dangerous. When I wasn't Christian and I didn't go [to gang meetings], they would beat me and six of them would follow me around.

> Now they see me and send me messages from Tabuco [the gang
> leader] that they will spy [*vijiar*] on me with their weapons, their guns,
> and I felt my heart [beat fast] but I began to pray and everything went
> away. You feel it in your heart, things have changed.

Amid the dislocation and inequity that characterize Latin America, sociologist David Martin argues, evangelical Christianity represents a "migration of the spirit" through which poor people break the ties that bind them to their precarious condition. In Martin's reading, Pentecostalism helps "to implant new disciplines, re-order priorities, counter corruption and destructive machismo, and reverse the indifferent and injurious hierarchies of the outside world. Within the enclosed haven of faith a fraternity can be instituted under firm leadership, which provides for release, for mutuality and warmth, and for the practice of new roles" (1990: 284). Pentecostalism indeed allows gang members like Pablo to break with their "communal hyper-individualism" and to articulate a new form of relational self. In other words, Pablo breaks with previous ties (i.e., the gang, with all its notions of loyalty and honor) and rebuilds new strong ties within the "enclosed haven of faith." There he learns about "mutuality and warmth" ("brotherhood and love," in his own words), as well as about discipline ("control," as he puts it). Pentecostalism has, in effect, redrawn Pablo's lived geography: now his new sanctioned territory is the church, as the community of the elect, and his body, over which he must establish sovereignty.

While Pentecostalism's reterritorialization is couched in the language of control and brotherly love, that language frequently includes vivid war imagery. The struggle to build a new self and community takes on the trappings of a cosmic war against evil, a Manichean conflagration that pits God and his armies (with a battalion under Pablo's command) against Satan and his minions. As Pablo puts it: "We are in a day-to-day struggle with the enemy, Satan. He's always trying to make us fall, to trick us, to get inside of us. Only strong prayer can defeat him." In El Salvador, this rhetoric of spiritual warfare displaces remnants of the civil war, such as crime and the culture of violence, to the symbolic field. Put another way, the physical violence that pervades everyday life in El Salvador as a result of sociopolitical change now finds a safe outlet in the struggle to produce controlled, disciplined subjects of a sovereign God. Through Pentecostalism, young people, the segment of the population with the greatest potential for violent, destructive behavior, can redirect their energy to the spiritual struggle of staying clean and of cleansing society.

Martin (1990: 44) argues that in Latin America, evangelical Christianity, particularly Pentecostalism, is contributing to, among other things, a "feminization of the male psyche." With its fierce moral asceticism, Pentecostalism is transforming the Hispanic-Catholic culture of machismo by helping create peaceable subjects who find the violence of the state or guerrillas, the Right and the Left, "deeply repugnant" (267). Roque, a twenty-two-year-old former gang member, now a youth pastor at the Assemblies of God in San Francisco Gotera, illustrates Martin's point. He characterizes his encounter with Jesus Christ in the following terms: "Since that moment there was total change, a radical change in my life. My nasty thoughts, my mind, everything that I had inside, the hatred [el rencor], the emptiness, all fell by the wayside."

Conversions to Pentecostalism among gang members have significant implications for the democratic transition in El Salvador. After all, democracy is not built just on free elections and a competitive party system. The foundations of democracy go beyond institutions like parliaments and court systems to what Jelin (1998) has called a "culture of citizenship," where all social actors, institutions, movements, and individuals share a civic, intersubjective world. From Pablo's testimony, it would seem that Pentecostalism is "domesticating" Salvadoran youths' most destructive behaviors in response to multiple transnational marginalities. Angel Reyes, a deacon at Prince of Peace, a Salvadoran Pentecostal church in Hyattsville, Maryland, puts it bluntly: "We started in an apartment in Virginia, and we were evicted after two services for singing and praying. It made no sense, because the building was full of people who drank and fought. The authorities should be grateful because we rescue so many people they can't control. In those two services, we saved five people" (Constable 1995). Along these lines, evangelical Protestant churches in El Salvador have formed a movement called "United Against Delinquency," which, in addition to organizing prayer vigils (jornadas de oración), stresses the need for prevention rather than harsher law enforcement. United Against Delinquency emphasizes the need to return to "moral and Christian values" and to strengthen institutions like families, schools, and churches, "in which the individual learns to socialize and integrate into society" (Diario de Hoy, July 27, 2000).

The work of Pentecostal churches among transnational youth gangs is helping to reweave the moral fabric of postwar El Salvador. Here our findings are in line with a growing literature that points toward the transformative potential of Pentecostalism in the Americas (Garrard-Burnett and Stoll 1993; Cleary and Stewart-Gambino 1997; Shaull and Cesar 2000). With its emphasis on the collective and personal experience of the sacred rather than on high theology, and its capacity to address the most pressing problems of the poor (illness, alcoholism, and the violence of everyday life), Pentecostalism is truly a grassroots religion. However, Pentecostalism among Salvadoran youth gangs is not without contradictions. Pentecostalism offers mara members a disciplinary and bellicose articulation of self and space that may hinder the production of a truly participatory and deeply rooted democracy in El Salvador.

The relation between religion and discipline has received substantial attention in the sociology of religion. Weber (1958) and Tawney (1926) explored how the notions of calling and this-worldly asceticism among Puritans and Calvinists gave rise to values such as self-discipline, individualism, and acquisitiveness that contributed to the emergence of modern capitalism. E. P. Thompson (1966: 361), in turn, documented how the Wesleyan call for a "methodical cultivation of the soul" served to discipline the English working class, helping the "millowner 'to organize his moral machinery on equally sound principles with his mechanical.'" Thompson's argument has been extended by Ong (1987) to analyze the role of Islamic revival in regulating sexuality and family life among female industrial workers in Malaysia. We go beyond these economy-based readings to suggest that the work of Pentecostal churches among youth gangs involves a deeper logic of discipline and domination, one that takes place at the level of "subjectivation," to borrow Foucault's term.

In his later work Foucault studied the link between Christianity and what he called "techniques of the self," practices that "permit individuals to effect, by their own means, a certain number of operations on their own bodies, on their own souls, on their own thoughts, on their own conduct, and this in a manner so as to transform themselves, modify themselves, and to attain a certain state of perfection, of happiness, of purity, of supernatural power, and so on" (Carrette 1999: 162). Among these techniques are confession and self-examination, part of a general "discourse of self-disclosure" that constitutes self around the need to "declare aloud and intelligibly the truth about oneself." Foucault ties these techniques to the rise of modern disciplinary society, which he documented in his works on prisons, hospitals, and asylums. While the testimonial, which is central to Pentecostalism, is different from confession, it is a technique of the self defined by the "tyranny of the gaze." The issue, then, is whether there is an elective affinity between self-surveillance in Pentecostalism and the panoptical society built by the Salvadoran military during the civil war. More concretely, we need to ask whether Pentecostalism, in appeasing the communal hyper-individualism of gang members, is not also producing "docile subjects" not empowered to participate fully in the democratic experiment. In other words, while Pentecostalism might be producing peaceable and disciplined subjects, it may be less successful at eroding the larger culture of domination and subordination that has plagued El Salvador. In fact, Pentecostalism may exacerbate and legitimize this culture by mapping the sacred onto it.

When asked why one of the groups in which he participates is called Castles of the King (*castillos del rey*), Pablo replies: "It is called like that because God is our true king. But his kingdom is not of this world, the world as we know it with all its sins. All we can do is be soldiers for him, fight Satan, and convince people to join his castle. And because we really know sin, ex-mara members are some of the best soldiers. But in the end it will only be him [Jesus Christ] who will build his kingdom with fire, when the wicked will be condemned and the righteous saved."

As a key eschatological image in Christianity, the notion of the kingdom of God has been the subject of multiple interpretations. Pohl (1999) shows how the kingdom of God has consistently been a metaphor of hospitality, reconciliation, and fullness in the Christian tradition. A particularly poignant example is the representation of the kingdom as a communal feast to which everyone is invited. Liberation theology, for its part, presents the kingdom of God as the telos, the divine fulfillment of human history. In contrast, among gang members who have become Pentecostals, the kingdom of God points to a time and space that is qualitatively different from, even opposed to, profane history. The kingdom of God is a sacred territory that, at the end of time, erupts into and cancels the fleeting and flawed world of human praxis. It is true that God acts in this world through the tangible gifts of the Holy Spirit, healing the bodies and psyches of gang members. These charismas, however, are but incomplete (albeit powerful) signs of an eschatological reality in which only those who have accepted Jesus as their savior will participate. In other words, for our informants, the inbreaking of the kingdom does not refer to a real but fragile "city on the hill" or "beloved community" on this earth, but to an individualized sense of redemption within a highly particularistic group.

Eladio, a former gang member now in the Assemblies of God in Gotera, offers a good example of how the notion of the kingdom of God operates among mara converts. When asked about his future, he states: "I don't know where I will be. If Jesus Christ has not come yet, maybe I'll be studying in another place or at the university. I really don't care. I'm in the things of God [*las cosas de Dios*]. If God wants something to happen in my life, it will happen. He is all-powerful in his majesty. Only that which pleases him happens." Eladio's sense of fate is predicated on the surrender of his agency, the exercise of which has, in his view, brought him only trouble. Eladio sets up a sharp dichotomy between his free will, which has led him to drugs and suffering, and God's will, which has given him peace and joy. In his words: "I lived in the world [*anduve por el mundo*], but God rescued me. I saw the things of the world and they were a hell, they were rotten to the core. The world is the path of death [*el camino de la muerte*]. But now I abide [*persevero*] in God's way and fulfill his commandments and his laws [*estatutos*]." Because the former gang members whom we interviewed construct a dichotomy between the "things of the world and the things of God," they attempt to establish an exclusionary territory that limits their participation in the outside world. Thus, when asked about the role of the church in politics, Juan José, whom we met before, answered: "No, the commitment [*compromiso*] of the church is to take the message, that is the one and only goal, to take the message of salvation, and the rest must be left alone. The world of corruption is something that must be forgotten. The world and people are going to stay just as they are now. It is their choice."

Prima facie, the rejection of "the things of the world" and the affirmation of the kingdom of God at the end of time appear to be a radical theological deterritorialization, marking the emergence of a new divine geography that puts an end to all human attempts at dominion. The deterritorialization enshrined in the notion of the kingdom of God represents an unequivocal refusal to partake in "principalities and powers" in the secular world, including globalization. The Pentecostal believer is ultimately not a citizen in any hegemonic nationalist or transnational project, but a subject of God's reign. What we have here is an "absolute space, the space of religion," consisting of "the places of what has no place, or no longer has a place—the absolute, the divine, or the possible" (Lefebvre 1991: 163–164).

There are nevertheless countervailing dynamics at play. The ex-gang members we interviewed also imagine the kingdom as a dominion under an utterly sovereign subject, *el "varón de varones,"* [the lord of lords], God. This dominion is territorialized in and mirrored by the hierarchical structures of the churches to which our informants belong. Despite claims of otherworldliness, converted gang members act as "territorial spirits," to borrow from evangelical Christian theologian George Otis, of a particular kind of rulership, commanders and soldiers in God's army in the struggle to defend and expand his kingdom in the here and now. Among the ex-mara Pentecostals we interviewed, the kingdom of God is an "ultralocalized extraterritoriality" (Hervieu-Leger 2002: 102).

As Adrian Hastings (1997) argues, this ultralocalized extraterritoriality can become associated with national projects of manifest destiny with potentially explosive effects. For example, notions of spiritual warfare and the kingdom of God were central in the discourse of nationhood articulated by middle-class charismatic Christians in Central America (Freston 2001). In Guatemala in the early 1980s, morality, order, and discipline became intertwined with right-wing nationalism and geopolitics under born-again general Efraín Ríos Montt. Ríos Montt saw himself as a latter-day King David battling the forces of evil to build a "New Jerusalem." In the construction of the new Guatemala, the struggle for "one soul at a time" and for a morally reformed society became "a divinely sanctioned 'final battle against subversion'" (Garrard-Burnett 1998: 138–161). In Ríos Montt's eyes, subversion, poverty, and violence "were not the product of inequality or class conflict, but the products of the 'rottenness of mankind.' This rottenness, he said in 1982 'has a name: communism, or the Antichrist, and all means must be used to exterminate it'" (148). This rhetoric justified a brutal scorched-earth campaign in the Guatemalan highlands, where many indigenous groups lived. We see how the radically deterritorializing thrust of the notion of God's dominion can lead to the literal obliteration of whole communities.

It has become common practice among secular Latin American intellectuals to raise the specter of Ríos Montt to disqualify Pentecostalism politically. Ríos Montt's case is unique, a peculiar combination of *caudillismo*, the Reagan administration's cold-war politics, and the premillenarianism of the Church of the Word (Verbo), to which the general belonged. Ríos Montt might have acted more as a soldier than as a Pentecostal, given that he did not grow up as an evangelical Christian (see Garrard-Burnett 1996). Even with these caveats, however, that the general was able to use the Pentecostal theology to frame his antiinsurgency campaign in cosmic terms is an indication of the dangers in Pentecostalism's rhetoric of discipline, war, and territory.

The language of dualism and spiritual warfare among Pentecostals may be attributed to their being embedded in the hostile context of chaotic transitions to democracy. Perhaps Pentecostal congregations are "experimental capsules" with a "latent capacity [for] cultural change held in religious storage to emerge over time when the circumstances are propitious to activate them, or when things are safe enough for people to make open political claims" (Martin 1990: 44). Or perhaps the opposite is true. Contrary to Martin's claims that Pentecostalism feminizes the psyche, we may hypothesize that the disciplinary and bellicose worldview among former gang members who have converted to Pentecostalism exacerbates the violent and exclusionary patterns that have characterized Salvadoran life by making them into a life-and-death struggle for souls. By displacing the war from the social to the spiritual, Pentecostalism turns the multiple marginalities experienced by transnational Salvadoran youths into a religious sectarianism grounded on a dualistic worldview. If to be a true Christian is to wage total moral war on an omnipresent satanic enemy, Pentecostalism can give rise only to narrow selves in tension with the cosmopolitan pluralism that, according to philosopher Charles Taylor (1998), is an essential ingredient of robust democracies. The words of César, a twenty-year-old former gang member now attending a Pentecostal church in Arlandria, are illustrative: "There are times when I wish that the angel of Jehovah would come down and burn the world in its wickedness [*inundicia*], and maybe then we Christians can finally be at peace, not tempted, as we always are, by all the vices of the world that made me fall and become a mara member."

RELIGION AND THE PRODUCTION OF HETEROGENEOUS SPACE

Despite sharp ideological differences, transnational Salvadoran gangs and Pentecostal churches exhibit many similarities. What we have here is a fierce competition between two polycentric, flexible transnational networks attempting to redraw cartographies for a displaced population. Gangs and Pentecostal churches simultaneously deterritorialize and reterritorialize, producing spaces that have contradictory consequences for individuals and their societies. Gangs reterritorialize, creating hybrid selves and subcultures anchored in marked bodies and geographically bounded spaces (the street or the neighborhood). While these personal and local spaces may serve to nurture "cartographies of resistance" (Harvey 1996: 290) against marginalization and exploitation, they can also become isolated islands of expressivism, mirroring the globalized culture of immediate gratification. Further, the incorporation of gangs as foot soldiers in the global drug trade points to the fragility and contradictory nature of their "militant particularism."

Scholars have shown that Pentecostalism in the Americas exhibits great diversity on the ground and sustains complex relations with society and culture. Single case studies thus can only tell part of the story.

Droogers (1991) characterizes Pentecostalism as a "paradoxical" religion that involves rupture as well as continuity, individualism as well as communitarism, otherworldly eschatology as well as this-worldly pragmatism, and ascetic discipline as well as psychosomatic release. Transnational Pentecostal churches working among Salvadoran gang members in the Washington, D.C., area evince similar paradoxes. At one level, they provide resources for less destructive spaces and subjectivities for gang members. In providing morally sanctioned territories to homeless transnational mara members, these churches "domesticate" the new converts. By mitigating the most damaging effects of multiple transnational marginalities, Pentecostalism might be helping reweave the Salvadoran fabric of sociality torn by centuries of violence.

At another level, however, Pentecostal churches reproduce the patterns of domination over the self and the body that have been central to Salvadoran authoritarian politics. Churches, with their language of spiritual warfare, inculcate a habitus of exclusionary difference that has potentially negative consequences for a sending society struggling to strengthen the values of solidarity, tolerance, and reciprocity among its citizens and for the migrants seeking full participation in the public sphere in United States. Among gang members who have turned to Pentecostalism, there is a destabilizing undercurrent of deep resentment and aggression, which, while justified by the multiple forms of marginality they suffer, rejects wholesale the "secular" world, including modernity's self-critical tools. This rejection is symbolically intensified by proclaiming a totally deterritorialized kingdom of God. Further, because the rhetoric of an ever-present spiritual warfare opens this eschatological notion to reterritorialization in this-worldly projects like national moral crusades, the rejection of modernity's critical reason leaves gang members unable to engage in a full critique of the power relations that have led to their disenfranchisement.

We have used the notion of territory to underscore the link between religion and the production of space in a transnational setting. Here the emic and the etic converge. For the notion of territory is in the discursive repertoire both of religious actors seeking to render meaningful personal conversion and institutional pastoral strategies, and of scholars trying to map out global processes. Critical geographers argue that space is a dynamic reality constructed and interpreted by subjects located at the intersection of multiple and shifting webs of social relations spanning the local and the global. Space is not opposed to time. Rather, space and time are intertwined in spatio-temporal "envelopes" through which subjects articulate identities and lived experiences

(Massey 1994: 5). Because "the spatial is socially constituted [and] . . . space is by its very nature full of power and symbolism, a complex web of relations of domination and subordination, of solidarity and co-operation" (264–265). As a source of narratives about home, community, selfhood, and utopia, religion is part of the symbolism and power involved in the construction of space.

In Pentecostalism we see religion contributing to the "dynamism of the spatial." Pentecostalism among Salvadoran gangs forces us to conceptualize space and time in terms of simultaneity and paradox. Pentecostalism articulates at least four "envelopes of time-space," which overlap and enter into tension with each other. One is the time-space envelope of the renewed self, the "remapped subject," whose history is now embedded in the narrative of conversion and whose body and soul are liberated from demonic rule and marked with the charismas and signs of salvation. This self is closely linked and supported by a second spatio-temporal envelope, that of the church as a local redeployment of the community life that has been undermined by geopolitical conflicts, transnational migration, and the restructuring of the Salvadoran economy. Despite its highly sectarian nature, this envelope is porous, in tension with various spaces and roles in secular life. Third, there is the transnational time and space in which the churches operate to minister to migrants across national borders. Finally, Pentecostalism involves a realm of life constructed at the end of time through the obliteration of all human-made boundaries. Building on Tweed's (1997: 91–98) work among Cuban Catholics in Miami, we can characterize these interacting and dynamic time-spaces as subjective, "locative," "translocative" (connecting sending and receiving societies horizontally), and "supra-locative" (linking human and divine histories).

As we argued in Chapter 2, religion is a source for "heterotopias" (Soja 1989: 16–21), the multiple, intersecting "envelopes of space and time" that accompany globalization. In the next chapter, we explore in more detail the relation among religion, lived space, and collective identity in the context of transnational migration.

6

A CONTINUUM OF HYBRIDITY
Latino Churches in the New South

In the southern United States, public transportation has never enjoyed great success. Atlanta, the South's unofficial capital, offers no exception to the rule. In recent years, however, Atlanta's two-line commuter train system has garnered some popularity among the city's newest residents. As the train runs north from downtown, its cars fill with Spanish-speaking and primarily Mexican immigrants. By the time the train reaches the northern end of the line, in the suburb of Doraville, these Spanish speakers usually comprise the majority of those who file off the train. On one such train, the profound impact of these immigrants on metro Atlanta's landscapes has been inscribed on the route map: armed with a ballpoint pen, someone has crossed a bold "X" through "Doraville" and scrawled "MEXICO" in its place.

The graffiti artist who defaced this map was onto something. Processes of economic globalization and their accompanying flows of migrants are remapping the city of Atlanta, and the new contours taking shape in the suburb of Doraville are being formed, in part, through the transposition of Mexican places onto metro Atlanta's spaces.[1] However, this transposition comprises only one phase in the complex projects through which Mexicans and other Latin American immigrants carve out places that feel like home on the landscapes of Doraville. This chapter relates how two Doraville churches provide immigrants with both the spaces and the materials to create miniature border zones, "hybrid sites and spaces on the global landscape" (Nederveen Pieterse

1995).[2] These hybrids are not deterritorialized, as some globalization theorists would argue, but rather anchored in a particular place that is being shaped by global economic change, transnational migration, and local historical factors.

DORAVILLE: THE GLOBAL IN THE LOCAL

Los Angeles is widely hailed (or derided) as the "quintessential post-modern metropolis" (Soja 1995). However, the City Too Busy to Hate (Atlanta's favorite nickname) certainly rivals the City of Angels in the degree to which it emplaces the restructured landscapes of postmodernity.[3] The central features of metro Atlanta's landscapes are not tall buildings but long roads: Peachtree Road, the Downtown Connector, Spaghetti Junction, the Perimeter, and, finally, Buford Highway, known as the place to go for "authentic" cuisine from around the globe. This sprawling six-lane highway, which bisects Doraville and comprises the town's somewhat misshapen heart, is lined with more than seven hundred immigrant-owned restaurants and businesses. Although native Atlantans occasionally venture to these spots in search of "authenticity," the businesses exist to serve immigrant Latinos and Asians from throughout metro Atlanta. Especially on weekends, places like the Mexican Flea Market in Doraville are so full that, as Lorena, a Mexican woman who came to Atlanta from Puebla eleven years ago, complained, "You can barely get inside! There are too many people.... You can't even walk!" Lorena recalled that when she arrived in Doraville, "in the flea market you didn't see lots of people. You'd go to the flea market and see maybe ten or fifteen cars." Indeed, Doraville's Latino population was so negligible that it was not counted in the U.S. census until 1980, when it registered at 2 percent (0.5 percent Mexican origin). By 1990, when Lorena moved to Doraville, the city's Latino population had increased to 9.2 percent (5 percent Mexican origin). In 2000, according to U.S. census data, Latinos comprised 43.4 percent of Doraville's population, and almost 30 percent of the city's population was Mexican. This demographic change has made Doraville one among a handful of metro Atlanta areas with a Hispanic population density of more than 20 percent. It also makes Doraville one among many towns and cities in the southeastern United States experiencing an explosion in immigration from Mexico and other parts of Latin America.[4]

Incorporated as a city in 1871, Doraville was a farming community until 1947, when General Motors built an assembly plant there. During the postwar economic boom of the next two decades, the city thrived as a center of manufacturing and transportation and, like many U.S. cities, it underwent massive physical restructuring. The sleepy rural town became a busy suburb filled with strip malls and split-level subdivisions (Rutheiser 1996). The mass production in Doraville's car-manufacturing plant went hand in hand with mass-marketed, homogenized suburban lifestyles. New neighborhoods emerged overnight with names such as Northwoods, Oakcliff, and Carver Hills, the latter designated exclusively for African Americans in a still-segregated South. These neighborhoods were filled with working-class General Motors employees who worshiped either in one of the city's three historically African American churches or in one of its dozens of newly built white Protestant churches.

In the 1970s, as the United States attempted to recover from severe recession and began to embrace more flexible forms of capitalism, metro Atlanta undertook a strategic shift in identity from a national to an international city. The city began to court international investment, offering an abundance of cheap nonunionized labor, vacant land, and access to air and rail transport (Rutheiser 1996). In so doing, it created linkages along which immigrants and refugees began to travel.[5] Atlanta, for the first time in its history, became a significant immigrant destination. Doraville's population actually decreased during this time. White flight emptied scores of ranch-style homes, garden apartments, and strip malls. Refugee resettlement agencies began filling apartments with refugees from Vietnam, Cambodia, and Laos, while immigrant entrepreneurs converted vacant malls into ethnic commercial enclaves. Atlanta's economy began to boom again in the 1990s, as the city led the nation in job growth (Rutheiser 1996) and garnered international attention as the site of the 1996 Olympic Games. Immigrants from Mexico and Central America, many of whom lived in the saturated economic markets and overcrowded barrios of southern California, heard of the job opportunities in Atlanta and began to join refugees in Doraville's cheap housing.

Today, instead of being a suburb centralized around one key manufacturing center, Doraville has been subsumed into a densely populated urban corridor extending along Buford Highway. Doraville emplaces many of the hallmarks of the current phase of globalization that we describe in Chapter 2: the transition from modern fixed economies of scale to postmodern flexible economies of scope (Harvey 1999), the urbanization of suburbia and formation of "edge cities" (Castells 1996; Garreau 1991; Soja 1995), the formation of global cities and increasing migration of both international capital and international migrants to their core (Sassen 1988), and the resulting development of new patterns of social segregation (Soja 1995). Doraville has experienced a localization of the global as its homes, restaurants, and businesses have filled with immigrants from throughout Asia and Latin America. Now most immigrants arrive directly from Mexico and Central America, joining family members already in Doraville or simply following the news of available work that travels across national borders by word of mouth. In the post-Fordist shift from the manufacture of durable goods to the production of fleeting services, Doraville has deindustrialized and reindustrialized by replacing large-scale manufacturing with niche-market production of goods and services. And as its neat suburban streets become increasingly chaotic, this peripheral suburb rapidly subsumes into a sprawling, fragmented urban core.

However, in "postmodern cities" like metro Atlanta, "there is not only change but continuity, as well, a persistence of past trends and established forms of (modern) urbanism amidst an increasing intrusion of postmodernization" (Soja 1995: 126). While much has changed in Doraville, much has stayed the same. First, the population of Doraville is still just under half white, and most of these white residents are aging working-class men and women who have lived in the city for decades. The local power structures in Doraville have remained remarkably consistent, with a mayor who has been in office since 1982 and in local government since 1971 and a city commission comprised entirely of aging Anglo men, many of whom trace their family lineage to Doraville's founding. Second, in Doraville, as throughout the South, residents continue to use their churches as the places in which they negotiate change and solidify patterns of segregation. Like the African Americans who preceded them, Doraville's newest residents, who face multiple forms of discrimination, turn to churches not only for refuge but also for places that provide the space and symbolic and material elements with which to engage a public sphere from which they are often excluded. However, unlike those predecessors, they also find in their churches support for the formation and maintenance of transnational, transregional, and translocal ties that shape the ways in which they negotiate the city's often inhospitable landscapes.

DORAVILLE'S CONTRASTING CARTOGRAPHIES

In September 1990 the International Olympic Committee selected Atlanta as the host city of the 1996 Olympic Games, a decision that would result in "the most important event in the city's history since General

Sherman burned it to the ground" (Rutheiser 1996: 228). It culminated the city's decades-long struggle to remake its image not only as the capital of the South, but also as "the world's *next* great international city" (Rutheiser 1996: 108). Those courting the Olympics touted the city's southern tradition of hospitality and civil rights history and worked hard to distance themselves from such unsavory characteristics as segregation. Atlanta was awarded the games in part because the city's advocates were able to create an image of community cohesiveness and enthusiasm for the event (Rutheiser 1996: 227–228). Notwithstanding these claims, durable southern patterns of segregation and discrimination had remained intact in Atlanta, as many longtime residents drew on racist ideologies to make sense of the demographic changes occurring around them.

In Doraville, the degree to which longtime residents resisted change was demonstrated when the Dekalb County Chamber of Commerce created a plan to construct the International Village for the Olympics. As imagined by the Chamber, the village would attract tourists and shoppers to the already multiethnic but dilapidated area by building tree-lined walkways, an open-air market, and mixed-use residential and business spaces. This attempt to tout Doraville and the adjacent town of Chamblee as evidence of metro Atlanta's status as a global city was categorically rejected by the Doraville City Commission, which in 1993 "blasted the project as a threat to jobs for longtime residents and the town's identity" (Fey 1993). The primary complaint of these commissioners, who fervently held to the outdated image of Doraville as an orderly middle-class suburb rather than part of a teeming global metropolis, was that housing would be located above shops and restaurants. The vice-mayor clearly articulated the commission's position on this prospect on December 13 of that year: "The international village wanted us to go after low rent housing to attract more immigrants. Why would we want to attract more immigrants when we got all we want? We got plenty. We got enough to go around. If you want some in your neighborhood, we'll send you some." He explained of the concept of mixed-use residential and business space: "That's just not our way of life here. We're basically Baptists and Methodists and Presbyterians. We don't believe in that" (Brice 1993). The vice-mayor turned to religious affiliation to anchor the identity of Doraville's residents, but while he was describing Doraville as mainline Protestant and uninterested in immigrants, the city's largest church, the Misión Católica de Nuestra Señora de las Américas, was attracting thousands of Mexicans with its annual procession in honor of Our Lady of Guadalupe. In so

FIGURE 6.1. A procession in December, 2002 to honor the Virgin of Guadalupe concludes in the parking lot of the *Misión Católica de Nuestra Señora de las Américas*.

doing, the church not only continued a long tradition of processions
in honor of the Virgin of Guadalupe but also claimed the city streets
for its members, remapping Doraville's space in ways that challenged
official understandings of the city. Such a divergence of events and interpretations of the city confirm that, contrary to the imaginings of the
city's longtime residents, Doraville had been subsumed into a postmodern cityscape, "a landscape filled with . . . peculiarly juxtaposed life-
spaces" (Soja 1995: 134).

How do Doraville's old-timers and most recent immigrants make
sense of the restructured landscapes on which they now reside? While
both longtime residents and immigrant newcomers consider churches
the city's most important places, two contrasting maps of the city
emerge. Longtime Anglo residents see Doraville's established Protestant
churches as its most important places: First Baptist, Northwoods
Methodist, First Presbyterian. This perception remains even as such
churches rapidly shrink and, in some cases, relocate to more remote
suburbs, leaving space for new immigrant churches to fill. Beyond
churches, Anglo community leaders see the city's many parks as, in the
words of the city librarian, among the most "important neighborhood

gathering places." Indeed, since the 1950s, the city government has invested significant capital and energy in the park system and has encouraged the formation of numerous youth sports leagues including basketball, baseball, and swimming teams and an extremely popular boxing club.[6] He explained that because the city government has been so heavily involved in organizing events and creating places like city parks that encourage community cohesion, there is little need for voluntary organizations, and historically there have been few in Doraville. Like many longtime residents of Doraville, he views the immigrant population as "transient" and therefore not to be taken into consideration when discussing community cohesion.

Perhaps this sentiment explains the very different maps of Doraville's public spaces drawn by Latino members of our two case churches. As one member of the Misión Católica explained: "In this area, it seems that there are no recreation areas, no parks where young people can go. . . . I don't know, there is a need for more space so that youngsters can have other options [besides gangs and drugs]." While these concerns may seem unfounded in light of the attention that Doraville's city government gives to public parks and recreation, they begin to make sense when examined in light of such material evidence as a sign next to a large playing field in a Doraville city park: "No soccer allowed on field. Strictly enforced." Playing soccer together is perhaps the most pervasive pastime among Mexican and Central American immigrants to the city, one of the few times in which they can gather with others from their hometown (since most of the teams are arranged according to locality of origin), watch or play a game, share a meal, exchange news from home, and make new friends.

Since Doraville's Latino and Latina newcomers have been implicitly excluded from the city's "important neighborhood gathering places," they have had to seek places in which to come together for recreation. This need is exacerbated by the fact that the vast majority of Doraville's Latinos are undocumented immigrants who live in constant fear of being detained by the police or the INS. Both in Doraville and in the Mexican sending community where we undertook research, the most common word used to describe life in metro Atlanta was "encerrado"—locked up or closed. This feeling emerges partly because the new immigrants have often moved from a rural community to an urban center and long for open spaces, but it also points to undocumented immigrants' insecurities about gathering in public places. Responding to the need for a safe place to gather, the Misión Católica recently renovated a small playing field and basketball court and began to organize sports leagues. The soccer league immediately attracted almost four hundred participants. Since the league is generally organized around hometown teams made up of immigrants from the various villages in Mexico and Central America represented in Doraville, it helps those immigrants maintain connections to their places of origin. In part because Misión Católica organizes a soccer league that affirms identities and localities far from Doraville, Latinos consistently identify it as one of the most important places in the city.

MISIÓN CATÓLICA DE NUESTRA SEÑORA DE LAS AMÉRICAS

Luz Maria is an undocumented Mexican immigrant to Atlanta who cleans homes for a living, but her vocation is her work as the organizer of the Misión's chapter of St. Vincent de Paul. Her dedication to this work has earned her the status of unofficial matriarch of the church. This founding member of the Misión explained why people feel "at home" there: "Here it feels like the town square [*plaza del pueblo*]. We come, we get to know each other, we mingle with each other. We listen to the word of God, but we also develop friendships. . . . It's like a vision of a plaza where people from all countries encounter each other."

The patroness of the Misión Católica is the Virgin of Guadalupe, "Queen of Mexico and Empress of the Americas." She has developed into Mexico's patroness over the course of centuries but only became the patroness of the Americas by papal decree in 1999 (Brading 2001). Like its patroness, the Misión Católica constantly negotiates its members' particular national identities with an emergent pan-Latino identity, and also like that of the Virgin, the broader identity is strongly encouraged by pastoral workers at the Misión and the church hierarchy.

Both the Misión's function as a *plaza del pueblo* and its dual identities are evident in and constructed through its landscapes, structures, and material artifacts. Directly adjacent to the Doraville station of Atlanta's rapid-rail system, the Misión Católica is a large former warehouse with brown vinyl siding that bears no resemblance to a traditional Catholic church structure. The only clue that it is a place of worship is a statue of Our Lady of Guadalupe in one of two plate-glass windows. She overlooks the small parcel of land between the warehouse and the street, most of which is paved with concrete. During the week this pavement is used as a parking lot, but on Sundays no cars are allowed to park there. Instead, the lot fills with people as men sell *paletas* (popsicles) from pushcarts, vendors sell food and religious articles from stands, music plays from loudspeakers, and the parking lot converts into the place to see and be seen. For most who worship at the mission, this is a familiar scene. In many pueblos and ranchos of Mexico and other parts of Latin America, local parishes stand adjacent to the town square, and on Sunday afternoons after mass, vendors gather to sell food and worshippers linger to chat with their neighbors and family members.

Even on weekdays, the Misión is a center of activity in Doraville. Beyond organizing masses, religious processions, and religious education, the Misión also hosts sports leagues, dances, parties, vocational-training classes, English classes, social service and healthcare providers, and advocacy groups. On weekday evenings, hundreds of people come to the Misión not only to attend English and vocational-training classes but also to find out about jobs through informal networks, get help filling out job applications, share information about housing and immigration issues, or simply hang out and drink coffee. Arturo, an elderly member of the church who now works in the maintenance department and whose adult children are very active members, proudly explained the Misión's draw as an alternative to illicit activities: "My children have a prayer group here. Three of my kids come on Fridays to sing praise to God, they come to participate here; . . . instead of going out to the bars or to dances, well, they come here."

The majority of those who gather here are Mexican (72.2 percent, joined by immigrants from all over the Americas, most notably Central America (8.9 percent) and Colombia (6.3 percent) (Rees and Miller 2002: 71). This national diversity is matched by the socioeconomic, ethnic, and generational diversity of the Misión's members. However, most Misión Católica members have in common their status as undocumented immigrants to the United States (again, approximately 70 to 80 percent, according to staff), which contributes to their feeling of exclusion from public spaces like parks, libraries, and community centers.

The range of roles the Misión plays is made concrete and visible in the nonworship spaces of the building's interior. On Sunday mornings, worshippers make their way from the bustling town square outside the sanctuary through one of two pairs of glass double doors, as they head toward the worship space at the rear of the building. Here, they are always greeted by volunteers who shake hands and say, "Welcome to the Misión Católica." They are also greeted by a range of materials, including informational flyers about everything from health issues to changes in immigration law, and bulletin boards with announcements about rooms for rent, items for sale, and upcoming events in the church and the wider community. As these materials make evident, one of the most important activities of the Misión is to provide services, informational material, and a site for the informal exchange of information for recent immigrants to metro Atlanta.[7]

Connecting these reception areas to the sanctuary are two adjoining hallways, where worshippers often find themselves standing during mass, since the sanctuary itself is too small to hold everyone on Sunday mornings. The decorations in each hallway both shape and reflect the two forms of collective identity that the Misión Católica constantly negotiates. Lining the walls of one hallway are posters of César Chávez, a Mexican American; Mama Tingo from the Dominican Republic; and Padre Rutilio Grande and Oscar Romero from El Salvador, as well as political posters like one from the organization Rights Without Borders proclaiming in Spanish, "No one is illegal." Flanking the entrance to the sanctuary stands a human-sized papier-mâché replica of the Statue of Liberty with a huge red question mark wrapped around its body. A youth group made the statue for a protest at the Capitol, and it has been used by the Misión in many other protest marches since that time. These items illustrate the Misión's role in building a hemispheric solidarity of resistance that revolves around support and advocacy for the newest immigrants to metro Atlanta.

The second hallway leading to the sanctuary is covered with maps of Latin American countries. People often gather around these maps, pointing out to others the places from which they have come or proudly describing the geography of their natal land. As one pastoral worker explained: "Because it's Our Lady of the Americas, . . . Father put the maps of the whole Western Hemisphere on the wall so that people would stand around them and talk, saying, 'This is where I'm from.' So that's another important thing because it promotes conversation and community. It gets people talking." Maps are among the Misión's most pervasive material artifacts. When the Misión organized relief efforts after natural disasters in El Salvador and Venezuela, volunteers painted huge maps of each country with its key cities and states to hang inside the sanctuary as a reminder for members to participate. These maps are the most explicit of many ways in which the Misión nurtures immigrants' connections to their place of origin by "transposing" those places onto the Misión's spaces (Brown 1999). In so doing, the Misión encourages "long-distance nationalism" (Glick Schiller 1999: 99), "a claim to membership in a political community that stretches beyond the territorial borders of a homeland."

On Sunday mornings, worshippers crowd the halls as they clamor toward the sanctuary, and the faux-wood portable pews with red vinyl kneelers fill rapidly. This large, drab, rectangular room with linoleum floor and ceramic tile ceiling was enlivened ~ the flags of every country in the Americas along the walls. The flags create a sense of pan-American identity, explains Francisco, a Mexican from Veracruz. "It is possibly the most important thing that Father was able to achieve," according to Francisco. "See, the Mexicans have one set of customs, the Guatemalans have other customs, Cubans and all different types of people, we all have different customs. And what he did, I believe it was something that would have been the most difficult to do. . . . He [put up the flags] so that we would all see one another as a community, we would all be one. This is what he was able to make us feel, that we are one, . . . that we wouldn't see each other as Mexicans or as Cubans, but that we would see each other as brothers."

Although the space is always circumscribed in a way that affirms a generalized pan-Latino identity (and the patroness's identity as "Empress of the Americas"), on special occasions artifacts fill the space that allow the sacred geography of a country of origin to be transposed onto the Misión's worship space. For instance, on the Feast of Our Lady of Guadalupe, a large papier-mâché sculpture of Tepeyac Hill (the site near Mexico City where the Virgin appeared in the 1500s) was constructed in one corner of the sanctuary. On other national feast days, members build small altars near the main altar with flowers, candles, and images of the particular Virgin being venerated on that day.

There is another, much smaller worship space at the Misión Católica: a tiny chapel housing images of Jesus, the saints, and, most notably, various manifestations of the Virgin Mary. These include Our Lady of Guadalupe, who is the largest of the images; Our Lady of Chiquinquirá, Colombia's patroness; Our Lady of Charity, Cuba's patroness; Our Lady of El Quinche, from Ecuador; and Honduras's Our Lady of Suyapa, among many others. Our Lady of Guadalupe long occupied a central position in the chapel, behind a pair of rough-hewn wood altar rails on which devotees knelt in prayer and adoration. Recently, however, pastoral workers at the Misión decided to move her to the side and replace her with the tabernacle, which houses the Blessed Sacrament. Unlike common ornate gold tabernacles, the Misión's is a straw hut made by a church member that represents the stable in which Jesus was born. As one pastoral worker explained: "The tabernacle is a grass hut because Jesus was poor, and if you're poor you identify with Jesus living in poverty. . . . He chose to be poor. He chose to be like me." The thatched hut highlights the Misión's generalized identity as a place that shelters all members, especially the *recién llegado* living in the most humble of conditions, and makes them feel at home. Also, the tabernacle,

transformed into the
versally Catholic and
nd the other national
ne Misión's role in af-
shed religious artifacts
onto its ~~~
otional practices. That
pastoral workers rearranged ~~
oritizing the more gen-
eralized and orthodox identity, suggests that, like that of Our Lady of
Guadalupe, the Misión's pan-Latino institutional identity is strongly encouraged and perhaps sometimes imposed by the Catholic hierarchy.[8]

In sum, the Misión Católica provides a space, a town square, that
encourages those who worship there to feel at home in two senses. First,
the Misión allows immigrants not only to bring key artifacts from their
home countries, but also to transpose the topography of their place of
origin onto its spaces. Second, like the simple thatched hut of its tabernacle, it provides a (perhaps temporary) home in which those who
have traveled far from their homeland are provided for, treated with
dignity, and, as we will illustrate, encouraged to participate more fully
in the Catholic Church while critically engaging the society in which
they find themselves.

SAGRADA FAMILIA LUTHERAN CHURCH

Sagrada Familia (Holy Family) is located around the corner from the
Misión Católica, sandwiched between a McDonald's and a busy Asian
shopping center on Buford Highway. Yet, most members describe it as
a peaceful place, a refuge. This has to do in large part with the landscapes surrounding the sanctuary. The lush lawn and mature shade trees
provide the only green space for miles along a road lined with strip
malls and gas stations. The sanctuary, set far back from the busy road,
resembles a ranch-style suburban home with a well-kept yard more than
a place of worship. One member explained, "I saw the sign that said
'Mass in Spanish,' but I had never gone because I thought it looked
like a house and nothing more." This church that so closely resembles
a household in its physical layout also functions like a household. As
its name would suggest, the congregation that gathers in this household serves as a second family. As one member explained, "In our
church, everyone is like a brother . . . and the father knows us all."

Unlike the Misión Católica, where worshippers must arrive very
early if they hope to find a place to sit in the sanctuary, Sagrada Familia seems to encourage late arrival, and the pastor rarely begins the

service within twenty minutes of its official starting time. Members take their time travelling down the concrete path that leads across the deep lawn to the entry. As they enter the church, they pause to hang jackets on coat racks and to exchange greetings. As in many households, this entryway is filled with photographs. Bulletin boards line the walls, and the photographs they display reveal that the most important events offered by Sagrada Familia are not protest marches, vocational-training classes, or big dances. Rather, they are Sunday potluck dinners, baptisms, confirmations, and retreats. Before and after Sunday services, church members often gather around these photos, sharing memories of events and commenting on how much some babies look like one or another parent. As members gather to discuss them, these photographs create tangible evidence of the intimate relationships that have formed in the congregation and also stimulate new relationships.

In most households, the second floor is a more intimate space than the first, and Sagrada Familia's upstairs sanctuary also encourages intimacy. At the top of the stairs, the pastor's wife always waits to welcome each person individually and hand out a weekly bulletin. As they pass into the sanctuary, worshippers go by a small table on which is displayed a large elaborately illustrated English Bible flanked by framed photographs of Martin Luther King Jr. and Oscar Romero. Above this table hangs a gilt cross with a Latin inscription, and next to the table

FIGURE 6.2. The Lutheran Church of *Sagrada Familia*, as viewed from Buford Highway. With the exception of the traditional red doors, the edifice more closely resembles a home or apartment complex than a typical Lutheran Church.

stands a very small Mexican flag. The use of an English-language "family Bible" and the choice of Martin Luther King Jr. as a key figure suggest the degree to which this church embraces an "American" identity, while the presence of a Mexican flag and a picture of Oscar Romero confirm the continuing importance of the places from which church members have come.

In the quiet, half-full sanctuary, an eight-foot U.S. flag stands to the right of the altar and next to a brightly painted Salvadoran-style cross. Above the altar hangs a crucifix, and behind it, placed among a row of tall white pilaster candles, is a devotional candle bearing the image of Our Lady of Guadalupe. Lining the walls of the sanctuary are framed prints representing the stations of the cross. Like the Misión Católica, Sagrada Familia houses some key artifacts that allow the transposition of other, in this case Latin American, places into its space. Sagrada Familia makes its sanctuary a comfortable, familiar place for the immigrants who worship here by making it resemble a Catholic church. A crucifix over the altar, the stations of the cross, and images of the Virgin Mary are all uncommon in Lutheran churches. The immigrants who worship at Sagrada Familia are Catholics who find the church appealing because of its intimacy but hesitate to break with the Catholic traditions of their places of origin. However, this place is also a uniquely "American" (i.e., U.S.) space in which immigrants can gather to learn how to construct new, "American" identities that embrace the discourse of multiculturalism.

A church that prominently displays the U.S. flag beside the altar clearly offers different kinds of collective identity than a church where the sanctuary contains a Statue of Liberty bearing a question mark and where the U.S. flag is only one among many representing the Americas. However, as Sagrada Familia encourages members to embrace multicultural "America" and the Misión Católica encourages them to unite in a pan-Latino solidarity of resistance, they both challenge some of the most common stories told by sociologists about contemporary religion in the Americas.

MISIÓN CATÓLICA: DEDIFFERENTIATION OF SPHERES AND THE FORMATION OF COUNTERPUBLICS

As it makes space on the inhospitable landscapes of Doraville, the Misión Católica creates a place that challenges the classical versions of secularization theory. For in this place, religion is not privatized and differentiated from other spheres of life, such as the economic and political. Instead, religious practices interact with multiple spheres under one roof. This has made it possible for the Misión to become, like many other immigrant congregations throughout the United States (Ebaugh and Chafetz 1999), a community center for Latinos in Doraville and throughout the Atlanta area. Beyond this, the Misión serves as a public sphere, an institutionalized setting in which a range of people come together to form both shared opinions and shared identities (Fraser 1997; Habermas 1989).

As Ammerman (1997a: 356–367) points out, this is not a new role for religious institutions but one that has simply been overlooked by secularization theorists who see religion as either so privatized that it has nothing to contribute to modern public discourse or so broadly generalized that it enters into the discursive interaction of the public sphere only in disguise, as broadly held values like human dignity. Meanwhile, liberal philosophers have ignored the role of religious institutions as public spaces because they have focused on the formation of a single public arena, distinct from both the state and the economy, in which citizens deliberate about their common concerns. In this liberal conception of the public sphere, a unified comprehensive public is preferable to a "nexus of multiple publics" (Fraser 1997: 77). Liberal philosophers further assume a radical opposition of reason and faith, which makes them loath to seek this public in a religious space.[9]

So what happens, for instance, in places like Doraville, where not all potential participants are "citizens" or even legal residents, and where legitimate public spaces subtly or explicitly exclude some of those who reside on the same terrain? Nancy Fraser argues that, in stratified societies, equal participation of all in one common public debate is not possible. Thus, true discursive interaction requires "contestation among a plurality of competing publics" (1997: 81). In settings such as Doraville, where the formation of a global metropolis has encouraged increasing fragmentation and the uneven juxtaposition of multiple lifeworlds, where a unified, centralized public space is impossible, subaltern counterpublics are vital. These are, in the words of Fraser (1997: 81), "parallel discursive arenas where members of subordinated social groups invent and circulate counter-discourses, which in turn permit them to formulate oppositional interpretations of their identities, interests, and needs." The Misión serves as a subaltern counter public in three ways. First, it provides space and resources for "everyday forms of resistance to oppression and demoralization" (Higginbotham 1993: 2) by offering dances, fund drives, and classes, as well as a wide range of services, such as a health clinic, a food pantry, clothing, showers, and apartments that temporarily shelter recently arrived immigrants. In particular, providing showers, clean clothing, and in some cases short-term housing to the newly arrived helps restore dignity to persons who have suffered difficult and demoralizing border crossings at the hands of unscrupulous *coyotes*. As one Misión Católica member succinctly put it: "Here we simply try to protect and defend everyone. . . . Here in the Misión what we're doing is defending people, defending human beings." Francisco explained that the need for these services is especially pronounced in the local context, and the significance of these services moves beyond practical considerations. Father Carlos, the former priest in charge,

> had more than enough . . . power to bring people together, and he also had so much love that he has given to us from the beginning. . . . Back then, people didn't come together, because they were afraid of the INS. He confronted so many problems, thousands of problems, and in all of this, he always *puso la cara* for all of us. Even with the police of Doraville and Chamblee, he always stood up for us . . . and that's why the community is so big and so strong. He was able to get everything that now we Hispanics—those who continue to arrive and those who were already here—are enjoying. We enjoy completely free computer classes; they give us welding classes, which is a great job; they give us electrician's classes and English classes that they teach us for free. . . . He was a great fighter for all of us.

Father Carlos, a Jesuit priest from the Antilles Province, had worked for decades in the Dominican Republic and was strongly informed by the theology of liberation. He was a highly charismatic leader, but he described his mobilization strategy as developing lay leadership and then becoming a servant of the community, assisting its members as they formulated strategies for responding to the needs and problems they identified. As a result, even though he left the Misión in the summer of 2000 and was replaced by a diocesan priest less concerned with social activism, the everyday workings of the church continue to be largely directed by lay members of the staff and volunteers.

The Misión Católica was not always a confident, lay-led collectivity. Francisco explained how less than a decade ago, in its early years, members lacked courage and trust:

> In those days Immigration was going around and detaining people . . . gathering people up. And those were, I think, those were the most terrible times, not just for me but for the community in general because we don't have documents; . . . these were really hard times because we were just waiting, wondering when someone was going to show up

and take us away. . . . There wasn't confidence among the people until a leader came—someone came to guide us and to give us this confidence to gather together here. And he told us that nothing was going to happen to us if we came together, because God loves us. Right? God wanted us to gather together. So then the people began to lose this fear because . . . in those days there weren't many people walking around or coming together at the Misión. . . . Now it's very different, everything's very different, because the community feels trust; . . . there's so much confidence.

His explanation highlights not only the central role of priests, but also the second way in which the Misión serves as a subaltern counterpublic: it helps construct identities that challenge the stereotypes of the broader public, grounding these identities in explicitly religious resources. Instead of self-identifying as illegal aliens, those who worship at the Misión have embraced a broader identity: beloved by God and willed by God to gather together in even the most inhospitable times and places. They act out this identity in concrete practices and settings. Many members of the Misión spend their days as laborers, nannies, housekeepers, dishwashers, and landscapers, lacking authority and visibility. Yet, these same people spend their evenings preparing for big events like protests, deciding how to distribute aid, teaching and taking classes, and making decisions about the fate of their community. Thus they subtly challenge identities assigned to them by the wider public.

In November 2000, volunteers at the Misión constructed an elaborate altar for the Day of the Dead. Around the edges of the altar were glued bright yellow fall leaves. The altar itself included *pan de los muertos*, tortillas, liquor bottles, a mug of beer, a cornucopia of fruit, flowers, a guitar, and framed photos of those whom it honored: Martin Luther King, Oscar Romero, César Chávez, Padre Rutilio Grande, and Guatemalan bishop Juan Gerardi. A sign posted next to the altar read: "This altar is dedicated to our martyrs who fought without arms for their brothers, for their people." The altar made tangible the third way in which the Misión acts as a subaltern counterpublic: it provides material and symbolic resources with which to engage in "agitational activities directed toward wider publics" (Fraser 1997: 82).

Father Carlos once explained that the lay council decided to offer computer classes, not because those who want to take them have a chance to get white-collar jobs and use computers in their work, but because the classes give members a sense of accomplishment and offer them tools, such as the Internet, for education, consciousness raising, and critical engagement with a broader public. Similarly, the Misión's English classes on weekday evenings do not aim to blend Latinos into the U.S. melting pot. Rather, they offer both opportunities to get better jobs and, especially, tools for critical engagement, as Latinos struggle against discrimination. As Oralia, a participant at the Misión since its founding, explains: "We have much more confidence to fight because now we are learning the language.... People no longer say, 'Oh, because I'm Hispanic, they're going to discriminate against me,' or 'I can't do this.' Instead, we can fight with what we have and, if we want to succeed in the fight, we can do it."

Members of the Misión Católica indeed fight. In recent years, the Misión has staged marches in protest of hunger, the INS, and the School of the Americas, and in honor of Martin Luther King and Oscar Romero. The Misión has also created and circulated letters to the editor of the local newspaper, protesting U.S. immigration policy and supporting the expansion of guest-worker programs. Just as a particular image of God provides those who worship at the Misión with resources for formulating alternative identities, a certain interpretation of God's will and of the Gospel gives them the courage to challenge the broader public. When we asked Luz Maria, unofficial matriarch of the Misión, about the question mark–bearing Statue of Liberty, she explained:

> We've done lots of things that some people think don't make much sense because they don't want to take risks. But also, see, [the pastor] always said, "The gospel is always telling us that for this Jesus was crucified." Right? We can never, never sit with our arms crossed and wait for God to help us. Instead, we have to help God. Because we're the ones that can do more than him. He will guide us, but we have to do it. . . . One time we went to protest at the Capitol, when they were trying to pass a law that would be deleterious to us. . . . And they made a Statue of Liberty with a sign. And we took it there and we also walked in the march against hunger with this statue . . . to make the people think. You know? That, so, yes, we are in a country of liberty, or of justice. We were in the Capitol and a ton of people got together to protest that there be true justice.

Luz Maria's statement reveals how, as a subaltern counter-public, the Misión provides space and resources to challenge the meanings assigned by the U.S. public to broadly held values like justice and liberty. After creating this challenge, discursively and also materially in the form of the resignified Statue of Liberty, members of the Misión were prepared to enter the discursive arena. They did so critically, "to make people think."

SAGRADA FAMILIA: A TRAINING GROUND
AND ALTERNATIVE TO PUBLIC SPACE

Worshiping at Sagrada Familia encourages an approach to political participation that diverges significantly from the contestatory approach taken at the Misión. Ana, one of three adult sisters from San Luis Potosi, Mexico, who are active in the congregation, offered a typical and pointed response to our question about political participation: "No, that's not something that the church is here to do. No, there are more important things than that—more important because we're Hispanics and we need, more than anything, to learn how to get by here. And politics just doesn't benefit us."

Conforming to the model of an ideal household, Sagrada Familia provides a space apart from the confusing, exhausting, and demanding outside world. The work done in this space is the work expected of a family. First, Sagrada Familia mediates between the outside world and members of the congregation, helping out in times of need, providing emotional support and encouragement. Second, as Ana's response suggests, Sagrada Familia trains members for a more smooth incorporation into this outside world. In a family, this would be called socialization. In this case, it might more appropriately be called inculturation.

When asked about the most important events in the life of the church, members of Sagrada Familia did not name protests, petition writing, or vocational-training classes. Rather, they described collective potluck dinners, Vacation Bible School, and retreats, since "every time we have gatherings like that, we get to know more about the people and their problems." Miguel and Olinda, a young couple from Acapulco, began attending Sagrada Familia shortly after their arrival in Doraville in large part because they were lonely and longed to be part of a community, and because they felt most of their neighbors and co-workers were uninterested in establishing new friendships. Miguel explained the appeal of retreats: "Through them, people communicate with each other more. In some places I've seen, let's say, the people go to church, go to mass, and you see each person in his own place and they don't get to know each other, they don't greet each other. And people who go to other churches have told me that it's like that. They just come to church and then they leave. They don't get to know each other. But here, yes. Here we come, we greet each other, we get to know each other." Retreats accomplish two of the key objectives of Sagrada Familia members: they assist in the formation of intimate relationships and they allow members to relax in a tranquil environment.

This dual focus suggests that, unlike the Misión, Sagrada Familia embodies many of the traits identified by secularization theorists as prototypical of modern religion. Some secularization theorists predicted that with the increasing differentiation of societal spheres, the shift from *Gemeinschaft* to *Gesellschaft*, religion would become increasingly privatized and affective, with religious institutions catering to the psychological needs of their "clients" and with "clients" picking and choosing between available options on the basis of their personal preferences (Berger 1967; Hunter 1983; Weber 1946). Indeed, Sagrada Familia members have chosen to worship here because it is a place to retreat from the confusing and exhausting outside world, an alternative to public spaces. However, in this nonpublic space, members do not simply nurture affective relationships. Rather, Sagrada Familia serves as a training ground for entering the public at large.

The pastor prepares the children by teaching them the Pledge of Allegiance and encouraging them to speak English. He also encourages their parents to learn English, interspersing it regularly into the worship service. (By contrast, at the Misión Católica the use of English during worship is explicitly prohibited.) He encourages parents to buy their children a Bible in English and he prays that children will "acculturate to the U.S. and learn the ways of this country." He also upholds the possibility of achieving the American dream. One week in his sermon the pastor explained to the parents that their children could achieve middle-class status through hard work: go to school, study hard, get an entry-level job and work hard, and you will move up. In addition, he uses church activities such as Halloween parties and Thanksgiving dinners to introduce his congregation to U.S. customs and norms. At Sagrada Familia, Thanksgiving dinner must include turkey and pumpkin pie, although beyond those staple dishes, members are encouraged to bring their favorite Mexican dishes or other foods from "home." In short, the church advances the notion of incorporation into a pluralist or multicultural United States, where immigrant identities are no longer expected to dissolve in the U.S. melting pot. Rather, "immigrant groups are encouraged to preserve their culture, custom, and identity yet be fully embedded in an American mosaic" (Glick Schiller, Basch, and Blanc 1995: 51).

The pastor also sometimes uses the pulpit to teach congregants about their rights, encouraging them to develop a strong voice against discrimination. For instance, one Sunday he explained to the congregation that, here in the United States, the Constitution and the Bill of Rights prevent the abuse of power. He explained that because of these, even undocumented persons have rights in this country. One right is that no one can enter one's house without a warrant. After explaining what a warrant was, he reminded the congregation, "If anyone comes to your door—even a policeman—remind him that you are a member of this church and you know what your rights are!" In short, Sagrada Familia prepares its members to enter the broader public and to protect themselves in that public by knowing what their rights and responsibilities are, according to U.S. law. Rather than contest the law, or contemporary perspectives on immigrants' rights and responsibilities, the pastor teaches them to understand these in order that they might participate more fully—and with less fear—in the broader U.S. public. Thus, much like members of the Misión Católica, those who worship at Sagrada Familia embrace an identity that allows them to engage with the broader public. However, at Sagrada Familia, this engagement does not challenge but rather embraces U.S. understandings of rights and responsibilities, justice and liberty.

THE POWERFUL INFLUENCE OF TRANSNATIONALISM

Despite the differences between the Misión Católica and Sagrada Familia, the vast majority of those who worship at either church are transmigrants who "live their lives across borders" (Glick Schiller and Fouron 2001). However, there are many ways to live as a transmigrant, and members of Sagrada Familia and the Misión Católica exhibit this range. Oscar is a twenty-nine-year-old single man from Guanajuato, Mexico, who goes to mass at the Misión Católica weekly when he is in Atlanta. Oscar has come to Atlanta to earn the money he needs to start a business back in Guanajuato. He works long hours in a furniture factory and lives in an apartment crowded with other single young men from his neighborhood in Guanajuato. Oscar has no family in the Atlanta area, and "every fifteen days" he dutifully sends his family in Mexico a money order. He does not strive to establish enduring ties in Doraville because he has no intention of staying very long. Nevertheless, when he feels lonely, he makes his way over to the Misión Católica, where "they give you a coffee and some bread, and then you feel like you're not alone."

Guadalupe, who arrived in Atlanta five years ago and now worships every Sunday at Sagrada Familia with her husband, three children, sister-in-law, niece, and nephew, has a very different life than Oscar's. Her husband has his own business as a stonemason and her children win awards for citizenship in school. After the World Trade Center collapsed in the fall of 2001, they put U.S. flags on their cars. In their living room, they hung a poster of the twin towers with a U.S. flag waving behind them and the caption "In God We Trust" printed below. To the degree that it is possible for undocumented immigrants to the United States, they are settled here. Yet, they are here in large part because their rancho in Mexico depends on it. Since her arrival in Atlanta, Guadalupe has desperately wanted to return home for visits, but the cost and risk of crossing the border are too high. Shaken by the terrorist attacks in New York, Guadalupe told us that she and her family would like to return home for good, but they must remain in Atlanta. Like most of their townspeople who live in metro Atlanta, they own a home in Mexico, and they have a responsibility not only to send money to the family members who remain in Mexico, but also to provide much-needed jobs (generally construction work on their homes) for the few working-age people who have remained in their town.

Guadalupe, Oscar, and countless other members of these Doraville churches live in a transnational social field: "the network of social relationships that link together an array of transmigrants and individuals in the homeland connected to each other through kinship, friendship, business, religion, or politics" (Glick Schiller and Fouron 2001: 3). These social fields are neither "autonomous cultural spaces outside of either sending or receiving states" nor closed "circuits" that preclude transmigrants from entering into the social and political life of the place to which they have migrated. Rather, they "maintain or establish familial, economic, religious, political, or social relations in the state from which they moved, even as they also forge such relationships in the new states in which they settle" (Glick Schiller 1999: 96–97). Sagrada Familia and the Misión participate in the formation of these social fields in complex ways. They help shape migrants' political relationship with the broader receiving context by encouraging among their members either a pan-Latino solidarity of resistance or a Hispanic multiculturalism. Further, they help migrants forge social relationships with other Latinos in metro Atlanta by creating either a town square or a household for the "second family." Finally, they encourage migrants to establish and maintain among themselves a national identity as Mexicans, Hondurans, Guatemalans, Salvadorans, Colombians, and so on. Both churches consistently use those labels as the primary markers of subgroups within the congregation and offer national symbols, such as flags, maps, songs, or national patron saints, around which identity crystallizes. Significantly, they do not understand this construction of national identity to contradict a pan-Latino or Hispanic multicultural identity. Rather they see strong national identity as complementing and in some ways constituting such generalized identities. For instance, many members of the Misión Católica describe the national flags lining the walls of the sanctuary as a key way in which the church encourages pan-Latino solidarity, and Sagrada Familia promotes multiculturalism by serving typical national dishes from each country at its potluck meals.

Finally, both churches offer multiple resources, such as the home-town soccer teams, with which their members can maintain relation-ships with particular places of origin and with others living in metro Atlanta from their hometowns. In the particular transnational social field that we researched between metro Atlanta and a village near the border between the states of Mexico and Hidalgo, these churches play an especially important role as the center of life-cycle events such as baptisms, first communions, and confirmations. These activities pro-vide an opportunity for extended family and friends from the village to come together in Doraville and reconstitute community through re-ligious rituals, meals together, and fiestas (complete with mariachi). Re-ligious celebrations also offer an opportunity for legal residents of the United States, who can travel freely, to visit home, sustaining a back-and-forth movement across national borders. These religious links across borders have material components, most notably *recuerdos* (souvenirs) from important religious life-cycle events. For instance, when Guadalupe baptized her daughter at Sagrada Familia, she passed out small framed photos adorned with religious images. These photos were made by friends in her rancho in Mexico and brought to the baptism by her mother, who visited for the occasion. Now, the *recuerdos* grace homes of friends and family members in both Mexico and metro Atlanta.[10]

When members of these churches travel back to their place of ori-gin to visit, they often return to Doraville with religious artifacts that they donate to the churches. This explains both why the Virgin of Guadalupe sits behind the altar at a Lutheran church and why the small chapel at the Misión Católica overflows with saints and Virgins. They also carry religious artifacts with them on visits, filling their homes and those of their relatives with paintings of the Last Supper, felt images of the Virgin of Guadalupe, and small statues of saints for home altars that they have purchased in Doraville. Even when they cannot return home physically, they maintain multiple links to their places of origin. Cer-tainly the most urgent ties are economic, visible in the form of numer-ous money wire centers in Doraville. These economic ties can also

FIGURE 6.3. A religious procession around the Catholic Church in the Mexican *rancho* from which Guadalupe and many members of her extended family have come. The sanctuary was built with donations of money earned by townspeople working in Doraville and surrounding areas.

support religious transnationalism, as when migrants in Doraville funded the construction of a church in their village in Mexico.

Perhaps most important for the daily lives of transmigrants are the affective ties that extend the boundaries of their imagined communities beyond the local. Events in Doraville at the Misión or Sagrada Familia matter to those with whom the churches' members are linked in their place of origin. The reverse holds, as well. Events two thousand miles away often seem more urgent than those down the street. At both churches, prayers and homilies regularly address crises in sending countries. Both churches also include in their prayers and concerns individual family members of congregants who live in sending countries and family members and friends who are undertaking the perilous journey across the border. In short, the Misión Católica's town square encompasses multiple communities that extend far beyond the boundaries of the church's parking lot, and Sagrada Familia's household symbolically shelters extended families much larger than the one that gathers beneath its roof on Sunday mornings.

A CONTINUUM OF HYBRIDITY

While both the Misión Católica and Sagrada Familia encourage a particular kind of engagement with U.S. society, each also allows for the maintenance of translocal, transregional, and transnational ties. As a result, these churches neither create pure U.S. or counter-U.S. identities, nor maintain only transnational identities. Rather, they nurture the fluid mixing and blending of multiple religious identities to create new hybrids, such as Lutherans who are devoted to the Virgin of Guadalupe or Catholics who build a Mexican Day of the Dead altar to honor Martin Luther King. These hybrid identities are shaped in hybrid organizations that are inevitably political in their effect.

As Nederveen Pieterse (1995: 56) argues: "We can construct a continuum of hybridities: on the one end, an assimilationist hybridity that leans over toward the center, adopts the canon, and mimics the hegemony, and, at the other end, a destabilizing hybridity that blurs the canon, reverses the current, subverts the center." Sagrada Familia's "assimilationist hybridity" encourages immigrants to become part of mainstream multicultural America, while the Misión's "destabilizing hybridity" provides them with tools for diverting the current and staying outside of the mainstream. However, both churches can and do shift from one end of the continuum to the other. When Sagrada Familia's pastor teaches undocumented immigrants that they have rights and encourages them to stand up for those rights, he may be embracing U.S. ideals, but he is also using those ideals to destabilize the status quo. Conversely, when pastoral workers at the Misión Católica decide to replace the beloved Virgin of Guadalupe with a more generalized image that will unify members into a pan-Latino Catholic identity, they encourage assimilation into the institutional Church and minimize the destabilizing influence of particular, localized, and often home-based popular devotions.

Moving beyond examinations of immigrant congregations as safe, clearly bounded spaces in which subcultural identities are formed to promote either adaptation (Ebaugh and Chafetz 2000) or liberal pluralism (Warner and Wittner 1998; Warner 1993), we have sought in this chapter to strengthen and deepen these approaches by emplacing two immigrant congregations in multiple and overlapping spatial scales. We found that, although participation in congregational life may allow some immigrant groups, such as well-educated middle-class Hindus, to "take their place at the multicultural table" (Kurien 1998), it works quite differently for Doraville's undocumented Latinos, who face

classism, racism, and geographic exclusion as a result of the global economic and social processes that have subsumed the particular town of
Doraville into a chaotic "postmodern cityscape."

First, close examination of the history and current configuration
of this particular place has demonstrated that in Doraville, there may
not be a multicultural table at all—and if there is, the places around it
are reserved for immigrants, such as the city's small-business owners,
with legal status and economic resources. In other words, local and regional dynamics of power, and the resistance to multicultural imaginings by the powers that be, cannot be overlooked. As Doraville emplaces
global trends, the city's longtime residents draw upon deeply engrained
traditions of discrimination and segregation to conceptually map their
changing city. As they do so, they exclude the city's immigrant newcomers from public spaces and gathering places. Second, careful attention to the ways in which members of two immigrant churches engage
the physical space and material artifacts of those churches reveals that
since immigrants in Doraville have not been invited to Doraville's
"table," they have turned to their churches as places in which to construct their own tables. The Misión Católica has created an alternative
public, a subaltern counterpublic, that challenges the discourses being
articulated around the table from which its members have been excluded. By contrast, Sagrada Familia has created an alternative to public
space that teaches its members "table manners," the rules of engagement in the larger public from which they have been excluded, in hopes
that such lessons will help members make a place for themselves at the
table. Finally, the multiple forms of transnationalism that members of
both churches exhibit suggest that Doraville's immigrants and
transmigrants are moving back and forth between more than one table.
As they participate in congregational life, members of both churches
create and sustain transnational ties and "long-distance national" (Glick
Schiller 1999) and regional identities. In so doing, they draw on a variety of resources for the construction of shifting identities, identities that
are not subcultural and clearly defined, but hybrid, overlapping, and
sometimes contradictory.

7

PREMODERN, MODERN, OR POSTMODERN?
John Paul II's Civilization of Love

Pope John Paul II has been variously described as "the first citizen of a global civil society," defending the universality of human rights against parochial nationalism, and as the "great disciplinarian," deeply concerned with institutional loyalty and purity of doctrine at the cost of Vatican II's spirit of openness.[1] On the one hand, the pope is one of the most vocal critics of the excesses of neoliberal capitalism, particularly its consumerism. On the other, he has become something of a global pop-culture hero. What accounts for these paradoxes? In this chapter, we argue that John Paul II's attempts to reposition the church in the context of globalization and the crisis of modernity have led to the emergence of a theology and pastoral practices which mix traditional, modern, and postmodern sensibilities. The pope's "hybrid" worldview and practices are best exemplified in his call to build a global "civilization of love and peace" through, among other things, a new evangelization.

To examine the tensions and contradictions within John Paul II's civilization of love and peace, we undertake a close reading of his encyclicals, apostolic letters, messages, and speeches on postmodernity, globalization, the role of the media, and the new evangelization. Since the pope sees globalization as one of the outcomes of modernity, we begin by outlining his view of the latter. Here, John Paul II's handling of the recent disclosure of the third and last secret of Our Lady of Fatima, who has been linked with some of the most catastrophic events in modern times, offers an excellent window onto his ambivalence toward modernity.

FATIMA, THE VATICAN, AND MODERNITY

Ever since she appeared to three shepherd children at Cova da Iria, Portugal, in 1917, Our Lady of Fatima has held special fascination for Catholics throughout the world. As Cuneo (1997: 134) writes: "Of the dozen Marian apparitions that have been reported worldwide over the past two hundred years, none has packed nearly as much dramatic punch as Fatima. Secret messages, apocalyptic countdowns, cloak-and-dagger intrigue within the highest echelons of the Vatican: not even Hollywood could ask for better material than this." Fatima's hold on the Catholic imagination is in large part due to the work of ultraconservative Catholics who saw in her messages an outright condemnation of secular modernity, particularly of "atheistic" socialism, and the restoration of Christendom.

In one of her apparitions, on July 13, 1917, the Virgin offered the children three visions. The first was a terrifying vision of hell, while the second, which was kept secret until 1941, predicted the end of World War I and the beginning of World War II under the reign of Pius XI. In this second vision, Mary also addressed the impending cold war, demanding that the pope consecrate Russia to her Immaculate Heart as a way to convert the godless nation and prevent Russia from spreading "her errors throughout the world, causing wars and persecution of the Church."[2] Once this was done, Mary predicted, a period of global peace would ensue. Lucia, the only one remaining of the three original seers, stipulated that the third secret be disclosed in 1960. When Pope John XXIII did not do so, conservative Catholics wondered whether the pope had betrayed the Church's true mission, striking a Faustian bargain with the Soviet Union. After all, in their view, the Second Vatican Council was a clear indication of Rome's surrender to secular modernity. "When Paul VI, too, failed to release [the third secret], an apocalyptic Catholic priest with a cult following argued that Paul was an imposter sneaked into the Vatican to advance the Communist cause" (Wills 2000: 51). What was this secret anyway? "Did the secret warn of some evil plot that was being hatched against Catholicism from within the church itself? Did it speak of an impending nuclear war in which entire nations, possibly even the United States, would be annihilated?" (Cuneo 1997: 136).

Against this historical background, the Congregation for the Doctrine of the Faith released the third secret on June 26, 2000, under John Paul II's instructions. Surprisingly, the event was rather anticlimactic in both the content of the secret and the way in which the Vatican handled the revelation.[3] First, upon disclosing the secret, Cardinal Angelo Sodano, the Vatican's secretary of state, declared "that the text contains a prophetic vision similar to those found in Sacred Scripture, which do not describe photographically the details of future events, but synthesize and compress against a single background facts which extend through time in an unspecified succession and duration. As a result, the text must be interpreted *in a symbolic key*." Second, it turns out that the third secret did not predict any cataclysmic events in the future. Instead the revelation told about the martyrdom of "bishops, priests, men and women religious, and various lay people of different ranks and positions." The vision placed the Holy Father passing through a "big city half in ruins," ascending to the top of a mountain covered with corpses, and finally falling "on his knees at the foot of the big Cross . . . killed by a group of soldiers who fired bullets and arrows at him." John Paul II and Vatican interpreters took this to be a reference to the 1981 attempt against the pope. John Paul attributes his survival to Mary: "It was a mother's hand that guided the bullet's path and in his throes the Pope halted at the threshold of death." This is the reason the pope sent the bullet that was removed from his body to Our Lady of Fatima's shrine to be exhibited as a testament to her miraculous intervention.

The move away from literal interpretations of dire predictions seems to break with the anti-modernist apocalypticism associated with the Fatima apparition. Cardinal Joseph Ratzinger's theological commentary appended to the revelation appears to confirm this conclusion. From the outset, the commentary acknowledges that the third secret "will probably prove disappointing or surprising after all the speculation it has stirred. No great mystery is revealed; nor is the future unveiled. We see the Church of the martyrs of the century which has just passed represented in a scene described in a language which is symbolic and not easy to decipher." The commentary goes on to endorse a view of human agency remarkably in tune with the spirit of Vatican II. "The vision shows the power which stands opposed to the force of destruction— the splendor of the Mother of God and, stemming from this in a certain way, the summons to penance. In this way, the importance of human freedom is underlined: the future is not in fact unchangeably set; and the image which the children saw is in no way a film preview of a future in which nothing can be changed. The purpose of the vision is not to show a film of an irrevocably fixed future. Its meaning is exactly the opposite: it is meant to mobilize the forces of change in the right direction."

Moreover, interpreting the specific symbols in the secret, Cardinal Ratzinger concludes that "the mountain and city symbolize the arena of human history: history as an arduous ascent to the summit, history as the arena of human creativity and social harmony, but at the same time a place of destruction, where man actually destroys the fruits of his own work. The city can be a place of communion and progress, but also of danger and the most extreme menace." This idea of the "Church's arduous path" in human history echoes John XXIII's view of the Church as "the pilgrim people of God," coparticipants in God's salvific work.

Prima facie, the Vatican's interpretation of the third secret of Fatima appears to endorse an Enlightenment-based notion of progress at odds with premodern Catholic understandings of history. After all, traditional Catholicism attributes agency to saints and the Virgin Mary and sees humanity as helplessly trapped in a cycle of sin. However, while the interpretation affirms human free will, it also reinforces the authority and hierarchy of the Church in ways that would certainly please traditionalists. Archbishop Tarcisio Bertone, the secretary of the Congregation for the Doctrine of the Faith, writes in the introduction to the Fatima dossier: "Now a veil is drawn back on a series of events which make history and interpret it in depth, in a spiritual perspective alien to present-day attitudes, often tainted with rationalism." In other words, while the Vatican's reading "disenchants" the third secret, stripping it of apocalyptic, overtly supernatural content, it preserves the Church's monopoly on interpreting a message that cannot be understood in purely rational, secular terms. This monopoly is clearly reaffirmed in Ratzinger's theological commentary, which highlights Lucia's assertion that "she had received the vision but not its interpretation. The interpretation, she said, belonged not to the visionary but to the Church."[4] The Church's interpretation, furthermore, stresses the need for personal conversion rather than for a transformation of unjust social structures. According to Ratzinger, "'to save souls' has emerged as the key word of the first and second parts of the 'secret,' and the key word of this third part is the threefold cry: 'Penance, Penance, Penance!'" What is central to the third secret, Ratzinger continues, is "the exhortation to prayer as the path of 'salvation of souls' and, likewise, the summons to penance and conversion."

On a more abstract level, by relating the third secret to John Paul II's papacy, Ratzinger has gone beyond "domesticating" the millenarian thrust of the message. He has effectively inserted John Paul II and his papacy into a grand historical narrative of martyrdom and redemption that begins with Golgotha and culminates with the twentieth century. As Ratzinger puts it, in the Church's "Via Crucis of an entire century, the figure of the Pope has a special role. In his arduous ascent of the mountain we can undoubtedly see a convergence of different Popes. Beginning from Pius X up to the present Pope, they all shared the sufferings of the century and strove to go forward through all the anguish along the path which leads to the Cross. In the vision, the Pope too is killed along with the martyrs."

This teleological vision not only legitimizes John Paul II's papacy, but also authorizes an ambivalent vision of modernity. On the one hand, there is a recognition of the value of human history "as the arena of human creativity and social harmony." On the other, modernity is construed as an exhausted, ultimately contradictory project in need of redemption. That is why in Ratzinger's interpretation of vision, at the summit of the mountain "stands the cross—the goal and guide of history. The cross transforms destruction into salvation; it stands as a sign of history's misery but also as a promise for history." And who can point the way toward modernity's redemption? "It is the suffering Church, a Church of martyrs, which becomes a sign-post for man in his search for God."

The Vatican's reading of the third secret of Fatima has interesting parallels with postmodernist critiques of modernity's entwinement with power, particularly with subject-centered nihilism and instrumentalism. In fact, John Paul II takes up this issue in his encyclical letter *Fides et Ratio*, in which he skillfully draws from postmodernist discourses to reappropriate a modernity at the service of traditional notions of authority.

THE "GREAT TRADITION" VERSUS POSTMODERNISM

Compared to the relatively one-dimensional view of Latin American progressive Catholicism in *Instruction on Christian Freedom and Liberation* (1986), *Fides et Ratio* (John Paul II, 1998a) is a sophisticated document.[5] John Paul II opens the encyclical letter with a clear acknowledgment of the virtues of philosophy as a secular discipline. "The Church cannot but set great value upon reason's drive to attain goals which render people's lives ever more worthy. She sees in philosophy the way to come to know the fundamental truths about human life. At the same time, the Church considers philosophy an indispensable help for a deeper understanding of faith and for communicating the truth of the Gospel to those who do not yet know it" (#5). For the pope, thus, the problem is not with rationality or philosophy itself. Rather, he is concerned with a "crisis of meaning" generated by "an increasing fragmentation of knowledge [that] makes the search for meaning difficult and often fruitless." This fragmentation, in turn, "serve[s] only to aggravate radical doubt, which can easily lead to skepticism, indifference or to various forms of nihilism" (#81). It is important to note here that the pope is not appealing to theology as the only legitimate source of truth, for he recognizes the significance of all disciplines in the humanities and social sciences. In other words, John Paul II acknowledges the reality and value of the autonomous spheres of human knowledge and action that characterize secular society. However, he believes that in the present age, "a legitimate plurality of positions has yielded to an undifferentiated pluralism based upon the assumption that all positions are equally valid." Contemporary rationality and philosophy have contributed to this undifferentiated pluralism by their "one-sided concern to investigate human subjectivity, [which] seems to have forgotten that men and women are always called to direct their steps towards a truth that transcends them. Sundered from that truth, individuals are at the mercy of caprice, and their state as persons ends up being judged by pragmatic criteria based essentially upon experimental data, in the mistaken belief that technology must dominate all."

The focus of John Paul II's critique, thus, is what he calls "a radically phenomenalist or relativist philosophy" that has lost its capacity to ask questions about Being itself, fundamental questions about ontology (#82–90). This philosophy is open to many dangers, including scientism, pragmatism, and historicism. First, this philosophy "refuses to admit the validity of forms of knowledge other than those of the positive sciences; and it relegates religious, theological, ethical, and aesthetic knowledge to the realm of mere fantasy." While recalcitrant positivism has been discredited, there is a new scientism "which dismisses values as mere products of the emotions and rejects the notion of being in order to clear the way for pure and simple facticity. Science would thus be poised to dominate all aspects of human life through technological progress." Second, there is the danger of pragmatism, a means-ends mentality that judges actions and makes choices purely on the basis of their practical consequences. This mentality is particularly reflected in the "growing support for a concept of democracy which is not grounded upon any reference to unchanging values: whether or not a line of action is admissible is decided by the vote of a parliamentary majority." Finally, there is the claim that "the truth of a philosophy is determined on the basis of its appropriateness to a certain period and a certain historical purpose. At least implicitly, therefore, the enduring validity of truth is denied." As contemporary philosophy falls prey to these "errors," nihilism sets in. Such nihilism is highly corrosive of human life. "It should not be forgotten that the neglect of being inevitably leads to losing touch with objective truth and therefore with the very ground of human dignity." Adrift in a sea of nihilism, human beings are led "little by little to a destructive will to power or to a solitude without hope. Once the truth is denied to human beings, it is pure illusion to try to set them free. Truth and freedom either go together hand in hand or together they perish in misery." More pointedly, "if technology is not ordered to something greater than a merely utilitarian end, then it could soon prove inhuman and even become [a] potential destroyer of the human race."

The pope's critique of the excesses of technology fits within Thomistic natural law. Nevertheless, John Paul II's words have a distinctive modernist flavor. In fact, they betray late modernity's consciousness of crisis. There are, for example, clear echoes of Nietzsche in the pope's concern for the destructive power of nihilism. Also prominent is the Weberian concern that our society is becoming an iron cage. John Paul II takes the critique of the increasing dominance of instrumental rationality in everyday life further, challenging scientific positivism in a fashion that resonates with the Frankfurt School. Like Theodore Adorno's and Max Horkheimer's *Dialectics of the Enlightenment*, *Fides et Ratio* carries a powerful indictment of modernity's naive notion of progress and of rationality's central role in it. As rationality becomes instrumentalized, its emancipatory impetus is not only exhausted but also impugned by its own actions. Rationality's disenchanting drive, which was supposed to make us more autonomous, ends up becoming a "will to power" that not only dominates nature but turns inward to destroy us, leading directly to the Holocaust. Moreover, John Paul's critique of "phenomenalist and relativist philosophy" and his concern for ontology echo Heidegger's critique of Sartrean subject-centered existentialism in *Letter on Humanism*. Like Heidegger, John Paul II wants philosophy to move from "phenomenon to foundation." While their methods and conclusions are quite disparate, they share a care for Being itself as the ground of meaningful human activity.

What have we here then? A postmodern pope? John Paul II acknowledges in *Fides et Ratio* that "the currents of thought which claim to be postmodern merit appropriate attention." Postmodernism's attack against all certainties "has been justified in a sense by the terrible experience of evil which has marked our age. Such a dramatic experience has ensured the collapse of rationalist optimism, which viewed history as the progress of reason, the source of all happiness and freedom; and now, at the end of the century, one of our greatest threats is the temptation to despair" (#91). In other words, like Nietzsche, John Paul II sees the aporias of modernity leading directly to nihilism. Postmodernity as nihilism run rampant is the radicalization of modernity's shortcomings.

In contrast to Nietzsche, however, the pope does not advocate a pragmatic perspectivism, the final rejection of the quest for Truth and the affirmation of those values that enhance power. To the contrary, building on *Veritatis Splendor* (1993), his encyclical letter on Catholic moral teaching, John Paul II advocates a return to ultimate truth as revealed by the Christian gospels. "The Truth, which is Christ, imposes itself as an all-embracing authority which holds out to theology and philosophy alike the prospect of support, stimulation, and increase" (1998a). What is needed, according to the pope, is "a philosophy of genuinely metaphysical range, capable, that is, of transcending empirical data in order to attain something absolute, ultimate, and foundational in its search for truth. This requirement is implicit in sapiential and analytical knowledge alike; and in particular it is a requirement for knowing moral good, which has its ultimate foundation in the Supreme Good, God himself" (#83). A return to universal foundations means a rejection of the implications of historicism and the linguistic turn. "The claims of historicism . . . are untenable; but the use of a hermeneutic open to the appeal of metaphysics can show how it is possible to move from historical and contingent circumstances in which the texts [gospels] developed to the truth which they express, a truth transcending those circumstances. Human language may be conditioned by history and restricted in other ways, but the human being can still express truths which surpass the phenomenon of language. Truth can never be confined to time and culture; in history it is known, but it also reaches beyond history" (#95). And because the Church has "received the gift of the ultimate truth about life, [she] has made her pilgrim way along paths of the world to proclaim that Jesus Christ is 'the way, and the truth, and the life' (John 14:6). It is her duty to serve humanity in different ways, but one way in particular imposes a responsibility of a quite special kind: the *diakonia of the truth*" (#2).

It may seem from these last remarks that, in the end, *Fides et Ratio* represents yet another attempt to return to premodern conceptions of ultimate truth and to the notion that the Church has a monopoly on that truth. Yet, something quite interesting is going on here. Borrowing from Hobsbawm and Ranger (1983), we might say that what the pope is doing here is "re-inventing tradition" by locating the Church's struggles to discern the foundational truth of Christianity within a grand narrative that includes modern thought. "I believe that those philosophers who wish to respond today to the demands which the word of God makes on human thinking should develop their thought . . . in organic continuity with the great tradition which, beginning with the ancients, passes through the Fathers of the Church and the masters of Scholasticism and includes the fundamental achievements of modern and contemporary thought. If philosophers can take their place within this tradition and draw their inspiration from it, they will certainly not fail to respect philosophy's demand for autonomy" (#85).

As in the case of Fatima, John Paul II's rereading of contemporary history within the "great tradition" places the Church, and his papacy more specifically, at the center. To do this John Paul II walks a fine line between Catholic anti-modernism and modernism. On the one hand, unlike Pius IX in his *Syllabus of Error* (1864), he does not reject modernity *tout court* in favor of tradition. On the other hand, he does not share Vatican II's optimistic endorsement of modern progress. For John Paul II, the task at hand is not to update a Church that has fallen behind the times, but to redeem a modernity that has lost its bearings. He uses tradition to rescue modernity from its impasse, to recover the best modernity can offer. Furthermore, the pope uses critical discourses of late modernity and postmodernity to show the contradictions of the modern project and open the way for the reinscription of tradition within this chastened modernity.

Fides et Ratio thus offers a peculiar theology that combines premodern, modern, and postmodern themes. On one level, this hybrid theology responds to the mixing of codes produced by globalization. As we shall see when we discuss John Paul II's reading of neoliberal capitalism, the pope sees the dangers of globalization—fragmentation, individualism, and consumerism—as a reflection of postmodernism's radical phenomenalism and nihilism, that is, its stress on depthlessness, ephemerality, and undecidability. Thus the tensions between the global and the local and between homogeneity and heterogeneity that characterize the present episode of globalization become a version of the tensions between universality and particularity and between phenomena and essences that are at the core of *Fides et Ratio*. On another level, though, the pope's hybrid theology mirrors the paradoxes of globalization, unintentionally serving as a vehicle for global processes that he seeks to name and control.

JOHN PAUL II AND GLOBALIZATION

Casanova (1997) argues that the Catholic Church has been in tension with the modern system of nation-states since the collapse of medieval Christendom. As the essential units of this system, nations-states derived legitimacy by asserting territorial sovereignty and claiming to represent the will of particular peoples. This order, built on self-contained nation-states connected by economic and geopolitical dynamics, left little room for the Catholic Church's claim to universality. With globalization challenging the primacy of the nation-state, the Catholic Church has the opportunity to reassert its claim to universality and thus place itself at the center of a new, still undefined world order. In this context, Casanova observes that the pope has become "the high priest of a new universal religion of humanity and . . . the first citizen of a global civil society" (1997: 125). Tracing the globalization of the papacy to the First Vatican Council's assertion of papal supremacy, Casanova notes how the pope has now come to assume "the vacant role of spokesperson for humanity, for the sacred dignity of the human person, for world peace, and for a more fair division of labor and power in the world system. The role comes naturally to the papacy since it is fully in accordance with its traditional claims of universal authority. In a sense the papacy has been trying to re-create the universalistic system of medieval Christendom, but now on a truly global scale" (133).

Given his stature on the world stage, John Paul II represents the pinnacle of this drive toward a global papacy. Building on *Rerum Novarum* and the Vatican II documents, the pope has seized issues connected to globalization to reposition the Church as the defender of the rights of the individual and of local cultures and the chief advocate of an overarching "civilization of love and peace." John Paul II's point of departure is the recognition that "a feature of the contemporary world is the tendency towards globalization. It is a process made inevitable by increasing communication between the different parts of the world, leading in practice to overcoming distances, with evident effects in widely different fields" (John Paul II 1999a: #20). A central player in the process of globalization is the new communication technology. "Ours is an era of global communication. . . . The free flow of images and speech on a global scale is transforming not only political and economic relations between peoples, but even our understanding of the world. It opens up a range of hitherto unthinkable possibilities, but it also has certain negative and dangerous aspects" (John Paul II 2000: #11).

The dangers that John Paul II sees in globalization provide a rationale for his defense of particularity and the context to understand the alternative universal frame he proposes. "If globalization is ruled merely by the laws of the market applied to suit the powerful, the consequences cannot but be negative. These are, for example, the absolutizing of the economy, unemployment, the reduction and deterioration of public services, the destruction of the environment and natural resources, the growing distance between rich and poor, unfair competition which puts the poor nations in a situation of ever increasing inferiority. While acknowledging the positive values which come with globalization, the Church considers with concern the negative aspects which follow in its wake" (1999a: #20).

John Paul II's reading of the potential negative effects of globalization is in line with Catholic social thought, particularly with its emphasis on the common good.[6] Rather than simply responding to narrow utilitarian values like efficiency and the maximization of profit, the emerging global economy "must express a concrete and tangible commitment to solidarity which makes the poor the agents of their own development and enables the greatest number of people, in their specific economic and political circumstances, to exercise the creativity which is characteristic of the human person and on which the wealth of nations too is dependent" (1999b: #17). It is clear, thus, that despite claims that John Paul II's conservatism translates into indifference toward issues of social justice, the pope articulates a pointed critique of the neoliberal ideology that free markets are not only necessary but also sufficient means to achieve human fulfillment. The pope even echoes liberationist social analyses when he highlights the potential for increased dependency and inequality in the global economy.

John Paul II engages in a similar defense of the uniqueness and creativity of the human person when discussing the cultural aspects of globalization. "The fact that a few countries have a monopoly on . . . cultural 'industries' and distribute their products to an ever growing public in every corner of the earth can be a powerful factor in undermining cultural distinctiveness. These products include and transmit implicit value-systems and can therefore lead to a kind of dispossession and loss of cultural identity in those who receive them" (2000: #11). Against this threat of cultural homogenization, John Paul II proposes the notion of communion, "which has its source in Christian revelation and finds its sublime prototype in the Triune God." Communion "never implies a dull uniformity or enforced homogenization or assimilation; rather it expresses the convergence of a multiform variety, and therefore is a sign of richness and a promise of growth" (#10).

John Paul II's defense of local cultures and situated individuals would seem to dovetail with the postmodern suspicion of grand narratives. However, this is only an apparent convergence, for the pope grounds his critique of globalization not on an appeal to postmodern fragmentation and indeterminacy, which, as we saw, he rejects in *Fides et Ratio* as conducive to nihilism. Instead, John Paul II reconfigures the Catholic notion of universal natural laws with the aim of building a global ethic. "Globalization, for all its risks, also offers exceptional and promising opportunities, precisely with a view to enabling humanity to become a single family, built on the values of justice, equity, and solidarity. For this to happen, a complete change of perspective will be needed: it is no longer the well-being of any one political, racial or cultural community that must prevail, but rather the good of humanity as a whole" (John Paul II 1999b: #5–6). John Paul II's call "to be one family" is grounded on a universal anthropology and ethics, "a consciousness of universal moral values," the basis of which is "the universal moral law written upon the human heart. By following this 'grammar' of the spirit, the human community can confront the problems of coexistence and move forward to the future with respect for God's plan" (18).

While John Paul II acknowledges that globalization leads to increased cultural pluralism, he does not fall into a celebration of postmodern depthlessness and ephemerality. Rather, he uses globalization's time-space compression to justify a renewed call for unity and transhistorical foundations. "The Church, looking to Christ, who reveals man to himself, and drawing upon her experience of two thousand years of history, is convinced that 'beneath all that changes, there is much that is unchanging.' This continuity is based upon the essential and universal character of God's plan for humanity. Cultural diversity should therefore be understood within the broader horizon of the unity of the human race. In a real way, this unity constitutes the primordial historical and ontological datum in the light of which the profound meaning of cultural diversity can be grasped" (2000: #7).

Of the moral foundations laid by John Paul II, "the dignity of the human person" is first among equals. It is an inalienable and "transcendent" value. "Indeed, the whole of human history should be interpreted in the light of this certainty. Every person, created in the image and likeness of God (cf. Gen. 1:26–28) and therefore radically oriented toward the Creator, is constantly in relationship with those possessed of the same dignity. To promote the good of the individual is thus to serve the common good, which is that point where rights and duties converge and reinforce one another" (1998b: #2). Placing the dignity of the human person at the center of his global ethics enables John Paul II to stand side by side with secular multilateral organizations such as the United Nations in defense of human rights. "Defence of the universality and indivisibility of human rights is essential for the construction of a peaceful society and for the overall development of individuals, peoples and nations. To affirm the universality and indivisibility of rights is not to exclude legitimate cultural and political differences in the exercise of individuals rights, provided that in every case the levels set for the whole humanity by the [United Nations'] Universal Declaration [of Human Rights] are respected" (#3).

If we are a single family that speaks the common language of human rights grounded on the principle that God created us in his image, "an offense against human rights is an offense against the conscience of humanity as such, an offense against humanity itself. The duty of protecting these rights therefore extends beyond the geographical and political borders within which they are violated. Crimes against humanity cannot be considered an internal affair of a nation" (John Paul II 1999b: #7). By deterritorializing human rights—making them part of the church's claim to universality—John Paul II has, in effect, pulled the rug from under the nation-state, challenging its claim to be synonymous with the democratic public sphere. As the pope writes, "human rights have no borders, because they are universal and indivisible." Once again, John Paul II has appropriated the values of modernity and reinserted them at the heart of Catholic thought. Gone are the days when the Catholic Church equated humanism with secularization and vehemently opposed the efforts of local elites to build secular nation-states upon the Enlightenment principles of fraternity, solidarity, and equality. Now, in light of atrocities committed in the name of the nation-state that range from the Holocaust to genocide in the Balkans and Rwanda, the Catholic Church presents itself as a transnational guarantor of modernity's humanism. Hervieu-Leger identifies John Paul II's approach to modernity as a subtle form of integralism. Rather than directly impugning modernity's ideals, this integralism "places a high negative value on them by pointing out that modernity itself has proved to be incapable of achieving them. It endorses the modern promises that the Western world fails to keep or only partly fulfills—solidarity, human rights, justice, and so on—in order to turn the tables on modernity. This integralism comes not to bury, but to praise, the illusory grandeur of the modern ideal of freedom, in order to reaffirm the inevitable subordination of that ideal to the liberation that comes from God alone, but which the Church . . . alone knows how to attain" (Hervieu-Leger 1997: 115–116).

John Paul II urges his Church to uphold the right to life as the single most important human right. While the pope often stresses the right to life vis-à-vis the fetus, he also extends it to the defense of the integrity of the human person against emerging medical technologies, capital punishment, and poverty, political repression, and environmental degradation. In the pope's eyes: "There is no better word than 'life' to sum up comprehensively the greatest aspirations of all humanity. Life indicates the sum total of all the goods that people desire, and at the same time what makes them possible, obtainable and lasting" (John Paul II 1992: #2). The overall aim thus becomes to develop a "global civilization of love and peace" that is "inspired by feelings of tolerance and universal solidarity" (John Paul II 1996: 211). It is difficult to find a specific definition of what John Paul II means by this phrase, but a civilization of love and peace is characterized by a "culture of life" that entails "respect for the natural world and protection of the work of God's creation. In particular, it means respect for human life from the moment of conception until its natural end. A culture of life means serving those who enjoy no privileges, the poor and oppressed, since justice and freedom are inseparable and only exist if they exist for all. The culture of life means thanking God every day for the gift of life, for our value and dignity as human beings, for the friendship he offers us as we perform the pilgrimage to our eternal destiny" (202–203).

The essential ingredient in constructing and sustaining a civilization of love and peace supported by a culture of life is what John Paul II calls an "openness to transcendence and the realm of the spirit" (1992: #1). We can only respect nature and all its creatures if we understand that they are part of a divine design. Humanity in particular, as "God's masterpiece," has special, irreducible value. However, this does not mean that John Paul is articulating a modern and secularized religion of humanity.[7] It is not a case of replacing theology with sacred anthropology. It is the other way around: "Christian anthropology is really a chapter of theology, and the Church's social doctrine . . . 'belongs to the field of theology and particularly moral theology'"(John Paul II 1991: #55).

Perhaps the best way to understand what the pope means by a civilization of love and peace is to define what it is not—the culture of death. For the pope, the conflict between the culture of death and the civilization of love and peace is played out with special intensity in the Americas, where economic and cultural globalization, religious pluralism, and the need for evangelization collide.

THE AMERICAS: THE STRUGGLE BETWEEN THE NEW EVANGELIZATION AND THE CULTURE OF DEATH

With the crisis of socialism, John Paul II has paid increasing attention to capitalism, especially to the claim that free markets provide the only viable alternative to organize not only the economy but society itself, including politics and culture.[8] As early as *Centesimus Annus*, published in 1991 before talk of globalization had become widespread, John Paul II asked:

> Can it perhaps be said that, after the failure of Communism, capitalism is the victorious system, and that capitalism should be the goal of the countries now making efforts to rebuild their economy and society? If by "capitalism" is meant an economic system that recognizes the fundamental and positive role of business, the market, private property, and the resulting responsibility for the means of production, as well as free human creativity in the economic sector, then the answer is in the affirmative. . . . If by "capitalism" is meant a system in which freedom in the economic sector is not circumscribed within a strong juridical framework that places it at the service of human freedom in its totality, and that sees it as a particular aspect of that freedom, the core of which is ethical and religious, then the reply is certainly negative. Vast multitudes live in conditions of great material and moral poverty. There is a risk that a radical capitalistic ideology could refuse to even consider these problems, blindly entrusting their solution to market forces.

As global economic processes have begun to challenge the sovereignty of nation-states and to affect everyday life for large sectors of the world's population, the pope has sharpened his attacks on this "radical capitalistic ideology." He is particularly concerned with neoliberalism, which is emerging as a hegemonic ideology capable of challenging his global ethics. In the pope's eyes, neoliberalism operates with a reductive anthropology built around a highly individualistic and utilitarian notion of the self—the human being as primarily *homo oeconomicus*. This anthropology all but ignores the spiritual needs of the individual. Moreover, despite the neoliberal claim that free markets automatically translate into individual rights and freedom, this anthropology fails to provide solid grounding for critical moral decisions. In fact, because global neoliberal capitalism defines selfhood by what the individual possesses and consumes, there is a danger of losing sight of universal values. Thus, when economic elites reduce globalization to the spread of neoliberal capitalism, they in effect link globalization with the moral relativism expressed and legitimized philosophically by postmodernism. Here, once again, the pope's discourse shows a late modern sensibility. This time, John Paul II links current changes in capitalism with our sense of depthlessness and ephemerality in ways that echo Fredric Jameson's claim that "postmodernism is the logic of late capitalism."

According to the pope: "Today an invasive materialism is imposing its dominion on us in many different forms and with an aggressiveness sparing no one. The most sacred principles, once a secure guide for the behavior of the individual and of society, have been completely eliminated by false claims concerning freedom. . . . Today many people are tempted by self-indulgence and consumerism, and people's identity is often defined in terms of what they've got" (1996: 174). Particularly vulnerable are young people. "There are teachers of the 'fleeting moment,' who invite people to give free rein to every instinctive urge or longing, with the result that individuals fall prey to a sense of anguish and anxiety leading them to seek refuge in false, artificial paradises, such as that of drugs" (1992: #3).

It is not just individuals that have been caught in the maelstrom of materialism and consumerism. John Paul II also decries "the slavish conformity of cultures . . . to cultural models deriving from the Western world. Detached from their Christian origins, these models are often inspired by an approach to life marked by secularism and practical atheism and by patterns of radical individualism. This is a phenomenon of vast proportions, sustained by powerful media campaigns and designed to propagate lifestyles, social and economic programmes and, in the last analysis, a comprehensive world-view that erodes from within other estimable cultures and civilizations" (2000: #9).

Reference to the media, consumerism, and Western values points in the direction of the United States, which John Paul II has placed at the center of the current episode of globalization. Prominent in *Ecclesia in America*, his most recent apostolic exhortation to the Americas, is the pope's recognition that "the complex phenomenon of globalization is one of the features of the contemporary world particularly visible in America." The pope regards the United States with a certain ambivalence. On the one hand, he admires the country's youthful potential, its diversity, and its contributions to democracy. For example, in his 1987 visit to Miami, John Paul declared that "among the many admirable values of this nation there is one that stands out in particular. It is freedom." This freedom allows the United States to carry out its "special vocation," which is to "work at the service of humanity." On the other hand, the pope is troubled by a widespread "culture of death" in the United States, which includes not only unabashed materialism and consumerism, but the death penalty, abortion, and, more recently, cloning and research on embryonic stem cells. "In America, as elsewhere in the world, a model of society appears to be emerging in which the powerful dominate, setting aside and even eliminating the powerless: I am thinking here of unborn children, helpless victims of abortion; the elderly and incurably ill, subjected at times to euthanasia; and the many other people relegated to the margins of society by consumerism and materialism. Nor can I fail to mention the unnecessary recourse to the death penalty. . . . This model bears the stamp of the culture of death, and is therefore in opposition to the Gospel message" (1999a: #63).

Because of its wealth and power, the United States is in danger of succumbing to this culture of death. The stakes are high in this struggle between life and death. In his most recent visit to the United States in 1999, John Paul II reached back to the Dred Scott case, in which the Supreme Court ruled that African Americans do not have constitutional rights, to dramatize the country's current moral predicament. "Today, the conflict is between a culture that affirms, cherishes, and celebrates the gift of life, and a culture that seeks to declare entire groups of human beings—the unborn, the terminally ill, the handicapped, and others considered 'unuseful'—to be outside the boundaries of legal protection. Because of the seriousness involved, and because of America's great impact on the world as a whole, the resolution of this new time of testing will have profound consequences for the century whose threshold we are about to cross" (1999c: #3). The pope has thus elevated the struggle for the United States's moral compass to the global plane, turning it into an epoch-making battle.

For resources to carry out this struggle, the pope turns to Latin America, where in 1983 he called for a new evangelization to commemorate the five-hundredth anniversary of a European presence in the New World (Peterson and Vásquez 1998). Although John Paul II recognizes national differences and acknowledges that the United States has its own moral and religious resources, he sees in Latin America a vast reservoir of intensely lived piety and popular forms of Christian religiosity. With the proper "purification," this widespread popular piety may help resacralize secular society in the United States. "A distinctive feature of America [the hemisphere] is an intense popular piety, deeply rooted in the various nations. It is found at all levels and in all sectors of society. . . . The Synod of Fathers stressed the urgency of discovering the true spiritual values present in popular religiosity, so that, enriched by genuine Catholic doctrine, it might lead to a sincere conversion and a practical exercise of charity. If properly guided, popular piety also leads the faithful to a deeper sense of membership of the Church, increasing the fervor of their attachment and thus offering an effective response to the challenges of today's secularization" (1999a: #16).

The pope's appeal to a purified traditional popular Catholicism in "communion" with the hierarchy allows him to develop flexible pastoral approaches that blend grassroots with institutional levels, the local with the global, the particular with the universal, in ways that resolve the tensions exacerbated by globalization. Popular piety is part of an inculturated Catholicism that recognizes the contributions of local indigenous cultures while introducing a global ethics based on unchanging principles to which the Catholic Church has special access.

Most prominent in this popular piety is Our Lady of Guadalupe, whom John Paul has recognized as "Queen of all America," "Patroness of all America and Star of the first and new evangelization," and "Mother and Evangelizer of America." Such recognition is unprecedented within the Catholic Church, as "no other Marian image has been accorded such universal honours" (Brading 2001: 341). The appeal to Our Lady of Guadalupe is very strategic. Besides dovetailing with the pope's stress on Marian devotions, it enables John Paul to embrace difference while bringing the Americas together under a single evangelization program. The pope observes how La Guadalupana's influence "overflows the boundaries of Mexico, spreading to the whole continent. America, which historically has been, and still is, a melting-pot of peoples, has recognized in the mestiza face of the Virgin of Tepeyac, 'in Blessed Mary of Guadalupe, an impressive example of a perfectly inculturated evangelization'" (1999a: 11). As a mestiza virgin who appeared to the humble native American Juan Diego, Our Lady of Guadalupe is an affirmation of locality and difference. For John Paul, however, what is more important is that this difference is resolved into a Catholic synthesis. Our Lady of Guadalupe brings conqueror and vanquished, European and native American cultures together in a single church of which the Pope is the head. Put in another way, what John Paul II chooses to underline in this *mestizaje* is its Catholicity, the fact that it is at the service of a hemispheric project of evangelization.[9] John Paul hopes that Mary "will by her maternal intercession guide the Church in America, obtaining the outpouring of the Holy Spirit, as she once did for the early Church (Acts 1:14), so that the new evangelization may yield a splendid flowering of Christian life." Here reference to the Holy Spirit deterritorializes Mary. She is no longer limited to a locality, Tepeyac, or even a nation, which embodies the contradictions and power relations that characterized the conquest and the first evangelization. Mary, as Guadalupe, is now linked to the intercontinental charismatic renewal movement, which the pope has privileged as one of his evangelizing strategies.

The new evangelization frames John Paul II's call for the unity of the Americas. He urged those gathered at the inter-American Special Assembly of the Synod of Bishops in Santo Domingo (1992) to "reflect on America as a single entity, by reason of all that is common to the peoples of the continent, including their shared Christian identity.... The decision to speak of 'America' in the singular was an attempt to express not only the unity which in some way exists, but also to point to that closer bond which the people of the continent seek and which the Church wishes to foster as part of her own mission, as she works to promote the communion of all in the Lord." The pope is well aware that one of the most powerful dynamics linking the Americas are immigrants moving from Latin America to the United States. These immigrants "often bring with them a cultural and religious heritage which is rich in Christian elements." Thus "church communities will not fail to see in this phenomenon a specific call to live in an evangelical fraternity and at the same time a summons to strengthen their own religious spirit with a view to a more penetrating evangelization." In ministering to these immigrants, John Paul notes that "cooperation between the dioceses from which they come and those in which they settle ... has proven extremely beneficial." Here, in effect, the pope is sanctioning transnational and transcontinental pastoral and organizational strategies, demonstrating once again that he is highly attuned to the challenges brought by globalization. As we saw in Chapter 2, one of the effects of the time-space compression brought about by globalization is regionalization, including the formation of trading blocs. By focusing on the Americas as a unit, John Paul II is in fact advocating a religious and moral bloc with global reach. "The particular churches of America are called to extend their missionary efforts beyond the bounds of the continent. They cannot keep to themselves the immense riches of their Christian heritage. They must take this heritage to the whole world and share it with those who do not yet know it" (John Paul II

1999a: 74). Once again, the pope places the Americas at the heart of his global pastoral and theological perspective. John Paul II hopes that "the American continent, in accordance with its Christian vitality, will play its part in the great task of the mission *ad gentes*."

In addition to advocating for a purified popular religiosity, as well as transnational apostolates and inter-American episcopal meetings and commissions, John Paul has stressed the importance of evangelizing the continent through the mass media (Della Cava 1992). "For the new evangelization to be effective, it is essential to have a deep understanding of the culture of our time in which the social communications media are most influential. Therefore, knowledge and use of the media, whether the more traditional forms or those which technology has produced in recent times, is indispensable. Contemporary reality demands a capacity to learn the language, nature and characteristics of mass media. Using the media correctly and competently can lead to a genuine inculturation of the Gospel" (John Paul II 1999a: 72).

Nevertheless, like his stand vis-à-vis modernity, capitalism, and globalization, John Paul II's view of the media is ambivalent. As we saw earlier, the pope is deeply concerned with the commodification of culture and the proliferation of the "Western values" of individualism, materialism, and short-term gratification through the media. More recently, he has criticized the mass media for blurring the "distinction between truth and illusion." Media culture, he argues, is "so deeply imbued with a typical postmodern sense that the only absolute truth is that there are no absolute truths or that, if there were, they would be inaccessible to human reason and therefore irrelevant. In such a view, what matters is not the truth but the 'story,' if something is newsworthy or entertaining" (2001b: #3). In view of this tendency toward nihilism, John Paul II calls for a "critical" use of the media that would entail the proclamation of "the Good News of salvation of Jesus Christ" to the entire world. In the case of the pope, this proclamation has included not just the publication of *Crossing the Threshold of Hope*, an autobiographical essay which became an instant best-seller in the United States and was translated into twenty-one languages. The pope has also recorded several compact discs, including a widely popular CD of him singing the rosary in Latin against a background of Bach and Handel. *Abba Pater*, released in March 1999, can be found at amazon.com along with other CDs by the "same artist."[10]

It is clear that John Paul II deftly uses global media to spread his global message. The question is whether this entwinement with globalization undermines his "critical" stance toward modernity and the media. For what is being purveyed is not just that Christ is the savior but also that the pope is a "hip" spiritual world figure. Here the distinction between truth and illusion, which John Paul II seeks to maintain, collapses in a postmodernist turn à la Baudrillard. For the message becomes the image and the medium itself (i.e., the novelty of a CD recorded by the pope singing in five languages against a hybrid background of world beat and Latin chants).

The commodification of the pope's authority to speak, to enter the field of global popular culture as a legitimate and bankable spokesperson, has led some in the Catholic Church to ask whether John Paul II is a servant or a superstar. Woodrow (1998: 74–89) draws a sharp contrast between Paul VI's modesty and hesitance and John Paul II's self-assuredness, as shown by the latter's "highly mediatized" and triumphalist trips around the world. Often these voyages become "one-man shows (the pope, omnipresent, is the only one to speak, to warn, to admonish, rarely to learn and listen)." And certainly, Catholic celebrations of World Youth Day have become Woodstock-like festivals in which the pope appears with all the trappings of a rock star. Woodrow is admittedly not an impartial critic; he has clear liberationist sympathies. Nevertheless, even more "neutral" observers such as Tad Szulc (1995: 468) note that "if commercialization reflects popularity, then John Paul II has no rivals in what has become the worldwide exploitation of his image, often vulgar and too frequently sanctioned by the Church to generate income."

There are two particularly dramatic examples of the commodification of John Paul II's image. The first is the recent publication of a Vatican-sanctioned children's magazine about the pope's life. In four episodes, Stanley (2001) observes, the magazine "turns the 80-year-old pontiff into a comic book superhero—one who relies on faith, not magical powers, to help the needy and combat evil (in this case, Communism)." What the comic book sells is a story of rags to riches, the story of a unique and rugged individual who stood up against and ultimately beat the system. This narrative has an obvious correlate in the neoliberal ideology of self-made success. Commenting on the comic book, Stanley calls us in jest to "make way for the Vatican's X-man: Il Papa." More seriously, she notes that the magazine is only "one example of the cult of personality around John Paul II, who was an actor before he became a priest, and who knows better than almost anyone how to captivate an audience." Such a cult of personality would appear to be implicated in precisely the kind of subjectivism that John Paul calls to task in *Fides et Ratio*.

The second poignant example is the use of John Paul II's likeness on euro coins, the new currency of the European Union. Tagliabue (2001) sees this as part of a larger attempt by the Vatican to increase John Paul II's visibility in popular culture and the media. "For the Vatican, spreading the pope's image abroad on things of value is a good thing. Last March, it signed a deal with Maxx International, a licensing company in Beverly Hills, Calif., to sell international telephone calling cards with photographs of the pope." Here the critic of the excesses of neoliberal capitalism becomes literally an exchange value in the emerging economic order of trade blocs and global telecommunications. It is a curious case of "contagion," as Durkheim would put it, where the sacred and the profane exchange energies, recharging each other: the pope gives value to the coins and cards, and the cards and coins link John Paul II to the world of commodities, with all its fetishisms.

These two examples show how John Paul II and the Vatican, in seeking to reposition the Church in a globalized context, generate contradiction and heterogeneity at the theological and pastoral levels. The tension between universality and particularity and the production of doctrinal and ritual hybridity are by no means new for the Catholic Church. The first evangelization in the Americas provides ample evidence of widespread religious mixing and local resistance to orthodoxy (Griffiths 1999; Espin 1997). The colonial experience also generated institutional fissures within Catholicism, as the debates on the humanity of indigenous populations demonstrate. Nevertheless, with John Paul II the Church's entwinement with the secular world reaches a qualitatively new level. More than ever, the pope's visibility and authority are predicated on the work of mass media and culture industries, which see in tradition a rich source of exotic narratives and practices of self-improvement and spiritual well-being that can be marketed worldwide. Here the pope's image and his incursions into commercial literature and music become unmoored from his ontological quest to redeem modernity, to recenter it around the "great tradition." They become mere products in a vast and amorphous "inspirational" culture industry, alongside books on New Age spirituality and how-to guides. This is the paradox of John Paul's papacy: while it has sought to tame the chaos and change generated by globalization, it has also had the unintended consequence of intensifying and disseminating global processes, even those the pope wishes to combat. To become a relevant figure on the world stage, the pope has adjusted to the logic of the mass culture that he impugns. In the process, he has both changed and reproduced that culture. The *New York Times* puts John Paul II's predicament well. In a

January 27, 1999, editorial on his last visit to Mexico, the newspaper notes that the pope

> sought to warn Mexicans of the dangers of technology, which can lead . . . to a world without a soul. His trip, however, inadvertently reveals the magnitude of what he is battling. He has always relied on modern media to enhance his extraordinary charisma and communication with the faithful. Before he spoke of technological dangers in Aztec Stadium, the arena's screen blazed with greetings to the Pope transmitted from all over the hemisphere. His criticisms of materialism were part of a trip underwritten by Pepsi-Cola and several other companies. John Paul won his battle with Communism, but his struggle to mount a spiritual critique of capitalism and a global commercial culture promises to be an even more complex task.

HYBRIDITY AND THE LIMITS OF INSTITUTIONAL DISCIPLINE

In this chapter we have analyzed John Paul II's vision of a global civilization of love and peace, highlighting the central role the Americas play in this project. We have shown how the civilization of love and peace is part of an effort to construct a new moral and religious metanarrative in the wake of the failure of modernity to meet its secular goals. Despite John Paul II's effort to present a seamless "great tradition" and place the Church as its anchor, the pope's project creates fault lines resulting from a mixture of premodern, modern, and postmodern discursive and nondiscursive strategies.[11] Rather than disciplining the fragmentation and fluidity produced by globalization and postmodernity, John Paul II's theology and pastoral practices add to the plurality and bricolage that characterize culture and religion today. In this sense, in spite of himself, John Paul is a vehicle for some of the global processes he seeks to contain.

Our analysis has been essentially textual, focusing on tensions in John Paul II's worldview as articulated in his encyclicals, letters, and messages. However, these disjunctures are expressed in real life, among specific Catholic institutions and communities. For instance, John Paul II's call to rely on a "properly guided" traditional popular Catholicism, particularly on the cult of the Virgin of Guadalupe, to build an inculturated new evangelization of the Americas is not without its pitfalls. The Asociación Tepeyac in New York City is a case in point. The last ten years have witnessed a dramatic influx of Mexican migrants to the city. According to the 2000 census, New York City's Mexican population has more than tripled in the last decade to 187,000. Mexicans are now the third-largest Latino group in the city, just behind the more established

Puerto Rican and Dominican communities. Confronted with the massive Mexican influx, local parishes, particularly in Brooklyn, Queens, and Staten Island, have struggled to minister to the new arrivals. According to a Latino priest in Brooklyn:

> The most difficult group to reach is the Mexicans, who have come to this diocese very recently and in great numbers. They bring great religious and cultural richness, but they tend not to participate in the day-to-day life of the parish. They only become involved for ritual events like the celebration of the *quinceañeras* or during the feast of Our Lady of Guadalupe, when they organize the activities, the mariachis, the cultural events, and the food, mostly by themselves, asking the priest just to come at the appointed time to say the mass. I know that the Feast of the Virgin of Guadalupe is a good opportunity to evangelize, to invite Mexicans to live their faith everyday. After all, because they do not have a solid religious education and are economically needy, Mexicans are among the Latino groups most vulnerable to the work of the "sects." I normally preach in my Guadalupe sermons that because the Virgin was mestiza, she was mother to all Latinos and wants us to work together for the good of the parish. But, you know, of the five hundred who come to the Guadalupe mass, maybe at most fifty come back on a regular basis.[12]

When the priest speaks of the Mexicans organizing the fiesta of the Virgin of Guadalupe "by themselves," he is referring to the activities of the Comités Guadalupanos (Guadalupan committees), small groups of Mexican Catholics, often hailing from the same village in the states of Puebla, Guerrero, or Oaxaca, which hold regular meetings at the members' homes to plan the festivities. Guadalupan committees became so prominent that in 1997 the Archdiocese of New York brought Father Joel Magallán, S.J., directly from Mexico to serve as liaison with these groups. With the help of Magallán, forty Guadalupan committees formed the Asociación Tepeyac, a transparish lay network that coordinates events ranging from the *Antorcha Guadalupana*, a marathon through the streets of Manhattan, to social services for undocumented Mexican workers (Herszenhorn 1998; D. Gonzales 1997).[13] In the wake of the attack on the World Trade Center, Asociación Tepeyac has emerged as a grassroots aid network, assisting the families not just of Mexicans, but also of Colombian, Dominican, and other Latin American immigrants who lost their lives. This network has been all the more critical in view of the undocumented status of many of the immigrants and the failure of mainstream media and institutions to recognize the impact of the tragedy for Latinos in New York City.

Despite its important contributions to immigrant rights and pan-

Latino identity, parish priests regard the Tepeyac Association with some ambivalence. In the eyes of a Euro-American priest with a long experience among New York City Latinos: "For all the good things they do, especially in making visible the plight of Mexican laborers in the city, Tepeyac tends to divert energy from our parishes. The loyalty of Mexican immigrants is primarily to Tepeyac, or at best to their small Comité Guadalupano, not to their neighborhood or to the parish. The bottom line is whether we can incorporate Mexicans into our diocese at all levels along with Puerto Ricans, Cubans, and Dominicans to some extent, who are now the leaders of the Latino Catholic church in New York. I have my doubts that Tepeyac can help us with that."

The Asociación Tepeyac clearly subverts the centralizing thrust of John Paul II's new evangelization, his vision of an inculturated trans-American popular piety in "full communion" with the hierarchical church. But is it possible that, notwithstanding its challenge to the parish structure and local ecclesial hierarchy, Asociación Tepeyac is another, more flexible, way to discipline popular piety in response to changing migration patterns? Indeed, during our fieldwork in New York, some lay leaders commented on Father Magallán's centralizing and hierarchical style, how he has become the spokesperson for Guadalupan committees citywide. There are already signs, however, that the association is losing its place as the hegemonic voice of the Mexican population in New York City, as lay leaders who have closer links with other Latino groups have begun to appear (Kinetz 2001).

As the literature on popular religions in Latin America makes clear, even the best efforts of religious institutions to discipline grassroots initiatives fall short, invariably encountering indigenous resistance. Global processes such as migration, the emergence of new communications technologies, and the autonomization and commodification of culture further complicate the imposition of top-down discipline, leading to paradoxical results, as strategies aiming to impose orthodoxy themselves become vehicles of globalization and hybridity. Influenced by Weber's work on bureaucratization, sociology has tended to stress the conservative functions of religious institutions. Since institutions are primarily concerned with their own reproduction—with sustaining orthodoxy—they generate change only at rare "breakthrough" moments (like Vatican II and its aftermath in liberation theology), when charismatic prophets rise to challenge the entrenched power of priests. As Clegg (1990: 4) argues, this view is part of a distinctively modern approach to organizations, one that seeks to sketch "a singular set of empirical tendencies which were irresistible and inevitable." Rational-choice theories fare no better, seeing change only as the result of strategic choices by religious elites (Gill 1998). Generally, these elites are seen as unitary, with a monolithic set of interests—normally to shore up or expand their clientele—and full understanding of the consequences of their actions. However, as the contradictions in John Paul II's civilization of love and peace demonstrate, Catholic elites are divided, forced to deal with the conflicting demands of pre- and anti-modern Marianism, post–Vatican II modernity, and global postmodernity. These elites also act with "bounded rationality," unable to know all their options and all the effects of their known alternatives. The result is a certain degree of institutional hybridity that adds to increasing diversity of the religious field in the Americas.

Modernist approaches to institutions ignore another important aspect of Weber's sociology of religion: the role of paradox and irony in social action. Weber's insight that Puritan worldly asceticism contributed to the rise of an instrumental capitalist spirit at odds with the enchanted world of religion shows how strategies deployed deliberately by religious elites to define and reproduce collective identity end up having unanticipated consequences.[14] The case of John Paul II's New Evangelization shows that the focus on authority, hierarchy, centralization, and discipline, which characterize classical Weberian theories of organization, is still warranted. However, the present episode of globalization, with its relentless dialectic of homogenization and heterogenization, heightens paradox and complexity and forces us to pay close attention to how institutions generate change, even when they do not expressly intend it.

8

"BLITZING" CENTRAL AMERICA
The Politics of Transnational Religious Broadcasting

On the evening of March 28, 1990, 4.5 million Guatemalans turned on their televisions to watch *Rescued from Hell* (Rescatados del Infierno), a soap opera–style tale (*telenovela*) of the true-life religious-conversion stories of five Latin Americans. The show, created by the U.S.-based Christian Broadcasting Network (CBN), captured 64 percent of the television viewing market in Guatemala, making it the most watched television program in the history of Central America—more popular even than soccer's World Cup.[1] At the end of *Rescued from Hell*, after narrating the stories of radical conversion, the host of the show asked viewers to pray with him to "receive Jesus Christ." Using survey research methods, CBN representatives determined that more than two million people—42.2 percent of viewers—joined the host in prayer.[2]

Rescued from Hell was a centerpiece of CBN's Proyecto Luz, or Project Light, an extensive evangelical campaign undertaken in the spring of 1990. Over the course of six months, the transnational broadcasting company staged a "media blitz," using $1.5 million worth of television, newspapers, radio, films, tracts, and billboards to reach CBN's goal of "taking the gospel to every person" in Guatemala. At the end of those six months, CBN representatives reported to U.S. supporters that the project was a fantastic success, claiming that "CBN's spring media blitz in Central America, Project Light, has far exceeded the ministry's goal of two million souls won for the Lord."[3] As one Guatemalan pastor explained in the March 20, 1990, issue of Project Light's *Headlines*, the

FIGURE 8.1. The opening scene of the Christian Broadcasting Network's successful television special, *Rescued From Hell*. The producer of the show was a popular *telenovela* actor.

project's evangelical tracts were so popular that "you'd think we were passing out dollar bills." On first glance, CBN's Project Light seems an exemplary case of the use of religion to strengthen hegemonic national and international projects and of the role the mass media play in processes of global cultural homogenization.[4] Indeed, in *Exporting the American Gospel*, Brouwer, Gifford, and Rose (1996: 11) characterize Project Light as a prime example of campaigns in which "even as Christian fundamentalism is purveyed by an aggressive international sales force, . . . the social product that they distribute so successfully around the world is clearly stamped 'Made in the U.S.A.'"

Such an argument merits attention. In Project Light, as in all of its worldwide evangelism campaigns, CBN disseminated a two-pronged message that promotes global neoliberal capitalism and U.S. geopolitical hegemony. The first prong, the gospel of health and wealth, asserts that those who accept God's grace through salvation and subsequently strive to establish God's kingdom will be rewarded with material blessing. Rather than advancing a traditional Protestant ethic that connects asceticism, hard work, and economic success, CBN offers a narrative more aligned with contemporary flexible forms of capitalism: be willing to take financial risks, perhaps even to borrow money and invest it in the market or in evangelization campaigns, knowing that God will reward these risks by multiplying your wealth.

CBN pairs this timely message with a dominion theology, the belief that Christ will return to the earth only after Christians have established a thousand-year reign of God on earth. To build this kingdom, Christians must be in positions of worldly authority. Pat Robertson, the founder and president of CBN, has made clear through his own political engagement that he understands the United States to be the crucial actor in establishing this kingdom on earth. During the Project Light campaign, he also described communism as the absolute enemy of the kingdom and vehemently argued that Central America was a crucial battleground for this war between good and evil. Although this construal of geopolitical struggle is no longer central in hemispheric relations, it remains an instructive historical precedent of the role of religion and the global media in the construction of local and national identities.[5]

Project Light, however, also reveals a more complex dynamic at play—one that challenges the claim that CBN's social product is "clearly stamped 'Made in the U.S.A.'" CBN couches its potentially homogenizing two-pronged message in a call for personal salvation and radical individual transformation. This call takes a particular shape in each context, as CBN uses sophisticated glocal techniques to tailor messages to local, national, and regional markets. Glocalization, as described in Chapter 2, refers to global approaches to marketing that do not impose a standard image of the product but rather shape advertising, and sometimes the product itself, in response to perceived demands of specific local markets (R. Robertson 1995). Glocalization allows organizations to produce "hybrid" cultural goods that are neither strictly global nor local. This hybridity, in turn, challenges simplistic arguments that global cultural production must be either homogenizing or heterogenizing.

We argue that, even in the context of profound power asymmetries between Guatemala and the United States, Project Light shows that globalized religions do not always impose hegemonic messages produced in "core" countries onto consumers in the "periphery." Our analysis reveals that Project Light was effective in large part because it was glocalized: CBN packaged its core message in a set of images and discourses that producers knew would appeal to viewers. After researching local, national, and regional markets, Project Light organizers created media that had "indigenous" content, constructing stories of situated individuals who achieved material success and personal transformation in the face of the sociopolitical chaos most Guatemalans confront in their everyday lives. Project Light also addressed issues surrounding the changing nature of gender roles and family life, at the same time appealing to the viewers' notions of what constitutes good entertainment.

Moreover, examination of responses to the campaign suggests that while many viewers found the packaging of CBN's core message appealing, they did not fully internalize the gospel of health and wealth and dominion theology. Rather, many viewers used the narratives and scripts provided by CBN to build their own individual and collective identities and to create hybrid religious forms. Rather than explicitly resisting the CBN campaign, as the Catholic hierarchy encouraged them to do, many Guatemalans acted as selective consumers. This selective consumption is itself a form of cultural production, since consumption always entails the creation of meaning (Fiske 1989: 35). Yet such productive consumption does not represent the pure agency of actors heroically defending the integrity of local practices against the impersonal external forces of globalization. Instead, we find situated actors who draw from multiple local and global resources to imagine individual and collective identities. In Project Light, Guatemalan viewers created hybrid religious forms from CBN media, but they did so within boundaries created by Guatemala's relationship with the United States, a relationship of profound geopolitical importance in the decade preceding Project Light.

THE GUATEMALAN CONTEXT

In 1990, as Project Light was winding down, another campaign got into full swing: a presidential campaign that would result in the election of Jorge Serrano Elías, a proponent of neoliberal economic policies and the first democratically elected evangelical president in Central America. Serrano and his mentor Efraín Rios Montt enjoyed a close friendship with Pat Robertson, CBN's founder and director. All shared the Reagan-era conviction that Central America was a key regional stage for a global struggle between democracy (often conflated with capitalism) and communism. During this era, leaders of the U.S. Christian Right often worked behind the scenes to influence the struggle, and their Central American collaborators played crucial roles as the drama unfolded. In 1982, when the neo-Pentecostal Rios Montt was called to power in the wake of a coup by reformist military leaders, Pat Robertson immediately flew to Guatemala to publicly embrace and congratulate his friend. A few years later, Serrano, then a protégé of Rios Montt, emerged as an outspoken supporter of Project Light and appeared on programs in the United States that CBN produced to illustrate the success of the campaign.

This was not the first time Guatemalans in political power had welcomed U.S. Protestants and their political and economic messages. More than a century earlier, in 1871, Rufino Barrios led a Liberal revolution, encouraging an "ideology of progress" (Steigenga 1999: 152) that would bring Guatemala in line with "modern" nations by opening the country to international trade and U.S. missionaries. By inviting U.S. missionaries to Guatemala, the Liberal government aimed to end the era of conservatism there, in which the Catholic Church held significant power. Protestant missionaries had limited success in converting Guatemala's Catholics, but they did establish a U.S. presence in Guatemala, accompanied by large-scale agricultural and business interests, that would spearhead resistance to the next phase of widespread political reform in Guatemala.

In 1944, after a period of heavy-handed rule by Jorge Ubico and the stagnation of Guatemala's economy, a military junta undertook the October Revolution, sending Ubico into exile and opening the way for the democratic election of Juan José Arévalo. Arévalo and his successor, Jacobo Arbenz Guzmán, instituted a decade of land reform and labor organizing. As a part of his land reform program, Arbenz redistributed a portion of the land owned by the U.S.-owned United Fruit Company (UFC), the largest single employer and landowner in Guatemala, offering recompense for the declared tax value of the land. He also legalized Guatemala's Communist Party and purchased arms from Czechoslovakia, causing increasing concern to the cold-war government of the United States. Both administrations were met with resistance by Guatemala's traditional elite, who saw the transformation of the country's power relations as a threat to their own hegemony. They were joined in their resistance by the UFC and the U.S. government. In June 1954, the United States planned Operation Success, bombing Guatemala's capital from planes while a military coup was undertaken by U.S.-trained troops on the ground. The operation ended Guatemala's short-lived experiment with democratic reform and ushered in thirty years of military dictatorship (Steigenga 1999; Garrard-Burnett 1998).

Although the Catholic hierarchy actively supported the "anticommunist" stance of the 1954 coup, during the next twenty years many Catholic clergy and lay leaders gradually moved away from the military and elite. Many of them undertook social and pastoral work in the countryside among indigenous Guatemalans. This shift began with the work of Catholic Action in the 1940s and 1950s, a movement that aimed to bring "orthodox" Catholicism to the indigenous Maya. After Vatican II (1962–1965) and Medellín (1968), the shift continued among progressive and activist Catholics, who established Ecclesial Base Communities and aligned with popular movements for justice and peace in the rural areas of the country.

At the same time, armed revolutionary movements began to pose a serious threat to the ruling elite, who initiated violent counterinsurgency campaigns in the 1970s and 1980s, often targeting Catholic clergy and lay workers. The most brutal phase of counterinsurgency was led by Efraín Rios Montt, who in 1982 was installed as Guatemala's president after a military coup. He immediately initiated a campaign to eradicate guerrilla activity in the Guatemalan highlands and other rural areas. During the first fourteen weeks of his tenure, this campaign killed more than two thousand men, women, and children (Stoll 1994: 102). In addition, the Rios Montt regime created "model villages," forcing peasants who lived in zones where guerrillas were strongly supported to relocate to areas controlled by the army. Combined with scorched-earth sweeps that destroyed local supplies of essential provisions as a means to cut off support to guerrillas, this policy made internal refugees entirely dependent on the army for basic necessities. To support Rios Montt's counterinsurgency campaign and the global challenge to communism that he understood it to represent, Pat Robertson raised millions of dollars for CBN's Operation Lovelift, a "humanitarian aid project" that provided food and supplies to some of the one million Guatemalans who were forced to leave their villages as part of the model-village policy (Brouwer, Gifford, and Rose 1996: 56).

Rios Montt remained in office only a short time. A 1983 coup brought to power another military leader, Humberto Mejía Victores, who continued the counterinsurgency campaigns while also strengthening the military presence in rural areas. By 1985, the military felt it had achieved sufficient control of insurgents that it could bow to international pressures and institute a democratic election process. In that year, Guatemala elected its first civilian president in twenty years. Nonetheless, the military continued to operate death squads in the countryside, and the fear of persecution remained. Into the midst of this turmoil, dislocation, and civil war, CBN brought Project Light.

In 1990 Guatemala, a country that many have dubbed the "New Jerusalem of the Americas" (Stoll 1994; Garrard-Burnett 1998), already led Latin America in Protestant growth (Stoll 1990; Martin 1990). Just thirty years earlier, in 1960, Protestants comprised as little as 1.5 percent of the country's population (Brouwer, Gifford, and Rose 1996: 47). By the early 1990s the proportion of Guatemalan Protestants had risen, in some estimates, to 35 percent (Brouwer, Gifford, and Rose 1996: 47; Stoll 1994).[6] In a simplistic reading, Dominguez and Huntington (1984) have attributed this astounding growth to precisely the type of campaign Project Light exemplifies: missionary activity by wealthy, ultra-conservative, U.S.-based Evangelicals and their followers.

Careful examination of the Guatemalan context in recent years suggests, however, that although the message of U.S. Evangelicals has been highly effective in reaching certain classes in Guatemalan society, it may not be responsible for a large proportion of that country's growth in Protestantism. Rather, the seeds of much Protestant growth outside urban areas in Guatemala were planted during the years of turmoil and dislocation accompanying civil war. Propelled not only by the promise of physical safety, but also by a need to reconstruct community in safe spaces removed from political maneuvering, small, indigenous-led congregations of Pentecostals sprouted in villages and towns throughout the Guatemalan countryside (Green 1999; Garrard-Burnett 1998). The most numerous Protestants in Central America, Pentecostals highlight dramatic personal transformation and focus on healing and the practice of speaking in tongues.

Members of the urban evangelical elite like Serrano and Rios Montt share little more than a name with these Pentecostals. They belong to urban "neo-Pentecostal" megachurches that emerged in the 1980s and 1990s as parallel movements to both rural Pentecostal and mainline Protestant churches (Garrard-Burnett 1998; D. Smith 1990). Neo-Pentecostals have been strongly influenced by U.S.-based religious broadcasting, and they share with CBN an emphasis on dominion theology and the gospel of health and wealth. To the urban middle and upper classes, they offer a means both to achieve upward mobility (primarily through networking) and to justify it (through a message of personal prosperity as evidence of God's grace in one's life). As Dennis Smith explains: "This theology apparently comforts middle-class believers and legitimates their position in a desperately polarized society. It also stimulates upwardly-mobile evangelicals as they battle to survive in an intensely competitive and unforgiving economic environment" (1990: 294).[7] Project Light offered programming that specifically targeted the urban middle and upper classes, but CBN reworked its message to appeal to a broad audience.

THE CHRISTIAN BROADCASTING NETWORK'S
TWO-PRONGED MESSAGE

When we asked the coordinator of Project Light why CBN undertook the campaign in Central America, he responded: "The choice was made by Pat Robertson. . . . He was interested in going into Latin American countries that were in turmoil and therefore the people would be . . . more sensitive to the spiritual message because their need was very obvious and perhaps it would be a place where the Gospel message could have a greater impact. Even . . . this could be a stabilizing element in society. If the Gospel messages were communicated and understood, it could help to raise countries out of their conflict."[8] Project Light was unique, in his view, because it was able to communicate its message to a broader spectrum than could most indigenous evangelical media. He explained that "it was a matter of having access to the upper classes, which you don't have if you're preaching in a small church in a humble neighborhood, or through many other normal ministry efforts of the evangelical church. But with the media, with the television, the radio, and the press, you are jumping over all the obstacles and getting into their homes—of the rich as well as the middle class and the poor." To understand why it was particularly crucial for the Project Light campaign to "have access to the upper classes" as a means to "raise countries out of their conflict," we must first understand the particular way in which CBN represents the "Gospel message."

A Project Light newspaper advertisement published in various Central American newspapers over the course of the project shows a photo of a smiling *ladino* family gathered around its expensive-looking wooden dining room table.[9] The father, who is wearing a suit, holds a handmade sign (presumably made by one of his children) paraphrasing a Bible verse: "The Lord is my shepherd, nothing will I need." A sun rises over the mountains in the background of the sign, conveying a message of tranquility and hope. The text of the advertisement states in bold print: "I can't manage on my salary." Below the photograph, as a response to this statement of despair, is printed: "And you, do you confront the problems of your daily life with anguish and desperation? Seek first the kingdom of God and all other things will be added unto you" (translation ours).

This advertisement presents a clear theological message: wealth will be added to those who turn to God. CBN's "health and wealth" gospel promises believers that they are entitled to receive material blessings from God (Stoll 1994; Brouwer, Gifford, and Rose 1996). This gospel often includes the notion that planting a "seed" through donations to an evangelist will eventually be rewarded by large financial return. Robertson preached this gospel in his annual Super Bowl weekend telethon in January 1989 when he campaigned in the United States for Project Light funding. He explained to viewers: "If you and I will do God's business, then God will do our business. That's the way it is. We help share extending his kingdom, He'll help share extending ours. He says, 'These things will be extended to you, they'll be heaped up on you. That's no problem. You'll have more finances than you know what to do with.'"[10]

For Robertson and CBN representatives, doing "God's business" means extending the kingdom of God as defined by dominion theology and Robertson's own understanding of the global order. As Robertson explained in the 1989 telethon campaign: "What's on the heart of God is extending the Kingdom of God, of seeing not just a few people or a few churches, but he wants to see nations come to him. He wants to see China, He wants to see Russia, He wants to see India, He wants to see Central and South America won to Jesus."

Understood within the framework of this dominion theology, the explicit focus on the elite of Guatemala begins to make sense. CBN must reach those in power if the organization wants to be able, in Robertson's words, to "take whole nations for Jesus Christ." Robertson made very explicit that when nations are taken *for* Jesus Christ, they will be taken *from* communism, constantly reminding U.S.-based sponsors that "we're using every available means to bring the light of Jesus . . . to a people long oppressed by the darkness of communism." As he explained in his January 1989 appeal for funding: "Not only is [Project Light] going to extend the Kingdom of God, it's going to stop communism in its tracks in Central America!"

One of the conversion stories highlighted in *Rescued from Hell*, a prime-time television show that anchored Project Light, tells how the "light of Jesus" transformed the heart of a man "oppressed by the darkness of communism." This compelling story of reconciliation between a member of the Salvadoran military and a former guerrilla begins with a fairly evenhanded treatment of El Salvador's civil war: a narrator reminds viewers of the popular phrase "War is hell," and he then introduces them to two men, equally committed to their cause, who fought on opposite sides in the country's civil war. The guerrilla first explains how he became attracted to communism during his university years and eventually "renounced my daughter, my wife, my mother, my house—I left everything to join the revolutionary cause." The military

FIGURE 8.2. Pat Robertson shaking hands with soldiers in El Salvador, after announcing that the popular CBN program *Rescued from Hell* would be sent to every military base in the country.

officer then begins to tell his own story, describing how he joined the army to gain discipline and leadership skills but found himself "lacing up my boots" and setting off for the war-torn countryside to engage in battle.

Though constructed as parallel stories, these accounts begin to diverge with the subtle message that the guerrilla chose to renounce commitment to values of family life while the military leader entered the army to strengthen the valued characteristics of order and discipline. The more clear divergence comes, however, when each begins to account for how he heard the message that "Christ loves you" and consequently asked Christ to enter his life. The guerrilla explains that, after a short imprisonment, he left the battlefield and returned to the city, where an evangelical pastor approached him and asked him to visit his church. He did visit but did not experience the moment of conversion until he returned to armed combat. As he prepared to begin his first assignment after hearing the message of Christ's love, he became paralyzed, fell to his knees, and asked Christ to cleanse him of his sins. He no longer felt compelled to fight among the guerrillas. Rather, he returned to the city to team up with the military officer and present the gospel at military bases throughout Central America.

Conversely, the military officer received the message of Christ's love through his best friend and fellow officer, "a great Christian and an excellent soldier," whose death in combat prompted the officer's conversion. The officer, encouraged by the example of his friend, continued to engage in warfare as a Christian and joined the ex-rebel in disseminating the message of Christ's love to fellow members of the military. Thus what appeared in the beginning to be an evenhanded story about the "hell" of war quickly developed into a story about where Christ stands in conflicts throughout Central America: if one is fighting against insurgents, one can be both a model Christian and a model soldier; if one is fighting as a guerrilla, one must renounce one's political commitments to enter a life with Christ.

This message comes as no surprise to those familiar with Pat Robertson's politics. In the 1988 presidential campaigns, Robertson was the only candidate who placed himself "firmly with Reagan in insisting that America must stand up against communism in Central America" (Hadden and Shupe 1988: 277). Historically, Robertson's explicitly political stance has not been well received by Guatemalans (Schultze 1992). Aware of this, CBN consistently chose not to foreground political and economic messages. Rather, the organization subtly incorporated these messages into stories about personal transformation. In so doing, CBN was able to particularize a universal message to appeal to local audiences.

LOCALIZING THE GLOBAL, OR TRANSFORMING SOCIETY ONE PERSON AT A TIME

While researching the project, we viewed uncut clips of interviews recorded for a television special about Project Light. In one of the clips, which was not used in the show's final cut, the interviewer asked CBN's director of international operations what impact the project should have on society. He began his response by saying: "We've committed to seeing a long-term spiritual revolution in these [Central American] countries and to reporting on the impact of this: people who, living their lives, how the country is administrated . . . " At this point, he abruptly stopped and asked for an opportunity to answer the question again. His second answer began in the same way, explaining a commitment to report to the CBN audience how the countries had changed, but this time his examples of change were "church attendance on the increase, growing numbers of people committing themselves to Christ, . . . less family problems, lower crime rates, less use of alcohol and drugs."

Inseparable from the social teachings of CBN, which are individualistic and deal primarily with moral issues, is an often unspoken political commitment. The director of international operations revealed his political focus through an instinctive reference to the intended correlation between the project and the civil governments of target countries. His revision suggests that this underlying political positioning is carefully controlled through self-censorship and edited out of CBN broadcasts.

CBN programming for the Project Light campaign focused on individual transformation as the foundation of societal transformation. As the coordinator of the Guatemala campaign put it: "It is our very firm belief that by changing the individual, you help to change the society. So, if you change the individual, you can change the family. If you change the family, you can change the neighborhood. If you change the neighborhood, you can change the city—you can change the country." To pursue individual conversion, Project Light edited CBN's global political and economic agendas by particularizing them in a discourse of transformation targeted at specific individuals. On August 28, 1989, during the planning phases of the project and before the Project Light idea was conceived, the coordinator faxed a memo to one of his colleagues at CBN proposing a slogan for the campaign: "Knowing how Latins appreciate pride in country . . . we've come up with a basic slogan that can have progressive endings or sub-slogans as the campaign goes on. The basic one is *"Por amor a Guatemala"* [For the love of Guatemala] . . . and with sub-slogans like 'let's care for our children,' 'let's build happy homes,' or 'let's reinforce our marriages' and finally 'let's follow Jesus Christ.' . . . I think it will work and give the feeling of being tailored just for each country."

Though "Por Amor a Guatemala" was eventually not chosen as the campaign slogan, the explanation of the appeal and rationale for such a slogan highlights two crucial points. First, it suggests an emphasis on nation, family, and success that emerges in neo-Pentecostal discourses in the United States and worldwide. Second, it reveals how CBN tailors this universal emphasis to particular populations, explicitly undertaking a glocal strategy. CBN used focus groups to develop and test the themes of the campaign and relied on Guatemalan writers and producers to create radio and television spots. Those themes, "taken out of situations of everyday life" for Guatemalans, were intended to get the attention of Guatemalans and subsequently focus that attention on the core salvation message of the campaign. Three of CBN's most important glocal themes were the possibility of socioeconomic mobility, the appeal of radical personal transformation, and the lure of improved family life.

In promoting socioeconomic mobility, CBN produced shows and television spots which portrayed the lives of middle- and upper-middle-class *ladinos* in Guatemala, virtually erasing the existence of indigenous persons, who comprise almost 60 percent of Guatemala's population. The Guatemala coordinator explained the decision to allow certain images to dominate the programming: "They're used to seeing telenovelas, for example, with very sophisticated people in rich settings. They identify with their struggles and their problems, jealousy and all those things that go along with telenovelas. So it doesn't matter that it is in a rich setting. As a matter of fact, most people would rather it be in a rich setting so they kind of have a 'want to' identity with that. So that's the same approach, pretty much, that we took." The telenovela format for *Rescatados del Infierno*, the most popular program in the campaign, was the most effective glocal technique employed by CBN representatives in Guatemala. *Rescatados del Infierno* was produced by a telenovela star and also included moderately well known telenovela actors. Ana López describes this "preferred" format: "The telenovela exploits personalization—the individualization of the social world—as an epistemology. It ceaselessly offers its audience dramas of recognition and re-cognition by locating social and political issues in personal and familial terms and thus making sense of an increasingly complex world" (1995: 261).

In *Rescatados del Infierno*, CBN framed stories of domestic violence, marital infidelity, alcoholism, and the suffering associated with war as personal. This discouraged viewers from considering the social and political issues underlying the struggles that it presented—such issues as machismo, trends of rural-urban migration, economic injustice, political corruption, and U.S. interventionism. Rather, CBN asked its viewers to recognize the presence of violence, infidelity, alcoholism, and suffering in their own lives, and then to "re-cognize": to see the problems through the lens of Jesus Christ's forgiveness and salvation.

Telenovelas function in the lives of Latin American viewers in ways similar to the way conversion to Pentecostalism functions in the lives of converts. First, they provide the material with which Latin Americans suffering multiple disruptions associated with modernization, urbanization, and economic and political turmoil can recreate community. In this case, community resides in the "tightly woven fabric of family relationships" (Martín Barbero 1995: 277) that always serve as the centerpiece of these dramas. Second, through the use of melodrama, telenovelas, like Pentecostal Christianity, present "terminal conflict between polarized moral forces" (Gledhill 1992: 107). In the case of neo-Pentecostalism, these are the forces of good and evil, equated during this era with democracy and communism, respectively. In telenovelas, such forces "run through the social fabric and are expressed in personal and familial terms extending beyond the biological family into all areas of social life" (Gledhill 1992: 107). Thus CBN could successfully use the telenovela format in Project Light not only because it was a preferred genre for many Guatemalan viewers, but also because its method of meaning making closely paralleled CBN's own.

One of the accounts dramatized in *Rescued from Hell* was that of a woman named Maydee Portillo, who was sexually abused by family members during her childhood and abducted and raped by strangers as an adult. She repeatedly attempted suicide, believing that her life had no value. When a woman from her neighborhood came to Maydee's home to talk to her about accepting Jesus into her life, Maydee prayed with this woman to receive Christ. She explains: "Immediately I was happy and felt a peace that I had never known." At the end of the show, after three more true stories of miraculous transformation, the host explains: "No human could possibly resolve these situations. Only Jesus is able to purify one's heart in just a few moments." Such testimonies served to illustrate the instantaneous change that is possible only through Christian salvation—the "radically new existence" afforded by conversion to Evangelicalism (R. Gonzalez 1991: 269).

In many instances, the focus on radical personal transformation required that CBN alter and even misrepresent the experiences of converts. The stories told in *Rescued from Hell* were based on personal conversion testimonies given to CBN representatives by Latin American Evangelicals. In fact, the transcript of Maydee Portillo's original testimony does not tell a story of dramatic transformation. Maydee had experienced conversion to Evangelicalism at the age of seventeen, but she became pregnant, had an abortion, and fell away from the Church. Throughout her traumatic life, she frequently considered returning to the Evangelical Church and actually did return at least once before the incident portrayed in *Rescued from Hell*. When reconstructed by CBN representatives to appeal to Guatemalan audiences, Maydee's lifelong struggles became a narrative of instantaneous and radical change.

In addition to reframing overwhelming political and economic issues as personal and reconstructing personal transformations as instantaneous, Project Light presented appealing images of family and of men's participation in family life. Like the process of creating a radical transformation package, this appealing image of men's involvement in family life often required that personal testimonies be reformulated for Project Light media. One story used in Project Light programming was based on a testimony in which a man named Dulio told in great detail how he and his wife, in search of meaning, became involved in subversive guerrilla activities, drugs, partying, and loose sexual behavior. Both eventually experienced conversions that radically changed their behavior. Significantly, Dulio converted first and later convinced his wife to join him in living an upright life.

After having been transformed into a script for Project Light programming, Dulio's testimony read differently: Dulio's wife stood by as an innocent victim of his debauchery, waiting for him to settle down. The story ended: "To Diana, love and peace have been returned, and for Dulio, his long search has ended." Dulio and Diana's story of a man converting and then convincing his wife to do the same was transformed by CBN into a story about men's return to family life and reconciliation with patiently waiting wives. The producers of Project Light media could make these alterations because they understood these locally salient themes to be the malleable packaging of CBN's core message, which itself was unchanging and unchangeable.

A more explicit example of CBN's attempts to deploy locally its universal, suprahistorical message of Christian salvation was "The Jesus Film," used in collaboration with the U.S.-based Campus Crusade for Christ. CBN had pledged to reach "every person in the . . . nation" with the film.[11] Translated into at least two indigenous languages, the film was sent into what the project coordinator called "tribal areas"—remote locations without televisions or newspapers and with few radios. CBN had originally planned to hold a series of evangelistic meetings led by local pastors in these rural areas, connecting with local networks to disseminate its global message of salvation. However, fearing heterodox readings by local pastors, the network eventually decided to show the Jesus film. As the coordinator for the Guatemalan project explained: "We realized very quickly that using the Jesus film as an evangelist could neutralize a lot of . . . potential problems and be a lot more effective. We knew exactly what the message was going to be, whereas working with local evangelists, the message might go in directions that we didn't want it to, or . . . it was just harder to control. We had a uniform message [with the Jesus film]."

Such a strategy reveals the tensions surrounding a glocal campaign.

Although willing to capitalize on the appeal of indigenous forms of evangelical Protestantism in Guatemala and to focus programming on issues Guatemalans themselves determined to be especially salient, CBN representatives did not want to encourage the heterogeneous salvation messages developed within those local forms and surrounding these local issues.

THE "BLITZ": VARYING DEGREES OF SUCCESS IN GLOCAL MARKETING

The centerpiece of the campaign, the so-called blitz, included three prime-time television shows aired on March 26, 27, and 28, 1990. The shows included *Fiesta Con el Superlibro* (Superbook party), a cartoon-format children's show; *No Me Preguntes, Preguntale a Dios* (Don't ask me, ask God), a question-and-answer session about "life's toughest questions"; and *Rescatados del Infierno*. At the end of each of the three shows, the audience was invited to pray with the host to "receive Christ." Using a strategy called "roadblocking," CBN aired each of these programs simultaneously on virtually every television station, meaning that if one watched television between eight and nine P.M. on March 26, 27, or 28, one had no choice but to watch one of these shows.

The three programs exhibit a range of strategies for the production of transnational media. Of the three shows that comprised the "blitz," two had been produced in the Virginia Beach studios of CBN before the campaign. *No Me Preguntes, Preguntale a Dios* was produced for U.S. audiences in the early 1980s. Because it featured well-known movie stars and had been extremely popular in the United States, CBN representatives assumed that it would be a popular program in Guatemala as well. For Project Light, CBN simply replaced U.S. hosts with Central American celebrities. These celebrities introduced each segment of the programs, all of which were translated into Spanish.

Fiesta con el Superlibro was also originally produced for viewers in the United States. This children's show used Bible stories to encourage the conversion of children to evangelical Protestantism. The *Superbook Party*'s adaptation illustrates especially well CBN's specific form of glocalization, the creation of a locally tailored package for a homogeneous core product. An internal CBN document, "Evangelistic Adaptation Philosophy," explicitly describes this process. In the document, CBN representatives discuss the glocal strategy they call "contextualization": They elect to rewrite the program's theme song and have a Central American children's choir record the new song. They also recon-

FIGURE 8.3. A scene from *The Superbook Party*, a children's program that CBN adapted for use in Central America

textualize the Bible stories by having a Spanish-speaking host frame them in ways they believed would be more appealing to Central American audiences. For instance, the document reads: "Central American children live in a world filled with fear and insecurity. Many don't have a father, or have several 'fathers' in succession; the rest know that they could lose their fathers at any time to war or emigration. The children of Central America need above all a *sense of security*. They need to be taught *that God the Father* CAN *be trusted*."

This "Evangelistic Adaptation Philosophy" not only aimed to make the show more appealing to Central Americans, it also worked to "correct doctrinal distortions" at the local level. The document called for a specific translation of the Virgin Mary as "the mother of Jesus" rather than the generally used "Mother of God" to combat what CBN representatives understood to be incorrect Catholic understandings of Mary's divine nature. It also called for the host of the show to reframe God's miraculous works in specific Bible stories so they would not appear to be magic, since "Latin American culture is steeped in ritual and magic. Ancient Indian customs and a syncretized form of Catholicism are never far from the surface."

The third prime-time show, *Rescatados del Infierno,* was scripted and filmed entirely in Central America. As we have explained, it used the telenovela-style "preferred format" of melodrama, and the producer was himself a telenovela star. Also, as an August 1989 CBN memo explained, the program focused on "areas of great concern in [Guatemala]: (a) alcoholism, (b) infidelity, and (c) Divorce/ marital problems," which CBN representatives had identified as central through the use of focus groups. Of the three programs, *Rescatados del Infierno* garnered the most viewers, followed by the *Superbook Party* and *Don't Ask Me, Ask God.*[12] The relative success of these shows reveals the effectiveness of CBN's glocal strategies: the show that was most informed by local concerns and produced in a "preferred format" for Guatemalans garnered the most viewers. Not surprisingly, the shows' relative success also challenges a strict U.S. cultural-imperialism reading of the campaign, since the program that had been especially popular in the United States because it featured U.S. celebrities actually garnered the least viewers of the three aired.

For CBN, proving success to U.S. supporters was crucial, since, through donations, those supporters must continue to provide funding for such campaigns as Project Light. Project organizers determined that a total of 42.2 percent of those who viewed their prime-time shows prayed with the host at the end of the programs to receive Jesus Christ. On this basis, they calculated that at least 20 percent of the total population of Guatemala prayed, and more than two million people were "saved."[13] However, it appears that the project's success, as measured in terms of conversions, was less than the organizers' numbers reveal.

First, conversion may not have meant for Guatemalans what CBN representatives intended it to mean. In his 1992 interviews examining the strengths and weaknesses of the project, Ben Frazer found that many informants reported "a Catholic mindset where you are never sure of your salvation" which resulted in "people [being] saved 4 or 5, even 10 or 12 times" (1992: 5). For Frazer, multiple salvations signified a failure for the project because of Guatemalans' failure to "understand" CBN's assertion that salvation is a one-time experience which leads one to become a practicing evangelical Christian. In his research among Guatemalan Evangelicals, David Stoll confirms that such a "misunderstanding" exists. He found that "the number of nominal evangelicals is growing rapidly, as is the number of Guatemalans straddling the fence with identities such as 'I'm a Christian' or 'I'm half-evangelical'" (1994: 105).

Second, there is evidence that fewer people converted than CBN representatives expected. One of the primary measures of response was the number of persons who called CBN's telephone counseling centers when prompted by television, radio, or print advertisements during the campaign. Trained volunteers talked with these callers to encourage them to pray a "salvation prayer." In a "Partial Statistical Summary" of the Project Light campaign, Stan Jeeter reported the total number of phone calls to CBN's telephone counseling centers over the course of the project (164,336) and the total number of salvations which occurred during phone-counseling sessions (10,711). These numbers reveal that, assuming each caller converted just one time, only 6.5 percent converted of those who called the counseling centers.

Thus those who called may have had a different understanding of what such an action meant. Frazer explained in a 1996 interview with Marie Marquardt that after having spoken with Guatemalans about their responses to Project Light, he was forced to reconsider why so many people called the counseling center: "The population of Guatemala is still steeped in Catholicism which is a confessional [religion]. . . . They're very used to saying they're a sinner . . . like when you go to confession. So, a lot of people were calling in to say 'yes, I've lived a bad life. . . . ' Let's don't pretend that this is . . . beginning a new life with an ongoing relationship with Jesus Christ." In CBN's terms, these people were not saved, because they did not pray the salvation prayer and consequently convert to evangelical Christianity. In other words, they did not accept CBN's universal core message but instead embraced and resignified this element of the glocal campaign.

RESPONSE RECONSIDERED

Notwithstanding these low conversion rates, the fact remains that on March 28, 1990, 4.5 million viewers tuned in to *Rescued from Hell*. On this night and throughout the campaign, Guatemalans could have turned off their televisions, changed the station on their radios, refused to read newspaper advertisements, or decided not to attend the Jesus film. Or, like many Catholics, they could have mounted explicit resistances. Instead, many listened, viewed, and read, reflecting CBN's success in appealing to local consumers through glocal marketing strategies. However, this does not necessarily signify that CBN succeeded in selling its core product: personal salvation attached to the two-pronged hegemonic message of Christian dominion and the promise of health and wealth.

As Ortner (1995) observes, much of the recent literature on popular response to global mass media has highlighted resistance—local cultures' ability to maintain their integrity or purity in the face of hegemonic mass-mediated cultural forms. In this view, media producers acting globally have almost complete control over programming, and their target audience has the limited choice of tuning in or not, and if people do watch, whether to accept the content or reject it (D. Smith 1990: 297). This dualistic approach faces increasing challenges from scholars who argue that, in a globalized setting, we need to rethink the concept of cultures as discrete bounded entities. As Abu-Lughod argues, television and other mass media have an extraordinary capacity to "unsettle the boundaries of culture," rendering "more and more problematic a concept of cultures as localized communities of people suspended in shared webs of meaning" (1997: 123).

Research on reception of mass media shows that as viewers watch programming, "the complex ways in which people are engaged in processes of making and interpreting media works in relation to their social, cultural, and historical circumstances" (Ginsburg 1994: 13). Mass-mediated messages enter peoples' everyday realities and can be interpreted only from within those realities (Yoshimoto 1989; Mankekar 1993). As Appadurai argues, electronic media offer "new resources and new disciplines for the construction of an imagined world" (1996: 3). The imagination is a constitutive element of the creation of individual and collective subjectivities, and in a globalized setting it becomes a space of contestation in which individuals and groups seek to "annex the global into their own practices" (4). As such, "the globalization of culture is not the same as its homogenization, but globalization involves the use of a variety of instruments of homogenization (armaments, advertising techniques, language hegemonies, and clothing styles) that are absorbed into local political and cultural economies, only to be repatriated as heterogeneous dialogues of national sovereignty, free enterprise, and fundamentalism" (42).

Close examination of Project Light *Headlines* makes clear that what emerged among Central American audiences of Project Light media were multiple meanings that sometimes complemented and sometimes contradicted CBN's intended meaning.[14] Located at particular intersections of gender, ethnicity, and class, viewers responded to those aspects of the programming that helped them make sense of everyday predicaments and gave them hope for improving their lives. Those aspects differed in relation to the social location of viewers, and they included specific images of class and status, means for escaping tradition in order to transform one's life radically, and attractive formulations of the role of women and family.

Many Guatemalans also tuned in to the shows simply because the programming was an entertaining and well-produced novelty. One set of Project Light *Headlines* reports that Catholic school teachers called the counseling center to say that for homework, they had assigned their students to watch the *Superbook Party* and other cartoon versions of Bible stories CBN broadcast over the course of the campaign. These teachers also requested copies of the comic-book versions of Bible stories that CBN was distributing to callers for free. They intended to use these texts in their religion classes as entertaining means to teach students biblical stories. However, as Catholic teachers, they did not intend to use the programming and texts to convert their students to evangelicalism. In other words, they found certain elements of the programming and publications appealing but did not passively accept CBN's core message.

Perhaps the most striking example of the simple entertainment value of Project Light's media campaign was the showing of the Jesus Film in remote areas of Guatemala. A CBN team would enter a small town with a huge portable screen, chairs, a projector, and a generator and set up an outdoor movie theater in the town square or even in the

FIGURE 8.4. A Central American child receiving a comic-book style Bible story, distributed without charge by CBN representatives during the Project Light campaign.

middle of the road. Project Light's coordinator explained the novelty of the Jesus film: "It was not the first consideration, but it became an obvious advantage in some rural areas. There were places that had no light, no power. So they would come crank up the generator, put up a string of lights, and people would stream in from around the mountainside . . . to see what was going on down there." In Project Light's *Headlines* for March 9, 1990, he reported that "in rural areas where films aren't common, the audience sometimes gets so involved with the film action that they throw stones at the screen when the Romans are about to crucify Christ."

This and other strategies, like Operation Blessing, which distributed five hundred tons of food and personal-hygiene products to poor Guatemalans, were sources of pride for CBN. The organization used footage from these events heavily in their reports to U.S. supporters, suggesting that Project Light worked to reach and civilize the "tribal" peoples of Guatemala. However, the most coveted audiences for CBN were not the disenfranchised, whom the network understood to be in need of entertainment, nutrition, and personal hygiene. Rather they were the urban middle and upper classes, who more closely resembled CBN's white middle-class U.S. supporters and who could bolster CBN's goal of "taking whole nations for Jesus Christ." These urban classes found CBN programming attractive because it offered the possibility of social mobility by way of association with sophisticated U.S. media and the high-powered Guatemalans who publicly supported it. A report in the Project Light *Headlines* for May 25, 1990, entitled "Jewish Merchant Opens Up to Gospel," reads: "A Jewish merchant in Guatemala City recently remarked to our media assistant, 'What a great campaign you did, the one about Jesus.' He quickly added that he was not going to become a Christian, but then confessed that because of the gospel message he is now regularly attending the Full Gospel Businessmen's Fellowship here in the capital."

The Full Gospel Businessmen's Fellowship is a U.S.-based network of men's clubs that brings charismatic Christians into fellowship (Stoll 1994: 105). In Guatemala, it functions much like a Rotary Club, hosting lunch meetings in expensive hotels. During these meetings members offer testimonies of how their lives have changed. Often, theology and biblical study become secondary to stories of worldly success. In Guatemala City, most of the elite members of the fellowship are charismatic Catholics rather than Evangelicals, and many non-Christians participate because of the networking opportunities the fellowship presents (Stoll 1994: 105). The Jewish businessman's decision to attend the

Full Gospel Businessmen's Fellowship suggests that, rather than convinced by CBN's message of personal salvation in Christ, he was attracted to the possibility of class mobility.

This is not to discount the capacity of CBN programming to produce radical personal transformation. The March 22, 1990, *Headlines* records a form of response that telephone counselors reported throughout the course of the campaign: "[An] owner of a Guatemala City nightclub where he has also been a musician for 22 years, called to say he had seen the Project Light TV spots and he felt something that he couldn't explain and began to cry. He said that he had knelt down by his TV set, weeping bitterly about the life he had led for so many years. Right then, on the phone, he accepted the Lord, and the very next day put his nightclub up for sale. He doesn't want to play worldly music anymore and he wants to turn his life over to the Lord completely." CBN's message offered the possibility of a radically new existence in which a nightclub owner could be freed of all his sins and imperfections and given the possibility of beginning a brand-new life. Moreover, Project Light *Headlines* reports that at least three suicides were prevented as a result of the programming, desperate alcoholics became sober and returned to their families, and disabled persons were physically healed. But even in many of these cases, personal transformations did not include conversion to Protestantism or affiliation with an evangelical church, once again illustrating viewers' ability to respond creatively to mass media without necessarily accepting the message intended by global media producers.

Among Guatemalan women, personal transformation had the most broad-ranging appeal. The May 5, 1990, *Headlines* reports:

> Union Leader's Wife Accepts Christ: The man was a union leader . . . and was strongly opposed to the CBN media blitz messages. It was an effort to deceive and distract the people so that they would not stand up and fight for their rights, he maintained. The gospel messages, he believed, were aimed at putting people to sleep. His arguments followed the Marxist line that religion is the "opiate of the people," but at the same time, he had no solution for the problems that had developed in his home. Because of his strong character, he and his wife were not getting along. At the same time, the Project Light messages dealing with family problems were tugging on his wife's heart. Sensing the opportunity, a Christian friend set up an appointment with her pastor, who led the union leader's wife to faith in Christ. Now this new convert is arranging for a Bible study in her home and hoping that her husband will also find the answer to his needs in Jesus.

The union leader's wife may have had a husband whose "strong character" was associated with *machista* cultural norms. She recognized that while her husband's union participation did nothing to convert machismo, the messages of Project Light could help her regain control of her home.

Elizabeth Brusco argues, based on a Colombian case study, that one of the most appealing elements of evangelical Protestantism in Latin America is its capacity to transform men from behaving according to standards of machismo, which discourage participation in the domestic sphere and concern with family issues, to behaving according to standards of *evangélicos*, whose primary concerns are "the quality of family life" (1995: 125). Brusco explains that in this new context, "the relative power positions of the spouses change. This is not to say that women now have power over their husbands. In evangelical households, the husband may be the powerful one, but his relative aspirations have changed to coincide with those of his wife" (122).

Interestingly, conversion may not be required for this message of the importance of men's domestic participation to take effect. *Headlines* for March 30, 1990, reports: "Wayward Husband Brought Home: [This woman] has good reason to be thankful for Project Light. . . . She called to say thank you for the media spots because her husband who had abandoned her and her two children had just seen the TV spot on the reconciled marriage and decided to return home. She declined to pray on the phone, but the counselor is praying that since the Lord has brought the couple back together, they will now open their hearts to Christ." The abandoned wife responded to Project Light, but not in the manner intended by CBN. She was not willing to pray with the counselor to "open her heart to Christ." Although she and her husband may have become Evangelicals after this experience, they were not willing to do so on the terms provided by CBN. They may also have simply incorporated the message about marital reconciliation into their lives without accepting the attached message of personal salvation and the core tenets to which it was connected. In other words, she and her husband acted as productive consumers, reinterpreting the message offered by CBN in ways that conformed to their own needs and corresponded to their own particular social location.

CONCLUSION

This chapter provides an "ethnography of production" (Abu-Lughod 1997), an analysis of the complex ways in which religious producers and consumers negotiate meaning in a globalized setting from within specific ethnic, class, gender, and national locations. Gupta and Ferguson (1997: 5) argue that "rather than opposing autonomous local cultures to a homogenizing movement of globalization," the task in cultural studies is "to trace the ways in which dominant cultural forms may be picked up and used—and significantly transformed—in the midst of the field of power relations that links localities to a wider world. The emphasis is on the complex and sometimes ironic political processes through which cultural forms are imposed, invented, reworked, and transformed." Indeed, Project Light simultaneously imposed hegemonic economic and political projects at the national and international levels and generated spaces and resources for the formation of hybrid forms of identity and subtle forms of resistance at the local level.

Project Light clearly illustrates the use of religious idioms to disseminate globally hegemonic nationalist projects and blitz viewers with a predominately "U.S." message. Project Light's two-pronged message of a gospel of health and wealth that supports neoliberal economic agendas and a dominion theology that bolsters U.S. geopolitical interests has been influential in nation building in Guatemala. This is confirmed not only by Serrano's election in 1990 but also by the election of Alfonso Portillo, another protégé of Rios Montt, a decade later.

Yet Project Light also illustrates the nuanced, sophisticated ways in which CBN disseminates its hegemonic core message: its glocal marketing strategy implicitly acknowledges the media's inability to erase local cultural and religious forms but uses this knowledge of heterogeneity to more successfully market its potentially homogenizing product. What on the surface looks like a case of U.S cultural imperialism at its most extreme and the dissemination of hegemonic discourses through the use of powerful and expensive media is in fact much more complex.

First, Project Light shows that the most successful transnational media are not those that emanate directly from the United States. The least successful of Project Light's television programs, *Don't Ask Me, Ask God*, was also the program with the most explicit connections to U.S. mass media. Conversely, such shows as *Rescued from Hell* garnered enormous popularity because CBN tailored the product's packaging to appeal to the particular context and because CBN used a telenovela format uniquely suited to carry its message.

Second, CBN's glocal marketing strategy opens the way for multiple interpretations of Project Light media. Responses to the campaign reveal that viewers embraced appealing elements of the campaign without accepting the core message of salvation and the attendant two-pronged agenda of CBN. Urban neo-Pentecostals in Guatemala do indeed espouse a gospel of health and wealth and a dominion theology that serves to advance neoliberal economic polity and the global dominance of U.S. political conservatism. Yet indigenous Pentecostals and other non-Evangelicals used elements of CBN programming to construct alternative hybrid religious forms.

In response to Project Light, Catholic teachers had students read and view the Bible stories from *Superbook Party* but did not heed the call to understand Mary as the "mother of Jesus" rather than the "Mother of God." A Jewish merchant joined a network of Evangelicals as a mark of status and a way to legitimize and advance his success but showed no desire to become evangelical. An abandoned woman embraced CBN's message of family reconciliation but did not pray the salvation prayer. These viewers responded to elements such as entertainment value, status conferral, and the presentation of appealing images of family but did not mechanically reproduce a global religious culture stamped "Made in the U.S.A." Rather, situated within intersecting class, gender, and ethnic hierarchies, Guatemalans selectively appropriated CBN's message to create hybrid religious forms, thereby reterritorializing or particularizing a message intended by CBN to be homogenous and universalizing.

CONCLUSION

This book asks how we can and should study religion in the Americas if we take globalization seriously. In Chapter 2, we offered some theoretical concepts that would help us understand the ways in which religious ideas, practices, and institutions interact with processes of economic, political, and cultural globalization. The concepts include de- and reterritorialization, transnational religious networks, glocalization, hybridity, and borders and borderlands. Rather than propose a full-fledged new New Paradigm that would supercede all that has gone before, we introduced these concepts to critique and relativize extant approaches, showing their shortcomings and opening new epistemological spaces to explore the richness of the changing religious field in the Americas. Drawing from transnational migration studies, critical postmodernism, postcolonial theory, and Latin American and Latino studies, we sought to overcome rigid and unproductive dichotomies—between modernity and tradition, the sacred and the profane, the local and the global, and domination and resistance—that have characterized modernist sociologies of religion. We have also demonstrated how even the most nuanced New Paradigm approaches draw on essentialist views of identity and locality. Although the NP has contributed to our understanding of the dynamics of religious pluralism and the enduring vitality of religion in the Americas, it overlooks the multiple and sometimes contradictory ways in which religions mix with each other and interact with "secular" phenomena like computer-mediated communications, economic transitions from Fordism to flexible production, and the redefinition of the nation-state to transform radically our notions of space, time, community, and identity.

In this conclusion, we highlight methodological corollaries of the concepts we employ. First, paying attention to religion's role in processes of de- and reterritorialization means examining the richness of place and locality and, at the same time breaking, the taken-for-granted "isomorphism (the congruence or one-to-one relationship)" among a territory, a people, and a culture (Lipsitz 2001: 5). In other words, while studying a particular place, we cannot be content to provide thick description of the internal dynamics of that place, or even of the immediate religious ecology that surrounds it. We must also pay attention to how that particular locale "emplaces" (Gieryn 2000) global processes and enters transnational fields. Chapter 6 illustrates such attentiveness: while the chapter offers a detailed description of two congregations located in Doraville, Georgia, it also reveals how this southern city has been reconfigured by global processes and how church members' transnational networks shape both the material elements and the activities of these particular religious communities. Conversely, while examining deterritorialized processes and practices, we must foreground how they are anchored, reproduced, and contested in and through particular places. For instance, while Chapter 4 focused on the quintessentially deterritorialized form of religion in cyberspace, it sought out the links between cyber-religion and specific, territorially bounded congregations.

This methodological corollary has important implications for the way we study religion as it is lived locally. In the United States, one particularly productive strand in the sociological study of local religion has concentrated on congregations (Wind and Lewis 1994; Ammerman 1997a; Warner and Wittner 1998).[1] This focus has been extremely valuable in moving the study of religion away from a narrow focus on texts, the ideas of the "great" religious men, and the evolution of denominations toward a textured and contextualized reading of religious practices and organizations. Among immigrants, congregational studies have allowed us to explore in detail "what new ethnic and immigrant groups [are] *doing together religiously* in the United States, and what manner of religious institutions they [are] developing *of, by, and for themselves*" (Warner 1998). This approach has allowed us to see that congregations are often safe and intimate spaces where immigrants can find voice, fellowship, and self-help networks and can learn values and practices, such as voluntarism and lay leadership, that ensure their integration into a robust pluralistic setting.

There are nevertheless some dangers in the congregational approach to religion and locality. By defining congregations as social realities sui generis and "particularistic spaces of sociality" (Ammerman 1997a: 355) that contain strong local cultures, there is a danger of sliding into Durkheimian functionalism and Geertzian cultural holism, which see congregations as relatively autonomous living organisms, animated by self-referential webs of meaning, whose interdependent operation guarantees the health of the overall social body. For example, Becker (1999), one of the most astute students of congregations, uses sociologist Gary Alan Fine's notion of "idioculture" to define the intersubjective reality within the congregation. An idioculture "is a system of knowledge, beliefs, behaviors, and customs shared by members of an interacting group to which members can refer, and that serve as the basis for further interaction. . . . This approach stresses the localized nature of culture, implying that it . . . can be a particularistic development of any group" (1987: 125). Becker critiques and augments Fine's ideographic approach by bringing in institutional analyses. These allow her to compare and contrast "bundles of core tasks and legitimate ways of doing things" among different congregational models, which are in turn shaped by the larger institutional environment.

In our view, globalization's time-space compression makes even this augmented view of congregation insufficient. As we have seen in our case studies and as recent debates in anthropology show, what is at stake is the nature of locality itself.[2] "The landscapes of group identity . . . around the world are no longer familiar anthropological objects, insofar as groups are no longer tightly territorialized, spatially bounded, historically unselfconscious, or culturally homogeneous" (Appadurai 1996: 48). In other words, the relation between culture and locality has been unsettled by the current episode of globalization, bringing particularistic difference into tension with hybridity and the global circulation of religious practices and narratives that stake universalistic claims. It is not that locality and face-to-face encounters do not matter anymore, but rather that they have become more unstable, stretched, and shot through with hybridity and disjunctures. In this context, we need to deepen and extend the stress on lived religion among congregational studies to account for fluidity, conflict, and paradox within religious localities and to capture the dialectic between de- and reterritorialization of religion. Thus, our cases demonstrate that congregations are not only sites of boundary formation and maintenance but also locales of mixing, multiplicity, overlap, and contradiction. They can also be liminal spaces of tension and transgression where the interplay of transculturation and exclusionary difference becomes localized. To avoid any potential functionalist bias, we must pay explicit attention to congregations as borderlands.[3]

Furthermore, we ought not to view congregations as the only significant locus for the study of the public face religion and disqualify all that falls outside them as "private devotions" or "individual meditation." If we take seriously the critique of the secularization paradigm, the blurring of the boundaries between the sacred and the profane, and "hybridity all the way down" (Rosaldo 1995), then we should see a congregation as one among many sites of lived religion in the Americas. Contemporary religion is not limited to visible architecture, to the cathedrals, temples, mosques, and synagogues that anchor congregational life. Religion with all its ambiguity and polyvocality is on the Internet, on the windows of a bank, in the body of the gang member whose tattoos have been removed, in the work of the *curandera* at the margins of an emerging basilica at the U.S.-Mexico border, and in telenovelas on Guatemalan TV.

To reiterate, it is not a question of jettisoning the study of congregations and the ethnographic methods associated with it. Rather, we need what Appadurai (1996: 48–65) calls a "cosmopolitan ethnography" or a "macroethnography" that recognizes the unstable and contested character of locality and that "captures the impact of deterritorialization on the imaginative resources of lived, local experiences." This cosmopolitan ethnography will have to be more refined at both the micro- and macrolevels. At the microlevels, it will have to explore religion in everyday life as it is lived in kitchens, clinics, social service centers, plazas, bars, restaurants—the multiple and interacting localities through which individuals navigate in their quotidian life. This can be done only through longitudinal fieldwork, requiring lengthy and close involvement in the day-to-day lives of our informants. Fieldwork would involve not just traditional techniques such as participant observation, focus groups, and in-depth interviews, but also the collection of detailed oral histories of physical and spiritual migration, and the use of projective social-psychological methods to elicit the changing cognitive and moral maps of our informants across various landscapes. Cosmopolitan ethnography is thus part of an anthropology of religion "on the move," a "traveling" anthropology conducting multisited fieldwork and mapping routes, pathways, and flows rather than describing fixed cultures (Clifford 1997; Marcus 1998). Robert Orsi (1999a), Karen Brown (1999), Colleen McDannell (1995), and David Hall and colleagues (1997) have already moved us in this direction. We need now to embed their insights about embodiment, everyday life, sacred space, and lived religion in the macro: in regional, national, transnational, and global processes of de- and reterritorialization. These processes invariably represent a complex mixture of geographic, economic, political, and cultural dimensions, necessitating a nonreductive materialist approach.

One way to address the "increasing porousness" of social and religious organizations (Wuthnow 1998b) is to shift the focus toward the dense networks deployed in daily life through which individual and collective identities are constructed. We are talking here of the links and exchanges people sustain not just with their immediate and extended families and in their churches, but at schools, in workplaces, on the Internet, and in the spaces of entertainment. In the study of these networks, as in the study of congregations, our task is to clarify the sites of overlap and elucidate the dynamics of intersection. We need to seek points of overlap between religious and nonreligious networks for a particular locality or population, and we must point out sites of intersection between relatively autonomous informal religious networks and formal/official networks, whether the latter be associated with the state or with a religious institution. Many of our case studies take as their point of departure the overlapping networks in which everyday religious actors are embedded. For instance, Chapter 5 examines not only specific transnational religious ties between Pentecostals in Washington, D.C., and Morazán, El Salvador, but also the ways in which these overlap with transnational gang networks and geopolitical projects.

What is the advantage of a focus on networks? It allows us to pursue thick descriptions of local everyday life without fixing us in the artificially bounded congregation. In this view, drawing on the work of Castells (1996), we can see congregations as relatively bounded terrains of interlocking networks, as nodes made up of intersecting networks, both real and virtual. The interpenetration that takes place at these nodes gives them relative stability and coherence. However, as Castells argues, networks are "open structures, highly dynamic." There are always disjunctures, fissures, and tensions within and among the networks "nucleated" at a given congregation. As nodes, congregations play an important role, not only providing maps and narratives to recenter self and reterritorialize community but also serving as sites of exchange and mixing. Like congregations, networks are rooted in particular places and constructed by situated actors. Nevertheless, because networks transgress borders and often link multiple spatio-temporal arrangements, a focus on them allows us to embed the personal and local in larger processes.

A final corollary of our globalization perspective emerges from our focus on glocalization, which points toward the need to rethink our understanding of religious institutions. We need to be wary of the populist fallacy that sees institutions as inevitably conservative forces that threaten to disenchant and bureaucratize the creativity and purity of religious passion at the grassroots. Our examination of "transnationalism from above" among corporate religious actors like the Vatican, in Chapter 7, and the Christian Broadcasting Network, in Chapter 8, sought to move beyond the homogenizing forces that these powerful institutions exert. We highlighted these institutions' sometimes strategic and sometimes unintended participation in the production of heterogeneity and hybridity. In so doing, we demonstrated that, when studying global religious institutions, we need not abandon the textual strategies and analyses of orthodox discourses and practices that have dominated the historical study of religion. Rather, since glocalization has made hybridity and borderlands part and parcel of institutional life, we should focus our attention once more on the sites of overlap and tension in these texts, discourses, and practices between the local and the global, the universal and the particular. As we revealed through our exploration of CBN's Project Light and the Vatican's New Evangelization, attempts to control, or make orthodox, the meanings of globally disseminated messages often lead to paradoxical results. Thus our cases suggest that when studying global religious institutions, we should also turn to how their orthodox discourses and practices are received, reinterpreted, indigenized, or made heterodox. In so doing, we see complex negotiations of power and meaning between the global/transnational institution and local actors.

In sum, we want to offer a new vision of the religious field in the Americas in which the "little religions" that Eliade (1959) dismissed as "aberrant aspects of pseudomorphs" are in fact the vital and public expressions of contemporary religion in a globalized setting. In the contemporary Americas, as throughout the world, these "pseudo religions" and "degenerated myths" are moving from the periphery of religious life to its very heart. To study religion in the Americas in all its "glorious impurity" (Warner 1997), we must develop interdisciplinary approaches in dialogue with critical cultural and area studies, approaches that combine deepened and decentered ethnographic field methods with a good grasp of political economy, as well as critical analyses of texts, lived space, popular culture, mass media, and computer mediated communications. Only through these interdisciplinary approaches will we be able to capture something of the sometimes paradoxical roles religion plays in border-making, border-blurring, and border-crossing processes. Our cases reveal that the religious field in the contemporary Americas is constituted through a complex interplay of these processes. They demonstrate not globalization's erasure of all boundaries but the ways in which globalization reconfigures the goals and actions of religious institutions and the everyday practices of the faithful to create new boundaries that are every bit as real, although more permeable and more often transgressed.

Notes

1. THE LIMITS OF DOMINANT AND EMERGING MODELS

1. Secularization is not only the result of the Protestant Reformation. Casanova (1994) identifies the formation of modern nation-states, the growth of modern capitalism, and the scientific revolution, as well as the Reformation, as key developments in the process. Moreover, Berger (1967) traces the development of this-worldly asceticism to ancient Judaism.

2. For a good overview of the ongoing debate about church attendance rates, see the symposium in *American Sociological Review* 63, 1 (1998).

3. In a survey of 1,500 Americans conducted by the nonprofit research group Public Agenda, 44 percent of respondents thought that it was a good idea to increase funding for faith-based social initiatives, even if they promoted a particular religious message; 23 percent said it was a good idea, but only if the programs were not connected to a religious message. Only 31 percent said outright that it was a bad idea. *New York Times*, February 4, 2001.

4. Derrida (2002: 82) expresses religion's ambivalence vis-à-vis late modernity well: "Religion today allies itself with tele-technoscience, to which it reacts with all its forces. It is, *on the one hand*, globalization; it produces, weds, exploits the capital and knowledge of tele-mediatization; neither the trips and global spectacularizing of the Pope, nor the interstate dimensions of the 'Rushdie affair,' nor planetary terrorism would otherwise be possible. . . . But, *on the other hand*, it reacts immediately, *simultaneously*, against that which gives it this new power only at the cost of dislodging it from all proper places, *in truth from place itself*, from the *taking-place* of its truth."

5. It should be noted that, as Warner (1993: 1053) remarks, "the new paradigm is not *defined* by economic imagery . . . but by the idea that disestablishment is the norm." In other words, the rational-choice model is but *one* deployment of the NP. It is a deployment, however, that has become increasingly dominant, which is why we concentrate on it here.

6. Stark and Finke critique rational-choice theorists who explain actions strictly according to mathematical models of maximization. Stark and Finke propose instead a "more subjective and bounded conception of rationality" in line with symbolic interactionism and other microsociologies. "Within the limits of their information and understanding, restricted by available options, guided by their preferences and tastes, humans attempt to make rational choices . . . [meaning] that they will attempt to follow the dictates of reason in an effort to achieve their desired goals" (2000: 38).

7. See Finke and Stark 1992 (252–255), Iannaccone 1997, and A. Gill 1998 (193–202) for good summaries of the key tenets of rational-choice theories of religion.

8. Chaves and Gorski (2001: 278–279) argue that the empirical evidence does not support the contention that religious pluralism and competition are always positively correlated with religious vitality, measured as religious participation. They argue that "the quest for a general law about the relationship between religious pluralism and religious participation should be abandoned." Rather, "the most valuable future work on this subject is likely to include investigations into the social, cultural, and institutional arrangements that determine, in part, religious pluralism's consequence for religious vitality."

9. To deal with this gap, Iannaccone (1997: 32) has introduced the concept of "religious human capital," which denotes "a person's accumulated stock of religious knowledge, skills, and sensitivities. It is an abstraction designed to encompass church ritual, doctrinal knowledge, friendships with fellow worshipers, and even faith (insofar as it is the product of experience)." In our view, even this conceptual tool fails to grasp the meso- and macrodynamics that shape and are shaped by the practices of situated individuals.

10. We agree with Bourdieu (1977: 72–95) on the need to construct a theory of practice that avoids, on the one hand, the "subjectivist illusion, which reduces the social space to the conjectural space of interactions" among unencumbered, decontextualized individuals, and on the other hand, "the realism of the structure, which hypostatizes systems of objective relations by converting them into totalities already constituted outside of individual history and group history."

11. We considered calling our approach the "New World" or "Third World" model. However, the time and space compression generated by globalization makes these labels too simplistic. Our approach shares with postcolonial critiques, including those of the subaltern school, a concern for voices at the margins and a stress on fluid and contested identities, especially among emerging hybrid postnational and transnational subjects. For a good introduction to postcolonial theory see Guha 1997, Spivak 1996, or Bhabha 1990, 1994.

12. As Lipsitz (2001: 17) puts it in criticizing the hegemony of the nation-state in American studies, "excessive focus on unilateral national histories and national cultures directs our attention away from the polylateral relations between sites, from the very circuits and network most likely to generate new imaginaries, identities, and intersubjectivities." For an attempt to write a "post or non-exceptionalist" U.S. history, see Bender 2002.

13. Hypodescent refers to practices and discourses that seek to affirm racial purity by setting a sharp dichotomy between whites and nonwhites. In the U.S. binary racial formation, whiteness is seen as a lack of black blood (the so-called one-drop rule). According to Roof (1998: 6), the stress on "the purity of religious categories is a hyper-Anglo concern which parallels the rise of racial categories" in the United States.

14. For a comparative perspective on race in the Americas, see Winant 1994. It is important to note that hypodescent is only a hegemonic ideology, which despite becoming embodied in schools, courts, and other political institutions does not succeed in forcing fixed identities on the entire population. As historian Neil Foley (1997) observes, drawing from African American novelist Ishmael Reed, the United States has always harbored the "secret of miscegenation." By the same token, in many Latin American nations, the state equated modernity and development with whiteness, actively seeking to "whiten" the population by encouraging immigration from Europe and by excluding "pure" blacks and indigenous people. Thus, the contrast between the United States and Latin America should not be overdrawn.

15. See Hexam and Poewe 1997; Heelas, Martin, and Morris 1998; and Voye 1995.

16. "Critical postmodernism preserves a continuity with 'rebellious modernism,' maintains a new cultural materialist conception of human rationality and subjectivity, adopts a multiperspective approach that avoids the twin extremes of absolutism and relativism, and sees politics everywhere, except in the formal political system" (Gabardi 2001: 15).

2.   THEORIZING GLOBALIZATION AND RELIGION

1. For a good overview see Held et al. 1999 and Hardt and Negri 2000.

2. See Wallerstein 1974; Braudel 1982, 1984; and Wolf 1982.

3. McAlister (1998: 156) suggests that we add "religioscapes" to Appadurai's list of global flows. Religioscapes would refer to "the subjective religious maps (and attendant theologies) of diasporic communities who are also in global flow and flux."

4. To counter the excesses of a rhetoric of circulation and deterritorialization, Tsing (2000: 327)

suggests that we consider that "world-making 'flows' . . . are not just interconnections but the recarving of channels and the remapping of the possibilities of geography." See Michael Smith 2001 for a critique of the failure to "locate globalization."

5. Data from the Census Bureau's "Current Population Survey" show that the income gap between the bottom and top 10 percent of earners is as wide as during the 1920s, the decade of robber barons and the market collapse. Similar concentrations of wealth are taking place in Latin American countries like Brazil and Mexico.

6. There is a thriving cyberspirituality that combines, among other things, Catholic ritual (transubstantiation), Gnostic philosophy, Jewish mysticism (Hasidism), Tibetan Buddhism, Native American cosmologies, and Hinduism (the concept of *prana*, or life force). See Zaleski 1997.

7. Eliade ontologized the sacred, turning it into a self-sustaining universal essence. Here we agree with Jonathan Smith (1987: 105) that "sacred and profane are transitive categories; they serve as maps and labels not substances; they are distinctions of office, indices of difference." For a discussion of Eliade and the future of the comparative study of religion, see Patton and Ray 2000.

8. McRoberts (2000: 96–126) uses Erving Goffman's concepts of framing and frame extension to show how migrants from Haiti, the West Indies, and the U.S. South use the biblical notion of exile to make sense of their experience of "being culturally and/or geographically out of place" in Boston. The Jewish exile in Babylon becomes an interpretive frame for the experiences of life at the margins in a bewildering city, for "the irony of faith in an apparently faithless world."

9. Simon Coleman (2000: 117–142) uses the term "narrative emplacement" to describe strategies of "scriptural incarnation" among evangelical Christians ("and the word became flesh and dwelt among us," John 1:14). Narrative emplacements like sermons and testimonies help articulate an "evangelical habitus in which the 'textualisation' of self is manifested in bodily dispositions and experiences." This habitus in turn is located in a global "landscape of evangelical action, ideals and characters."

10. Hardt and Negri (2000: xii, 143–146) argue that the new global order, which they call empire, "manages hybrid identities, flexible hierarchies, and plural exchanges through modulating networks of command." Thus, it is naive to assume that an attack on binary oppositions and a stress on hybridity will subvert the emerging power configuration. For us hybridity is purely a heuristic, conceptual tool to explore social complexity beyond the limitations imposed by modernist social science. We do not make a claim as to its universal emancipatory potential. "The politics of hybridity is conjunctural and cannot be deduced from theoretical principles. In most situations, what matters politically is who deploys nationality or transnationality, authenticity or hybridity, against whom, with what relative power and ability to sustain a hegemony" (Clifford 1997: 10).

---

3. MIRACLES AT THE BORDER

1. Our examination relies heavily on archival material gathered during two visits to San Juan, Texas, that includes newspaper articles, brief histories of the shrine written by members of the staff, and a collection of letters written by the faithful to the Virgin of San Juan and the rector of the shrine. We also quote extensively from six interviews conducted in November 2001. Half of these were conducted with priests currently assigned to the shrine; one is a native of the Lower Rio Grande Valley and another has been in the valley since 1961. The remaining interviews were with current or former members of the staff who have been associated with the shrine for more than twenty years. One of these, Pablo Villescas, is the grandson of Bernardino and Bernardina Villescas, the laypeople instrumental in the shrine's founding. Another, Bridgit Vela, became an employee of the shrine in 1950, shortly after the Virgin of San Juan arrived in Texas.

2. This and subsequent unattributed citations about the history of the Shrine of Our Lady of San Juan del Valle were taken from the anonymous history of the San Juan Shrine written in the 1970s and currently in the personal archives of Bridgit Vela.

3. Novenas entail leaving nine photocopied sheets of prayers to a certain saint (often San Judas Tadeo) in nine churches for nine consecutive days.

---

4. CROSSING THE ELECTRIC FRONTIER

1. For theoretical and philosophical approaches to cyberspace, see Heim 1993, 1998; Rheingold 1990; Hillis 1999; and Poster 2001. For ethnographic and psychological studies of Internet

users, see Rheingold 2000, Turkel 1995, Hine 2000. On religion and the Internet, see Cobb 1998; Zaleski 1997; Dawson 2000, 2001; Brasher 2001; and O'Leary 1996.

2. We studied both the structure and the content of web pages of a variety of congregations in a college town with a population of 120,000 and a major urban center, both in the U.S. South—Catholics, mainline Protestant churches, such as Presbyterians and Lutherans, and Pentecostal congregations. We also took size into account—from relatively small to megachurches—and the type of clientele served, whether middle-class suburban whites or urban African Americans or a multicultural student population. In addition, we studied the Hillel Student Center, as well as the local chapter of the Bahá'í, because both have active and complex web pages and are involved in many global projects. In each congregation, we engaged in participant observation of key activities to get a taste of community life and conducted in-depth interviews with the congregations' leaders, particularly those in charge of constructing web pages. The interviews focused on how the congregations use the Internet and the effects this use has on their organization, practices, and mission. More specifically, we asked our informants about the positive and negative aspects of the electronic media in the congregations' efforts to build community, reaffirm locality, and generate the "moods and motivations," to draw from Geertz's famous definition, that accompany religious experience. We have omitted the names of the congregations and have changed those of our informants in response to several requests for anonymity.

3. As a counterpoint to Putnam, Lin (2001: 214–215) uses the example of Falun Gong to illustrate how the Internet supports global social movements in the face of repressive state apparatuses.

4. Castells (2001: 132) argues that the Internet encourages a "network individualism," whereby individuals develop "portfolios of sociability, by investing differentially, at different points in time, in a number of networks with low entry barriers and low opportunity costs."

5. Slater (1998) found a similar affirmation of authenticity and traditional identities among on-line groups trading sexpics. In a context that allows maximum anonymity and has the potential for transgressive behavior, participants follow the norms of standard pornography and male heterosexuality. Participants also put "considerable energy into the project of re-fixing bodies and identities."

6. Castells has moved away from his earlier language of radical rupture. "In contrast to claims purporting the Internet to be either a source of renewed community or a cause of alienation from the real world, social interaction on the Internet does not seem to have a direct effect on the patterning of everyday life, generally speaking, except for adding on-line interaction to existing social relationships" (2001: 119).

7. The Kumbh Mela example also shows how the state capitalizes on the Internet to reassert nationhood abroad. Sponsorship of the web site by the government of Uttar Pradesh occurs in the context of the Bharatiya Janata Party's nationalist drive. The city of Ayodya, where in 1992 Hindu nationalists destroyed a Muslim temple, triggering deadly interreligious riots, is located in Uttar Pradesh.

---

5   SAVING SOULS TRANSNATIONALLY

1. Since Salvadoran gangs had their origins in the United States and now operate transnationally, we draw from fieldwork and in-depth interviews conducted in 1996 and 1997 in Morazán, an area in eastern El Salvador deeply affected by the war, and in Washington, D.C., where many Salvadorans, particularly from the eastern part of the country, fled during the armed conflict. The names of our informants have been changed to protect their anonymity.

2. For an overview of recent Salvadoran history see Montgomery 1995.

3. See Matthei and Smith 1998 for a similar case among Belizeans in the United States.

4. Salvadoran officials estimate more than twenty thousand gang members in San Salvador alone (Wallace 2000).

5. Wallace (2000: 54) argues that still dominant reactionary forces within El Salvador "might see the perpetuation of gang warfare as a useful mechanism for blunting whatever danger of revolution might remain," as well as a smoke screen for their own corrupt activities.

6. Some churches go even further, offering tattoo removal programs as part of their pastoral work among former gang members. Often the removal procedure leaves visible scars, which help those converted to illustrate in their testimonies the mark of sin and the spiritual struggles they have endured. Latino Pastoral Action Center (LPAC) in the South Bronx offers a striking

example how the body is reconstituted in the process of religious conversion. Part of LPAC's youth outreach includes a fully equipped gym set against the backdrop of a large mural of a muscular Christ rising from the streets of the barrio, carrying on his back a cross representing the sin of the world. For an interesting discussion of Christ as "body builder" within the context of the health and wealth gospel, see S. Coleman 2000.

6. A CONTINUUM OF HYBRIDITY

1. Recent work by Karen McCarthy Brown (1999) has highlighted how religion helps those who are "out of place," especially migrants and exiles, feel "in place" by transferring the natal terrain onto the terrain of residence, or the transposition of home places onto host spaces.
2. Names of places in this chapter have not been changed, but we have used pseudonyms to protect the anonymity of church members. Data for the chapter come from two years of field research in Doraville, Georgia. The research included thirty brief interviews with pastors of Doraville's churches, ten interviews with community leaders in the city, twenty-five interviews with members of two Doraville churches and approximately one year of participant observation in those churches. The Doraville research was supplemented with one month of research in a Mexican sending community, which included fifteen in-depth interviews with priests, pastoral workers, transnational migrants, and their family members. This research was supported by the Social Science Research Council. Also, a significant portion of the research was done as part of project supported by the Lilly Endowment entitled "Responding to Community Crisis." The project was codirected by Elizabeth Bounds and Nancy L. Eiesland, who gave permission for inclusion of material here.
3. The term "emplace" comes from Gieryn (2000: 466), who uses it to draw attention to the fact that "place is not just a setting, backdrop, stage, or context for something else that becomes the focus of sociological attention, nor is it a proxy for demographic, structural, economic, or behavioral variables. . . . Everything that we study is emplaced; it happens somewhere and involves material stuff. . . . The strong form of the argument is this: place is not merely a setting or backdrop, but an agentic player in the game."
4. The 2000 U.S. Census shows that the most significant change in Hispanic/ Latino population has been in the Southeast, where six of the seven states that have experienced a more than 200 percent increase in Hispanic population since 1990 are located (North Carolina, South Carolina, Georgia, Alabama, Tennessee, and Arkansas). For more detail, see Brewer and Suchan 2001.
5. See Sassen 1998 for a description of the tight linkage between international flows of capital and international flows of migrants.
6. As Orsi (1999a: 40) explains, city planners for more than a century have used the development of parks as "carefully cultivated nature" to realize the "modernist dream" of "bring[ing] order out of chaos, unity out of diversity, whiteness out of color."
7. As Ebaugh and Chafetz (2000) note, many contemporary immigrant churches are assuming the function of community centers.
8. We should note that there is some tension at the Misión between Mexicans, who comprise the majority of the congregation and whose numbers are steadily increasing, and other national groups. Such tension crystallizes around the image of Our Lady of Guadalupe, whom pastoral workers have attempted to tout as patroness of the Americas and thus the foundation of a pan-Latino community. Nevertheless, many non-Mexican members of the church resent the centrality of her image in the sanctuary and the fact that she remains, in the rearranged chapel, behind the altar rails with the tabernacle, in a place of honor separate from the images of other virgins and saints.
9. Charles Taylor's recent work is a clear example of this presupposition. He argues that secularism is "a necessity for the democratic life of religiously diverse societies" and that religion threatens the vibrant public sphere that forms the foundation of a thriving democracy (Taylor 1998: 46).
10. The other key life-cycle events in which these churches participate are funerals. The churches not only provide religious services but also invite their members to contribute toward the thousands of dollars needed to send the body of the deceased back to his or her homeland to be buried.

7. PREMODERN, MODERN, OR POSTMODERN?

1. See Casanova 1997 and Libânio 1984.
2. All quotes related to the Fatima messages and their interpretations are taken from a dossier at the Vatican official Web site, *www.vatican.va/roman_curia/congregations/cfaith/documents*.
3. For a fuller treatment of the third secret's disclosure, see Matter 2001.
4. In all fairness, Ratzinger is careful to point out that his theological interpretation was deemed correct by Lucia.
5. All quotes from *Fides et Ratio* are taken from *http://www.vatican.va/holyfather/johnpaulii*.
6. See *Centesimus Annus* (John Paul II 1991: #30–43).
7. Robertson (1991: 188) argues that one of the processes accompanying globalization is humanization. With the relativization of self and nation there has been a "diffusion of a conception of a homogeneous, but gender-distinguished humankind." While John Paul II does indeed refer to a unified human family in the single place that globalization is creating, his suspicion of subject-centered thinking precludes the sacralization of humanity. Humanity is ultimately valuable not as an autonomous product of global modernity, but because it is grounded in divinely sanctioned universals.
8. According to Coleman (1991: 25), Catholic social thought is a "distinct and original social ideology, with a sort of unity based on its Janus-faced opposition to both liberalism and socialism." Catholic social thought rejects both "the excessive individualism, voluntarism, and positivism of liberalism" and materialist reductionism, the notion of class conflict as the motor of history, and the abolition of private property espoused by radical versions of socialism. John Paul II clearly stands within this neither-nor tradition.
9. For an alternative, "declericalized and decentralized" reading of inculturation, see Richard 1998 and Schreiter 1997.
10. A reviewer for amazon.com writes: "Accompanied by a resplendently rhythmic score and including an intriguing blend of classical, world, and contemporary western music, *Abba Pater* is Pope John Paul II's uplifting message to the faithful everywhere. *Abba Pater* is the first musical CD ever to feature the most famous man in the world."
11. As Bhabha (1994: 2) writes: "Restaging the past" to make sense of the present "introduces other incommensurable cultural temporalities into the invention of tradition. This process estranges any immediate access to an imaginary identity or a 'received' tradition."
12. Interviews in New York City were conducted by Manuel Vásquez, December 10–12, 1999, as part of a study on the status of Catholic ministry among U.S. Latinos undertaken by the Life Cycle Institute at Catholic University.
13. In 2002, the *Antorcha Guadalupana* traveled from the Basilica of the Virgin of Guadalupe in Mexico City to St. Patrick's Cathedral in New York. As it passed through cities and towns along the way, rallies and masses were held at local churches, including the Misión Católica de Nuestra Señora de las Americas, in Doraville, Georgia, which is the subject of Chapter 6. Wearing tee-shirts with the motto "Messengers for the dignity of a people divided by the border," young people ran a route that spiritually linked Mexicans on both sides of the *frontera* with the "light of hope," traced the migration trajectories of Mexicans, and carved religious networks linking various localities with the goal of "uniting a divided people." The Asociación Tepeyac's explicit use of Guadalupe in the service of "long-distance nationalism" (Glick Schiller and Fouron 2001) exemplifies the group's resistance to Guadalupe as creator of a pan-American Catholicity.
14. There is a rich strand in sociology that focuses on internal complexity, the role of ritual and myth in institutional life, the interaction between organizations and their environments, and the disjuncture between organizational goals and outcomes. Particularly promising are "organized anarchy" models, which posit that problems, solutions, participants, and decisional events in an organization are "loosely coupled" rather than linked in a linear and causal chain. See Demerath et al. 1998.

8. "BLITZING" CENTRAL AMERICA

1. "Guatemala National Survey Reports," an internal CBN memo, November 13, 1990. Subsequent quotations without publication information refer to unpublished materials and video clips in the authors' personal collections. Our data include the campaign's visual and print media materials, such as newspaper advertisements, scripts for radio spots and television commercials, a prime-time show produced for the campaign, and testimonies aired on CBN's *700*

Club in Guatemala during the blitz. Research has also included analysis of CBN television and print media produced for U.S. audiences. In addition, we examined thirty-six internal documents describing various facets of the project and articles published in major Central American newspapers during the campaign. Information on the responses of Guatemalans comes from interviews conducted in Guatemala by Ben Frazier in 1992, which were intended to measure the success of the project. Frazier is a professor at Regents University, which is associated with CBN. Other sources include personal interviews conducted by Marie Marquardt in 1996 with the coordinator of Project Light, the coordinator of Latin American operations for CBN, and Frazier. We also rely on video footage that features interviews with Guatemalans and Salvadorans, and Project Light *Headlines* sent from Central America to the United States during the campaign. These *Headlines* were short reports on individual responses to the campaign written by the director of Project Light in Guatemala for possible inclusion in CBN's U.S. publication the *Flame*.

2. "Guatemala National Survey Reports."

3. "Project Luz Leads Millions to Christ," promotional tract published and distributed by CBN in 1990.

4. We focus here on CBN's case as an instance of the institutional "disciplining" of religion in a global context. CBN should not be taken as paradigmatic of the whole evangelical Christian scene in the Americas. As we saw in Chapter 5, on the ground Pentecostalism is a heterogeneous, sometimes paradoxical, phenomenon.

5. CBN's work in Guatemala in the 1990s may also shed light on ongoing evangelization campaigns in Russia and Eastern Europe. Here, again, global religious proselytism goes hand in hand with the penetration of neoliberal capitalism in the area.

6. Levine and Stoll (1997) offer a much more conservative estimate: that 20 percent of Guatemala's population was Protestant in the early 1990s.

7. Recent research by Steigenga reveals that in the mid–1990s neo-Pentecostals exhibited higher approval ratings of Rios Montt (71.9 percent) and Serrano (21.9 percent) than any other religious group he surveyed (1999: 171). Neo-Pentecostals were also more likely than any other group to label themselves "right" on an ideological scale (172).

8. This and subsequent quotes that are not otherwise documented were taken from personal interviews conducted by Marquardt in November 1996 at CBN's headquarters in Virginia Beach, Virginia.

9. In Guatemala, "*ladino*" is used in place of "mestizo" to signify people who are of "mixed" Spanish and indigenous descent.

10. Transcript of "Long Beach Saturday Night Appeal," January 1989.

11. Project Light video report to U.S. *700 Club* audiences.

12. "Project Luz Leads Millions to Christ," CBN promotional tract, 1990.

13. Dennis Smith explains the "technical-marketing oriented terms" under which most mass evangelists define their goal of religious conversion: if viewers understand and respond affirmatively to such questions as "(1) Do you believe you are a sinner? (2) Do you believe God loves you and wants to save you? (3) Do you believe that Jesus is God's son and that he died for your sins? and (4) Are you willing to confess your sin, ask God for forgiveness, and ask Jesus to be your Lord and Savior?" then they are considered to be "evangelized." If certain viewers respond yes to all of them and also repeat a short prayer, they are "saved" (1990: 296–297).

14. Content analysis of Project Light *Headlines* reveals the four primary appeals of the programming to Guatemalans: entertainment value (17.7 percent), the possibility of radical personal transformation (16.7 percent), appealing images of family life and the promise of marital reconciliation (11.5 percent), and the promise of increased status and economic prosperity (2.1 percent). Promises of radical personal transformation and improved family relations have been broadly identified as appeals of evangelicalism to Latin Americans (Burdick 1993; Brusco 1995; Stoll 1994), and our evidence supports these arguments. However, the relatively low appeal of economic prosperity for Guatemalans in this case challenges the vast amount of literature which has highlighted the importance of economic mobility for Latin American converts to Evangelicalism (Stoll 1990; Brouwer, Gifford, and Rose 1996; Brusco 1995).

CONCLUSION

1. In contrast, the study of local religion in Latin America has not focused on single congregations but on movements (like liberation theology) and tensions among the evolving religious

field, the state, civil society, and socioeconomic hierarchies. Ethnographies of local religious communities have consistently been situated within the national and international contexts (Ireland 1991; Burdick 1993; Vásquez 1998). So here we find another way in which the field of religion in Latin America can contribute to U.S. scholarship: the need always to take into account the larger context.

2. We do not want to imply that ethnographers of religion are unreflexive. Spickard, Landres, and McGuire (2002) offer an insightful collection of essays addressing issues like the position of the researcher and the power effects of his or her interventions. Still, the implications of globalization's time-space compression for the study of lived religion remain unexplored.

3. Of course there have been excellent studies of conflict within and among congregations, and between congregations and their immediate social environment, such as Warner 1988, Nelson 1997, Becker 1999, and Eiesland 2000. However, these studies have not directly addressed global and transnational dynamics, which not only are played out locally but also alter the nature of locality itself. To the extent that these dynamics have been explored, as in the case of Yang and Ebaugh 2001, it has been within the framework of adaptation.

Works Cited

Abu-Lughod, Lila. 1997. "The Interpretation of Culture(s) after Television." *Representations* 59: 109–134.

Adorno, Theodor. 1982. "On the Fetish-Character in Music and the Regression of Listening." In *The Essential Frankfurt School Reader*, ed. Andrew Arato and Eike Gebhardt. New York: Continuum.

Alder, Daniel. 1994. "Crime Gangs Replace Death Squads in El Salvador." *San Francisco Chronicle*, August 23.

Alvarez, Robert R. 1995. "The Mexican-US border: The Making of an Anthropology of Borderlands." *Annual Review of Anthropology* 24:447–470.

Ammerman, Nancy. 1997a. *Congregation and Community*. New Brunswick: Rutgers University Press.

———. 1997b. "Organized Religion in a Voluntaristic Society." *Sociology of Religion* 58:203–215.

Anderson, Benedict. 1983. *Imagined Communities: Reflections on the Origin and Spread of Nationalism*. London: Verso.

Anzaldúa, Gloria. 1987. *Borderlands/La Frontera: The New Mestiza*. San Francisco: Spinsters/Aunt Lute.

Appadurai, Arjun. 1996. *Modernity at Large: Cultural Dimensions of Globalization*. Minneapolis: University of Minnesota Press.

———. 2000. "Grassroots Globalization and Research Imagination." *Public Culture* 12, 1:1–19.

Asad, Talal. 1993. *Genealogies of Religion*. Baltimore: Johns Hopkins University Press.

Barre, Laura, and Ken Barre. 1995. *The History of Doraville, Georgia*. Roswell, Ga.: Wolfe.

Basch, Linda, Nina Glick Schiller, and Cristina Szanton Blanc. 1994. *Nations Unbound: Transnational Projects, Postcolonial Predicaments, and Deterritorialized Nation-States*. Amsterdam: Gordon and Breach.

Basilica and National Shrine of Our Lady of San Juan del Valle. 2001. "The History of the Shrine." http://www.sanjuanshrine.org.

———. 1999. "Welcome to the Basilica of the National Shrine of Our Lady of San Juan del Valle."

Bastide, Roger. 1978. *The African Religions of Brazil*. Baltimore: Johns Hopkins University Press.

Baudrillard, Jean. 1981. *For a Critique of the Political Economy of the Sign*. St. Louis: Telos.

———. 1993. *Symbolic Exchange and Death*. London: Sage.

———. 1994. *Simulacra and Simulation*. Ann Arbor: University of Michigan Press.

Bauman, Zygmunt. 1998. *Globalization: The Human Consequences*. New York: Columbia University Press.

Becker, Penny. 1999. *Congregations in Conflict: Cultural Models of Local Religious Life*. Cambridge: Cambridge University Press.

Bellah, Robert. 1970. "Civil Religion in America." In *Beyond Belief: Essays on Religion in a Post-Traditional World*. Berkeley: University of California Press.

_____. 1980. "Religion and Legitimation in the American Republic." In *Varieties of Civil Religion*, ed. R. N. Bellah and P. E. Hammond. San Francisco: Harper and Row.

Bender, Thomas. 2002. *Rethinking American History in a Global Age*. Berkeley: University of California Press.

Berger, Peter L. 1967. *The Sacred Canopy: Elements of a Sociological Theory of Religion*. Garden City, N.Y.: Doubleday.

_____. 1997. "Epistemological Modesty: An Interview with Peter Berger." *Christian Century* 114:972–975, 978.

_____. 1998. "Protestantism and the Quest for Certainty." *Christian Century*, August 26–September 2, 782–796.

_____. 2001. "Reflections on the Sociology of Religion Today." *Sociology of Religion* 62, 4: 443–454.

Berryman, Phillip. 1999. "Churches as Winners and Losers in the Network Society." *Journal of Interamerican Studies and World Affairs* 41, 4:21–34.

Beverley, John. 1999. *Subalternity and Representation: Arguments in Cultural Theory*. Durham, N.C.: Duke University Press.

Bey, Hekim. 1998. "The Information War." In *Virtual Futures: Cyberotics, Technology, and Post-Human Pragmatism*, ed. Joan Broadhurst Dixon and Eric Cassidy. London: Routledge.

Beyer, Peter. 1994. *Religion and Globalization*. London: Sage.

Bhabha, Homi K. 1990. *Nation and Narration*. London: Routledge.

_____. 1994. *The Location of Culture*. London: Routledge.

Blakemore, Bill. 2001. "Holy Water: Millions of Hindus Seek Absolution in Holy Ganges River." *World News Tonight*, January 24.

Brice, Arthur. 1993. "Metro's Melting Pot: Struggling with Ethnic Change: Chamblee and Doraville Face Immigrant Tide." *Atlanta Journal and Constitution*, December 13.

Bourdieu, Pierre. 1977. *Outline of a Theory of Practice*. Cambridge: Cambridge University Press.

_____. 1991. *Language and Symbolic Power*. Cambridge: Polity.

_____. 1998. *Acts of Resistance against the Tyranny of the Market*. New York: New Press.

Bowman, Glenn. 1985. "Theoretical Itineraries towards an Anthropology of Pilgrimage." In *Dimensions of Pilgrimage: An Anthropological Appraisal*, ed. Makhan Jha. New Delhi: Inter-India.

Brading, D. A. 2001. *Mexican Phoenix, Our Lady of Guadalupe: Image and Tradition across Five Centuries*. Cambridge: Cambridge University Press.

Brasher, Brenda. 2001. *Give Me That On-line Religion*. San Francisco: Jossey-Bass.

Braudel, Fernand. 1982. *The Wheels of Commerce*. London: Collins.

_____. 1984. *The Perspective of the World*. London: Collins.

Brewer, Cynthia, and Trudy Suchan. 2001. *Mapping Census 2000: The Geography of U.S. Diversity*. Washington, D.C.: U.S. Government Printing Office.

Brouwer, Steve, Paul Gifford, and Susan D. Rose. 1996. *Exporting the American Gospel: Global Christian Fundamentalism*. New York: Routledge.

Brown, Karen McCarthy. 1999. "Staying Grounded in a High-Rise Building: Ecological Dissonance and Ritual Accommodation in Haitian Vodou." In *Gods of the City*, ed. R. Orsi. Bloomington: Indiana University Press.

Brusco, Elizabeth E. 1995. *The Reformation of Machismo: Evangelical Conversion and Gender in Colombia*. Austin: University of Texas Press.

Burawoy, Michael, et al. 2000. *Global Ethnography*. Berkeley: University of California Press.

Burdick, John. 1993. *Looking for God in Brazil: The Progressive Catholic Church in Urban Brazil's Religious Arena*. Berkeley: University of California Press.

Carrette, Jeremy. 1999. *Religion and Culture: Michel Foucault*. NewYork: Routledge.

Casanova, José. 1994. *Public Religions in the Modern World*. Chicago: University of Chicago Press.

_____. 1997. "Globalizing Catholicism and the Return to 'Universal Church.'" In *Transnational Religion and Fading States*, ed. Susanne Hoeber Rudolph and James Piscatori. Boulder, Colo.: Westview.

Castells, Manuel. 1996. *The Rise of the Network Society*. Oxford: Blackwell.

_____. 1997. *The Power of Identity*. Oxford: Blackwell.

_____. 1998. *End of Millennium*. Oxford: Blackwell.

_____. 2001. *The Internet Galaxy*. New York: Oxford University Press.

Chaves, Mark. 1994. "Secularization and Declining Religious Authority." *Social Forces* 72:749–774.

Chaves, Mark, and Philip Gorski. 2001. "Religious Pluralism and Religious Participation." *Annual Review of Sociology* 27:261–281.

Cleary, Edward, and Hannah Stewart-Gambino, eds. 1997. *Power, Politics, and Pentecostals in Latin America*. Boulder, Colo.: Westview.

Clegg, Stewart. 1990. *Modern Organizations: Organization Studies in the Postmodern World*. London: Sage.

Clifford, James. 1997. *Routes: Travel and Translation in the Late Twentieth Century*. Cambridge: Harvard University Press.

Cobb, Jennifer. 1998. *Cybergrace: The Search for God in the Digital World*. New York: Crown.

Coleman, John. 1991. "Neither Liberal nor Socialist: The Originality of Catholic Social Teaching." In *One Hundred Years of Catholic Social Thought: Challenge and Celebration*, ed. John Coleman. Maryknoll, N.Y.: Orbis Books.

Coleman, Simon. 2000. *Globalization of Charismatic Christianity*. Cambridge: Cambridge University Press.

Comaroff, Jean, and John Comaroff. 2001. "Millennial Capitalism: First Thoughts on a Second Coming." In *Millennial Capitalism and the Culture of Neoliberalism*, ed. Jean Comaroff and John Comaroff. Durham, N.C.: Duke University Press.

Constable, Pamela. 1995. "Moved by the Spirit." *Washington Post*, August 12.

Cuneo, Michael. 1997. *The Smoke of Satan: Conservative and Traditional Dissent in Contemporary American Catholicism*. New York: Oxford University Press.

Danner, Mark. 1994. *The Massacre at El Mozote: A Parable of the Cold War*. New York: Vintage Books.

Dawson, Lorne. 2000. "Research Religion in Cyberspace: Issues and Strategies." In *Religion and the Internet: Research Prospects and Promises*, ed. Jeffrey Hadden and Douglas Cowan. Greenwich, Conn.: Elsevier.

———. 2001. "Doing Religion in Cyberspace: The Promise and the Perils." *Council of Societies for the Study of Religion Bulletin* 30, 1:3–9.

Dawson, Lorne, and Jenna Hennebry. 1999. "New Religions and the Internet: Recruiting in a New Public Space." *Journal of Contemporary Religion* 14, 1:17–39.

DeCesare, Donna. 1998. "The Children of War: Street Gangs in El Salvador." *NACLA Report on the Americas* 32, 1:21–29.

Deleuze, Gilles. 1993. *The Deleuze Reader*. Edited by Constantine Boundar. New York: Columbia University Press.

Della Cava, Ralph. 1992a. "The Ten-Year Crusade towards the Third Millennium: An Account of Evangelization 2000 and Lumen 2000." In *The Right and Democracy in Latin America*, ed. Douglas Chalmers et al. New York: Praeger.

———. 1992b. "Vatican Policy 1978–1990: An Updated Overview," *Social Research* 59, 1:171–199.

Demerath, N. J. 2000. "Secularization." *Encyclopedia of Sociology*. 2d ed. Edited by Edgar F. Borgatta. New York: Macmillan.

———. 2001. *Crossing the Gods: World Religions and Worldly Politics*. New Brunswick: Rutgers University Press.

Demerath, N. J., Peter Hall, Terry Schmitt, and Rhys Williams, eds. 1998. *Sacred Companies: Organizational Aspects of Religion and Religious Aspects of Organizations*. New York: Oxford University Press.

Derrida, Jacques. 1974. *Of Grammatology*. Baltimore: Johns Hopkins University Press.

———. 2002. *Acts of Religion*. New York: Routledge.

Diamond, Sara. 1988. "Holy Warriors." *NACLA Report on the Americas* 22, 5:28–38.

———. 1989. *Spiritual Warfare: The Politics of the Christian Right*. Boston: South End.

DiMaggio, Paul, Eszter Hargittai, W. Russell Newman, and John P. Robinson. 2001. "Social Implications of the Internet." *Annual Review of Sociology* 27:307–336.

Dobbelaere, Karel. 1999. "Towards an Integrated Perspective of the Processes Related to the Descriptive Concept of Secularization." *Sociology of Religion* 60:229–247.

Dolan, Jay P. 1985. *The American Catholic Experience: A History from Colonial Times to the Present*. Garden City, N.Y.: Doubleday.

Dominguez, Enrique, and Deborah Huntington. 1984. "The Salvation Brokers: Conservative Evangelicals in Central America." *NACLA Report on the Americas* 18, 1:2–36.

Droogers, André. 1991. "Visiones paradójicas sobre una religión paradójica." In *Algo más que opio*, ed. Barbara Boudewijnse, André Droogers, and Frans Kamsteeg. San José, Costa Rica: DEI.

———. 2001. "Global Pentecostalism: The Expansion of the Spirit–The Spirit of Expansion." Lecture presented at University of Florida Center for Latin American Studies, November 11, Gainesville.

Durand, Jorge, and Douglas S. Massey. 1995. *Miracles on the Border: Retablos of Mexican Migrants to the United States*. Tucson: University of Arizona Press.

Durkheim, Emile. 1995. *The Elementary Forms of Religious Life*. New York: Free Press.
_____. 1984. *The Division of Labor in Society*. New York: Free Press.
Eade, John. 2000. "Introduction to the Illinois Paperback." In *Contesting the Sacred: The Anthropology of Christian Pilgrimage*, ed. John Eade and Michael Sallnow. Urbana: University of Illinois Press.
Eade, John, and Michael Sallnow. 2000. "Introduction" to *Contesting the Sacred: The Anthropology of Christian Pilgrimage*, ed. John Eade and Michael Sallnow. Urbana: University of Illinois Press.
Ebaugh, Helen Rose, and Janet Salzman Chafetz. 1999. "Agents for Cultural Reproduction and Social Change: The Ironic Role of Women in Immigrant Religious Institutions." *Social Forces* 78:585–613.
_____. 2000. *Religion and the New Immigrants: Continuities and Adaptations*. Walnut Creek, Calif.: AltaMira.
Effendi, Shoghi. 1938. *The World Order of Bahá'u'lláh*. Wilmette, Ill.: Bahá'í Publishing Trust.
Eiesland, Nancy. 2000. *A Particular Place: Urban Restructuring and Religious Ecology in a Southern Exurb*. New Brunswick: Rutgers University Press.
Eliade, Mircea. 1959. *The Sacred and the Profane: The Nature of Religion*. New York: Harcourt Brace Jovanovich.
Elster, John. 2000. "Rationality, Economy, and Society." In *The Cambridge Companion to Weber*, ed. Stephen Turner. Cambridge: Cambridge University Press.
Erikson, Erik. 1968. *Identity: Youth and Crisis*. New York: Norton.
Espín, Orlando. 1997. *The Faith of the People: Theological Reflections of Popular Catholicism*. Maryknoll, N.Y.: Orbis Books.
Farah, Douglas, and Tod Robberson. 1995. "U.S.-Style Gangs Build Free Trade in Crime." *Washington Post*, August 28.
Featherstone, Mike. 1995. *Undoing Culture: Globalization, Postmodernism, and Identity*. London: Sage.
Featherstone, Mike, and Scott Lash. 1995. "Globalization, Modernity, and the Spatialization of Social Theory: An Introduction." In *Global Modernities*, ed. Mike Featherstone, Scott Lash, and Roland Robertson. London: Sage.
Fey, Tim Shannon. 1993. "Doraville Blasts 'Village' Project: Plan for Immigrants Seen as Job Threat." *Atlanta Journal and Constitution*, July 6.
Fine, Gary Alan. 1987. *With the Boys: Little League Baseball and Preadolescent Culture*. Chicago: University of Chicago Press.
Finke, Roger, and Rodney Stark. 1992. *The Churching of America, 1776–1990: Winners and Losers in Our Religious Economy*. New Brunswick: Rutgers University Press.
Fiske, John. 1989. *Understanding Popular Culture*. Boston: Unwin Hyman.
Foley, Neil. 1997. *The White Scourge: Mexicans, Blacks, and Poor Whites in Texas Cotton* Culture. Berkeley: University of California Press.
Foner, Nancy. 2000. *From Ellis Island to JFK: New York's Two Great Waves of Immigration*. New Haven: Yale University Press.
Foucault, Michel. 1978. *Discipline and Punish: The Birth of the Prison*. New York: Vintage Books.
Fox, Richard, and Orin Starn, eds. 1997. *Between Resistance and Revolution: Cultural Politics and Social Protest*. New Brunswick: Rutgers University Press.
Fraser, Nancy. 1997. *Justice Interruptus: Critical Reflections on the 'Postsocialist' Condition*. New York: Routledge.
Frazer, Benjamin. 1992. *Case Study of Project Light*. Author files.
Freston, Paul. 2001. *Evangelical Politics in Asia, Africa, and Latin America*. Cambridge: Cambridge University Press.
Freyre, Gilberto. 1986. *The Masters and the Slaves*. Berkeley: University of California Press.
Friedman, Jonathan. 1997. "Global Crisis, the Struggle for Cultural Identity, and Intellectual Porkbarrelling: Cosmopolitans versus Locals, Ethnics, and Nationals in an Era of De-homogenization." In *Debating Cultural Hybridity*, ed. Pnina Werbner and Tariq Modood. London: Zed Books.
_____. 1999. "The Hybridization of Roots and the Abhorrence of the Bush." In *Spaces of Culture: City-Nation-World*, ed. Mike Featherstone and Scott Lash. London: Sage.
Fukuyama, Francis. 1992. *The End of History and the Last Man*. New York: Free Press.
Gabardi, Wayne. 2001. *Negotiating Postmodernism*. Minneapolis: University of Minnesota Press.
García Canclini, Néstor. 1995. *Hybrid Cultures: Strategies for Entering and Leaving Modernity*. Minneapolis: University of Minnesota Press.
_____. 1999. *La globalización imaginada*. Buenos Aires: Paidós.
_____. 2001. *Consumers and Citizens: Globalization and Multicultural Conflicts*. Minneapolis: University of Minnesota Press.

Garrard-Burnett, Virginia. 1996. "The Resacralization of the Profane." In *Questioning the Secular State: The Worldwide Resurgence of Religion and Politics*, ed. David Westerlund. London: Hurst.

———. 1998. *Protestantism in Guatemala: Living in the New Jerusalem*. Austin: University of Texas Press.

Garrard-Burnett, Virginia, and David Stoll, eds. 1993. *Rethinking Protestantism in Latin America*. Philadelphia: Temple University Press.

Garreau, Joel. 1991. *Edge City: Life on the New Frontier*. New York: Doubleday.

Gauchet, Marcel. 1997. *The Disenchantment of the World: A Political History of Religion*. Princeton: Princeton University Press.

Geertz, Clifford. 1973. *The Interpretation of Cultures: Selected Essays*. New York: Basic Books.

Gellner, Ernest. 1983. *Nations and Nationalism*. Ithaca, N.Y.: Cornell University Press.

Gibson, William. 1984. *Neuromancer*. New York: Ace.

Giddens, Anthony. 1990. *The Consequences of Modernity*. Cambridge: Polity.

———. 2000. *Runaway World: How Globalization Is Reshaping Our Lives*. New York: Routledge.

Gieryn, Thomas F. 2000. "A Space for Place in Sociology." *Annual Review of Sociology* 26:463–496.

Giffords, Gloria F. 1974. *Mexican Folk Retablos: Masterpieces on Tin*. Tucson: University of Arizona Press.

Gill, Anthony James. 1998. *Rendering unto Caesar: The Catholic Church and the State in Latin America*. Chicago: University of Chicago Press.

———. 1999. "The Economics of Evangelization." In *Religious Freedom and Evangelization in Latin America: The Challenge of Religious Pluralism*, ed. P. E. Sigmund. Maryknoll, N.Y.: Orbis.

Gill, Sam. 1998. "Territory." In *Critical Terms for Religious Studies*, ed. Mark C. Taylor. Chicago: University of Chicago Press.

Ginsburg, Faye. 1994. "Culture/Media: A (Mild) Polemic." *Anthropology Today* 10, 2:5–15.

Gledhill, Christine. 1992. "Speculations on the Relationship between Soap Opera and Melodrama." *Quarterly Review of Film and Video* 14: 103–124.

Glick Schiller, Nina. 1999. "Transmigrants and Nation-States: Something Old and Something New in the U.S. Experience." In *Handbook of International Migration*, ed. Charles Hirschman, Philip Kasinitz, and Josh DeWind. New York: Russell Sage Foundation.

Glick Schiller, Nina, and Georges Eugene Fouron. 2001. *Georges Woke Up Laughing: Long-Distance Nationalism and the Search for Home*. Durham, N.C.: Duke University Press.

Glick Schiller, Nina, Linda Basch, and Cristina Szanton Blanc. 1995. "From Immigrant to Transmigrant: Theorizing Transnational Migration." *Anthropological Quarterly* 68:48–63.

Goldring, Luin. 1998. "The Power of Status in Transnational Social Fields." In *Transnationalism from Below*, ed. Michael Peter Smith and Luis Guarnizo. New Brunswick: Transaction.

Golledge, Reginald G. 1999. *Wayfinding Behavior: Cognitive Mapping and Other Spatial Processes*. Baltimore: Johns Hopkins University Press.

Gómez-Peña, Guillermo. 1996. *New World Border*. San Francisco: City Lights.

Gonzales, David. 1997. "In Hard Lives of Mexicans, Day of Mercy." *New York Times*, December 13.

Gonzalez, Roberto O. 1991. "The New Evangelization and Hispanics in the United States." *America*, October 19, 268–269.

Green, Linda. 1999. *Fear as a Way of Life: Mayan Widows in Rural Guatemala*. New York: Columbia University Press.

Griffiths, Nicholas. 1999. Introduction to *Spiritual Encounters: Interactions between Christianity and Native Religions in Colonial America*, ed. Nicholas Griffiths and Fernando Cervantes. Lincoln: University of Nebraska Press.

Guarnizo, Luis. 1997. "Going Home: Class, Gender, and Household Transformation and Dominican Return Migrants." In *Caribbean Circuits: New Directions in the Study of Caribbean Migration*, ed. Patricia Pessar. New York: Center for Migration Studies.

Guarnizo, Luis, and Michael Peter Smith. 1998. "The Locations of Transnationalism." In *Transnationalism from Below*, ed. Michael Peter Smith and Luis Guarnizo. New Brunswick: Transaction.

Guha, Ranajit. 1997. *A Subaltern Studies Reader, 1986–1995*. Minneapolis: University of Minnesota Press.

Gupta, Akhil, and James Ferguson. 1992. "Beyond 'Culture': Space, Identity, and the Politics of Difference." *Cultural Anthropology* 7:6–23.

———. 1997. "Culture, Power, Place: Ethnography at the End of an Era." In *Culture, Power, Place: Explorations in Critical Anthropology*, ed. Akhil Gupta and James Ferguson. Durham: Duke University Press.

Habermas, Jürgen. 1989. *The Structural Transformation of the Public Sphere: An Enquiry into the Category of Bourgeois Society*, trans. T. Burger and F. Lawrence. Cambridge: MIT Press.

Hadden, Jeffrey K., and Anson Shupe. 1988. *Televangelism: Power and Politics on God's Frontier*. New York: Holt.

Hall, David, ed. 1997. *Lived Religion in America: Toward a History of Practice*. Princeton: Princeton University Press.

Hammond, Phillip E. 1992. *Religion and Personal Autonomy: The Third Disestablishment in America*. Columbia: University of South Carolina Press.

Hannerz, Ulf. 1996. *Cultural Complexity: Studies in Social Organization of Meaning*. New York: Columbia University Press.

Hardt, Michael, and Antonio Negri. 2000. *Empire*. Cambridge: Harvard University Press.

Harrison, Bennett. 1994. *Lean and Mean: The Changing Landscape of Corporate Power in the Age of Flexibility*. New York: Basic Books.

Harvey, David. 1989. *The Condition of Postmodernity: An Enquiry into the Origins of Cultural Change*. Cambridge, Mass.: Blackwell.

———. 1996. *Justice, Nature, and the Geography of Difference*. Oxford: Blackwell.

Hastings, Adrian. 1997. *The Construction of Nationhood: Ethnicity, Religion, and Nationalism*. Cambridge: Cambridge University Press.

Heelas, Paul. "On Differentiation and Dedifferentiation." Introduction to *Religion, Modernity, and Postmodernity*, ed. Paul Heelas, David Martin, and Paul Morris. 1998. Oxford: Blackwell.

Heidegger, Martin. 1996. "Letter on Humanism." In *From Modernism to Postmodernism: An Anthology*, ed. Lawrence Cahoone. Oxford: Blackwell.

Heim, Michael. 1993. *The Metaphysics of Virtual Reality*. New York: Oxford University Press.

———. 1998. *Virtual Realism*. New York: Oxford University Press.

Held, David, Anthony McGrew, David Goldblatt, and Jonathan Perraton. 1999. *Global Transformations: Politics, Economics, and Culture*. Stanford: Stanford University Press.

Herskovits, Melville. 1966. *The New World Negro*. Bloomington: Indiana University Press.

Herszenhorn, David. 1998. "Mexicans Unite to Honor Their Spiritual Mother." *New York Times*, December 13.

Hervieu-Leger, Daniele. 1997. "Faces of Catholic Transnationalism: In and beyond France." In *Transnational Religion and Fading States*, ed. Susanne Hoeber Rudolph and James Piscatori. Boulder, Colo.: Westview.

———. 2002. "Space and Religion: New Approaches to Religious Spatiality in Modernity." *International Journal of Urban and Regional Research* 26, 1:99–105.

Hexam, Irving, and Karla Poewe. 1997. *New Religions as Global Cultures: Making the Human Sacred*. Boulder, Colo.: Westview.

Higginbotham, Evelyn Brooks. 1993. *Righteous Discontent: The Women's Movement in the Black Baptist Church, 1880–1920*. Cambridge: Harvard University Press.

Hillis, Ken. 1999. *Digital Sensations: Space, Identity, and Embodiment in Virtual Reality*. Minneapolis: University of Minnesota Press.

Hine, Christine. 2000. *Virtual Ethnography*. London: Sage.

Hinojosa, Gilberto M. 1994. "Mexican-American Faith Communities in Texas and the Southwest." In *Mexican Americans and the Catholic Church, 1900–1965*, ed. G. M. Hinojosa and J. P. Dolan. Notre Dame, Ind.: University of Notre Dame Press.

Hobsbawm, Eric. 1994. *The Age of Extremes: A History of the World, 1914–1991*. New York: Vintage.

Hobsbawm, Eric, and Terence Ranger, eds. 1983. *The Invention of Tradition*. Cambridge: Cambridge University Press.

Horkheimer, Max, and Theodor W. Adorno. 1987. *Dialectic of Enlightenment*. New York: Continuum.

Hunter, James Davidson. 1983. *American Evangelicalism: Conservative Religion and the Quandary of Modernity*. New Brunswick: Rutgers University Press.

Iannaccone, Laurence. 1997. "Rational Choice: Framework for the Scientific Study of Religion." In *Rational Choice Theory and Religion: Summary and Assessment*, ed. L. A. Young. New York: Routledge.

Instituto de Opinión Pública (IUDOP). 1997. *Sondeo sobre la juventud organizada en pandillas*. San Salvador: IUDOP/UCA.

Ireland, Rowan. 1991. *Kingdoms Come: Religion and Politics in Brazil*. Pittsburgh: University of Pittsburgh Press.

Jameson, Frederic. 1991. *Postmodernism: Or, the Cultural Logic of Late Capitalism*. Durham, N.C.: Duke University Press.

Jankowski, Martín Sánchez. 1991. *Islands in the Street: Gangs and American Urban Society*. Berkeley: University of California Press.

Jelin, Elizabeth. 1998. "Toward a Culture of Participation and Citizenship: Challenges for a More Equitable World." In *Cultures of Politics, Politics of Culture: Re-Visioning Latin American Social Movements*, ed. Sonia Alvarez, Evelina Dagnino, and Arturo Escobar. Boulder, Colo.: Westview.

John Paul II. 1987. *Sollicitudo Reis Socialis*. (All documents listed by John Paul II may be found at www.vatican.va/holy_father/john_paul_ii/index.htm.)

_____. 1991. *Centesimus Annus*.

_____. 1992. "Message of the Holy Father John Paul II for the Eighth World Youth Day."

_____. 1993. *Veritatis Splendor*.

_____. 1996. *Agenda for the Third Millennium*. London: HarperCollins.

_____. 1998a. *Fides et Ratio*.

_____. 1998b. "Message of His Holiness Pope John Paul II for the Celebration of the World Day of Peace."

_____. 1999a. *Ecclesia in America*.

_____. 1999b. "Message of His Holiness Pope John Paul II for the Celebration of the World Day of Peace."

_____. 1999c. "Speech at Arrival to St. Louis."

_____. 2001a. "Dialogue between Cultures for a Civilization of Love and Peace. Message for World Peace Day."

_____. 2001b. "Message for Thirty-fifth World Communications Day."

Juergensmeyer, Mark. 2000. *Terror in the Mind of God: The Global Rise of Religious Violence*. Berkeley: University of California Press.

Kaiser, Laura. 2001. "God Sitings: Searching for Faith." *Yahoo! Internet Life* 7, 12: 96–100.

Kant, Immanuel. 1991. "An Answer to the Question: 'What is Enlightenment?'" In *Kant: Political Writings*, ed. H. Reiss and H. B. Nisbet. Cambridge: Cambridge University Press.

Kapchan, Deborah, and Pauline Turner Strong. 1999. "Theorizing the Hybrid." *Journal of American Folklore* 112, 4/5:239–253.

Kearney, Michael. 1991. "Borders and Boundaries of State and Self at the End of the Empire." *Journal of Historical Sociology* 4: 52–73.

Keck, Margaret, and Kathryn Sikkink. 1998. *Activist beyond Borders: Advocacy Networks in International Politics*. Ithaca, N.Y.: Cornell University Press.

Kinetz, Erica. 2001. "Parade Dispute Is a Rite of Passage for Mexicans." *New York Times*, August 12.

King, Jack. 1970. "Friends Paint Picture of Alexander as Complex Individual." *Monitor* (McAllen, Tex.), October 25, A1.

Kraft, Charles. 1992. *Defeating Dark Angels: Breaking Demonic Oppression in the Believer's Life*. Ann Arbor: Servant.

Kselman, Thomas A. 1983. *Miracles and Prophesies: Popular Religion and the Church in Nineteenth-Century France*. New Brunswick: Rutgers University Press.

Kurien, Prema. 1998. "Becoming American by Becoming Hindu: Indian Americans Take Their Place at the Multicultural Table." In *Gatherings in Diaspora: Religious Communities and the New Immigration*, ed. R. Stephen Warner and Judith Wittner. Philadelphia: Temple University Press.

_____. 2000. "The Emergence of American Hinduism: Genteel Multiculturalism and Militant Fundamentalism." Paper presented at the annual meeting of the Association for the Sociology of Religion, August 11–13, Washington, D.C.

Lash, Scott. 1988. "Discourse or Figure? Postmodernism as a 'Regime of Signification.'" *Theory, Culture, and Society* 5, 2/3:311–336.

_____. 1999. *Another Modernity, a Different Rationality*. Oxford: Blackwell.

Lash, Scott, and John Urry. 1987. *The End of Organized Capitalism*. Madison: University of Wisconsin Press.

Lavie, Smadar, and Ted Swedenburg. 1996. Introduction to *Displacement, Diaspora, and Geographies of Identity*, ed. S. Lavie and T. Swedenburg. Durham, N.C.: Duke University Press.

Lechner, Frank. 1991. "The Case against Secularization: A Rebuttal." *Social Forces* 69:1103–1119.

Lefebvre, Lucien. 1991. *The Production of Space*. Oxford: Blackwell.

Levine, Daniel H., and David Stoll. 1997. "Bridging the Gap between Empowerment and Power in Latin America." In *Transnational Religion and Fading States*, ed. Suzanne Hoeber Rudolph and James Piscatori. Boulder, Colo.: Westview Press.

Levitt, Peggy. 2001. "Between God, Ethnicity, and Country: An Approach to the Study of Transnational Religion." Paper presented at Social Science Research Council workshop, "Transnational Migration: Comparative Perspectives," June 29–July 1, Princeton.

Libânio, J. B. 1984. *A volta à grande disciplina*. São Paulo: Edições Loyola.

Lin, Nan. 2001. *Social Capital: A Theory of Social Structure and Action*. Cambridge: Cambridge University Press.

Lipsitz, George. 2001. *American Studies in a Moment of Danger*. Minneapolis: University of Minnesota Press.

López, Ana M. 1995. "Our Welcomed Guests: *Telenovelas* in Latin America." In *To Be Continued . . . : Soap Operas around the World*, ed. Robert C. Allen. London: Routledge.

Luckmann, Thomas. 1967. *The Invisible Religion: The Problem of Religion in Modern Society*. New York: Macmillan.

Luke, Timothy. 1996. "Identity, Meaning, and Globalization: Detraditionalization in Postmodern Space-Time Compression." In *Detraditionalization: Critical Reflexions on Authority and Identity*, ed. Paul Heelas, Scott Lash, and Paul Morris. Oxford: Blackwell.

Mahler, Sarah. 1995. *American Dreaming: Immigrant Life on the Margins*. Princeton: Princeton University Press.

_____. 2001. "Bringing Religion to a Transnational Perspective: Clarifications and Initial Ideas on the Viability of the Framework." Paper presented at the University of Florida, April 2, Gainesville.

Malkki, Liisa. 1997. "National Geographic: The Rooting of Peoples and the Territorialization of National Identity among Scholars and Refugees." In *Culture, Power, Place: Explorations in Critical Anthropology*, ed. Akhil Gupta and James Ferguson. Durham, N.C.: Duke University Press.

Mankekar, Purnima. 1993. "National Texts and Gendered Lives: An Ethnography of Television Viewers in a North Indian City." *American Ethnologist* 20, 3:543–563.

Marcus, George. 1998. *Ethnography through Thick and Thin*. Princeton: Princeton University Press.

Marfleet, Phil. 1998. "Globalisation and Religious Activism." In *Globalisation and the Third World*, ed. Ray Kiely and Phil Marfleet. London: Routledge.

Martin, David. 1990. *Tongues of Fire: The Explosion of Protestantism in Latin America*. Oxford: Basil Backwell.

Martín-Barbero, Jesus. 1995. "Memory and Form in the Latin American Soap Opera." In *To Be Continued . . . : Soap Operas around the World*, ed. Robert C. Allen. New York: Routledge.

Marx, Karl. 1978. *The Marx-Engels Reader*, ed. Robert Tucker. New York: Norton.

Massey, Doreen. 1994. *Space, Place, and Gender*. Oxford: Blackwell.

Matter, E. Ann. 2001. "Apparitions of the Virgin Mary in the Late Twentieth Century: Apocalyptic [sic], Representation, Politics." *Religion* 31:125–153.

Matthei, Linda Miller, and David Smith. 1998. "Belizean 'Boyz 'n the 'Hood'? Garifuna Labor Migration and Transnational Identity." In *Transnationalism from Below*, ed. Michael Peter Smith and Luis Guarnizo. New Brunswick: Transaction.

Mazón, Mauricio. 1985. *The Zoot Suit Riots: The Psychology of Symbolic Annihilation*. Austin: University of Texas Press.

McAlister, Elizabeth. 1998. "The Madonna of 115th Street Revisited: Vodou and Haitian Catholicism in the Age of Transnationalism." In *Gatherings in Diaspora: Religious Communities and the New Migration*, ed. R. Stephen Warner and Judith Wittner. Philadelphia: Temple University Press.

McCutcheon, Russell. 1997. *Manufacturing Religion: The Discourse on Sui Generis Religion and the Politics of Nostalgia*. New York: Oxford University Press.

McDannell, Colleen. 1995. *Material Christianity: Religion and Popular Culture in America*. New Haven: Yale University Press.

McLuhan, Marshall. 1964. *Understanding the Media: Extensions of Man*. New York: Signet Books.

McMullen, Michael. 2000. *The Bahá'í: The Religious Construction of a Global Identity*. New Brunswick: Rutgers University Press.

McRoberts, Omar. 2000. "Saving Four Corners: Religion and Revitalization in a Depressed Neighborhood." Ph.D. diss., Harvard University.

Melander, Veronica. 1998. *The Hour of God? People in Guatemala Confronting Political Evangelicalism and Counterinsurgency (1976–1990)*. Stockholm: Uppsala University.

Melton, Gordon. 1993. "Another Look at New Religions." *Annals, AAPSS* 527:97–112.

Mitchell, Katharyne. 1997. "Transnational Discourse: Bringing Geography Back In." *Antipode* 29, 2:101–114.

Mittleman, James. 2000. *The Globalization Syndrome: Transformation and Resistance*. Princeton: Princeton University Press.

Montgomery, Tammie Sue. 1995. *Revolution in El Salvador: From Civil Strife to Civil Peace.* Boulder, Colo.: Westview.

Moore, James Talmadge. 1992. *Through Fire and Flood: The Catholic Church in Frontier Texas, 1836–1900.* College Station: Texas A&M University Press.

Moreno, Edgardo. 1990. "CBN Central America Outreach under Fire in Nicaragua: Salvadoran Broadcasts More Popular Than Soccer's World Cup." *News Network International,* April 5, 3–4.

Morley, David. 2000. *Home Territories: Media, Mobility, and Identity.* London: Routledge.

Morley, David, and Kevin Robins. 1995. *Space of Identity: Global Media, Electronic Landscapes, and Cultural Boundaries.* London: Routledge.

Morse, Margaret. 1998. *Virtualities: Television, Media Art, and Cyberculture.* Bloomington: Indiana University Press.

Nederveen Pieterse, Jan. 1995. "Globalization as Hybridization." In *Global Modernities,* ed. Mike Featherstone, Scott Lash, and Roland Robertson. London: Sage.

Nelson, Timothy. 1997. "The Church and the Street: Race, Class, and Congregation." In *Contemporary American Religion: An Ethnographic Reader,* ed. Penny Becker and Nancy Eiesland. Walnut Creek, Calif.: Altamira.

Oblate Fathers. 1980. *Virgen de San Juan Shrine.* Hackensack, N.J.: Custombook.

O'Connor, Mike. 1994. "A New U.S. Import in El Salvador: Street Gangs." *New York Times,* July 3.

O'Leary, Stephen D. 1996. "Cyberspace as Sacred Space: Communicating Religion on Computer Networks." *Journal of the American Academy of Religion* 64:781–808.

Ong, Aihwa. 1987. *Spirits of Resistance and Capitalist Discipline: Factory Women in Malaysia.* Albany: State University of New York Press.

Orsi, Robert. 1994. "'Have You Ever Prayed to Saint Jude?': Reflections on Fieldwork in Catholic Chicago." In *Reimagining Denominationalism: Interpretive Essays,* ed. Robert Mullin and Russell Richey. New York: Oxford University Press.

———. 1996. *Thank You, St. Jude: Women's Devotion to the Patron Saint of Hopeless Causes.* New Haven: Yale University Press.

———. 1997. "Everyday Miracles: The Study of Lived Religion." In *Lived Religion in America,* ed. David D. Hall. Princeton: Princeton University Press.

———. 1999a. Introduction to *Gods of the City: Religion and the American Urban Landscape,* ed. Robert Orsi. Bloomington: Indiana University Press.

———, ed. 1999b. *Gods of the City: Religion and the American Urban Landscape.* Bloomington: Indiana University Press.

Ortner, Sherry. 1995. "Resistance and the Problem of Ethnographic Refusal." *Comparative Studies in Society and History* 37, 1:173–193.

Otis, George. 1999. *Informed Intercession.* Ventura, Calif.: Renew Books.

Otto, Rudolph. 1923. *The Idea of the Holy.* London: Oxford University Press.

Papastergiadis, Nikos. 2000. *The Turbulence of Migration: Globalization, Deterritorialization, and Hybridity.* Cambridge: Polity.

Parsons, Talcott. 1968. "Christianity." In *International Encyclopedia of Social Sciences,* ed. D. Sills. New York: Free Press.

Patton, Kimberley, and Benjamin Ray, eds. 2000. *A Magic Still Dwells: Comparative Religion in the Postmodern Age.* Berkeley: University of California Press.

Peterson, Anna, and Manuel Vásquez. 1998. "The New Evangelization in Latin American Perspective." *Cross Currents* 48, 3: 311–329.

———. 2001. "'Upwards, Never Down': The Catholic Charismatic Renewal in Transnational Perspective." In *Christianity, Social Change, and Globalization in the Americas,* ed. Anna Peterson, Manuel Vásquez, and Philip Williams. New Brunswick: Rutgers University Press.

Peterson, Anna, Manuel A. Vásquez, and Philip J. Williams, eds. 2001. *Christianity, Social Change, and Globalization in the Americas.* New Brunswick: Rutgers University Press.

Pile, Steve, and Nigel Thrift. 1995. Introduction to *Mapping the Subject: Geographies of Cultural Transformation,* ed. Steve Pile and Nigel Thrift. London: Routledge.

Poewe, Karla O. 1994. *Charismatic Christianity as a Global Culture.* Columbia: University of South Carolina Press.

Pohl, Christine. 1999. *Making Room: Recovering Hospitality as a Christian Tradition.* Grand Rapids, Mich.: Eerdmans.

Portes, Alejandro, Luis Guarnizo, and Patricia Landolt. 1999. "Introduction: Pitfalls and Promise of an Emergent Research Field." *Ethnic and Racial Studies* 22, 2:217–237.

Poster, Mark. 2001. *What's the Matter with the Internet?* Minneapolis: University of Minnesota Press.

Powell, Walter, and Paul DiMaggio, eds. 1991. *The New Instutionalism in Organizational Analysis.* Chicago: University of Chicago Press.

Pratt, Geraldine. 1999. "Geographies of Identity and Difference: Marking Boundaries." In *Human Geography Today,* ed. Doreen Massey, John Allen, and Philip Same. Cambridge: Polity Press.

Putnam, Robert. 1993. "The Prosperous Community: Social Capital and Public Affairs." *American Prospect* 13: 35–42.

_____. 2000. *Bowling Alone: The Collapse and Revival of American Community.* New York: Touchstone.

Raub, Susan. 1980. "Thousands Attend Shrine Ceremonies." *Corpus Christi Caller Times,* April 20.

Rees, Martha Woodson, and T. Danyael Miller. 2002. "Quienes Somos? Qué Necesitamos? Needs Assessment of Hispanics in the Archdiocese of Atlanta." Archdiocese of Atlanta, March 25.

Rheingold, Howard. 1990. *Virtual Reality.* New York: Simon and Schuster.

_____. 2000. *The Virtual Community: Homesteading on the Electronic Frontier.* Cambridge: MIT Press.

Richard, Pablo. 1998. "The South Will Judge the North: The Church between Globalization and Inculturation." In *The Papacy and the People of God,* ed. Gary MacEoin. Maryknoll, N.Y.: Orbis Books.

Robertson, Pat. 1991. *The New World Order.* Dallas: Word.

Robertson, Roland. 1991. "Globalization, Modernization, and Postmodernization: The Ambiguous Position of Religion." In *Religion and the Global Order,* ed. Roland Robertson and William R. Garrett. New York: Paragon House.

_____. 1992. *Globalization: Social Theory and Global Culture.* London: Sage.

_____. 1995. "Glocalization: Time-Space and Homogeneity-Heterogeneity." In *Global Modernities,* ed. Mike Featherstone, Scott Lash, and Roland Robertson. London: Sage.

Roof, Wade Clark. 1998. "Religious Borderlands: Challenges for Future Study." *Journal for the Scientific Study of Religion* 37:1–14.

_____. 1999. *Spiritual Marketplace: Baby Boomers and the Remaking of American Religion.* Princeton: Princeton University Press.

Rosaldo, Renato. 1989. *Culture and Truth: The Remaking of Social Analysis.* Boston: Beacon.

_____. 1995. Foreword to *Hybrid Cultures: Strategies for Entering and Leaving Modernity,* by Nestor García Canclini. Minneapolis: University of Minnesota Press.

Rosen, Jonathan. 2000. *The Talmud and the Internet: A Journey between Worlds.* New York: Farrar, Straus and Giroux.

Rouse, Roger. 1991. "Mexican Migration and the Social Space of Postmodernism." *Diaspora* 1, 1: 8–23.

Rudolph, Susanne Hoeber. 1997. "Religion, States, and Transnational Civil Society." Introduction to *Transnational Religion and Fading States,* ed. Susanne Hoeber Rudolph and James Piscatori. Boulder, Colo.: Westview.

Rudolph, Susanne Hoeber, and James Piscatori, eds. 1997. *Transnational Religion and Fading States.* Boulder, Colo.: Westview.

Rutheiser, Charles. 1996. *Imagineering Atlanta: The Politics of Place in the City of Dreams.* London: Verso.

Said, Edward. 1993. *Culture and Imperialism.* London: Chatto and Windus.

Saldívar, José David. 1997. *Border Matters: Remapping American Cultural Studies.* Berkeley: University of California Press.

Sandoval, Moises. 1991. *On the Move: A History of the Hispanic Church in the United States.* Maryknoll, N.Y.: Orbis.

Sassen, Saskia. 1988. *The Mobility of Labor and Capital: A Study in International Investment and Labor Flow.* Cambridge: Cambridge University Press.

_____. 1991. *The Global City: New York, London, Tokyo.* Princeton: Princeton University Press.

_____. 1998. *Globalization and Its Discontents.* New York: New Press.

_____. 2000. "Digital Networks and the State: Some Governance Questions." *Theory, Culture, and Society* 17, 4:19–33.

Schreiter, Robert. 1997. *The New Catholicity: Theology between the Global and the Local.* Maryknoll, N.Y.: Orbis Books.

Schultze, Quentin, J. 1992. "Catholic vs. Protestant: Mass-Mediated Legitimation of Popular Evangelicalism in Guatemala." *Public Relations Review* 18, 3:257–263.

Shaull, Richard, and Waldo Cesar. 2000. *Pentecostalism and the Future of the Christian Churches.* Grand Rapids, Mich.: Eerdmans.

Sherkat, Darren, and Christopher Ellison. 1999. "Recent Developments and Current Controversies in the Sociology of Religion." *Annual Review of Sociology* 25:363–394.

Slater, Don. 1998. "Trading Sexpics in IRC: Embodiment and Authenticity on the Internet." *Body and Society* 4, 4:91–117.

Smith, Anthony. 1991. *National Identity*. Reno: University of Nevada Press.

Smith, Christian. 1996. *Resisting Reagan: The U.S. Central America Peace Movement*. Chicago: University of Chicago Press.

_____. 1998. *American Evangelicalism: Embattled and Thriving*. Chicago: University of Chicago Press.

Smith, Dennis A. 1990. "The Gospel According to the United States: Evangelical Broadcasting in Central America." In *American Evangelicals and the Mass Media*, ed. Quentin J. Schultze. Grand Rapids, Mich.: Academie Books.

Smith, Jonathan Z. 1978. *Map Is Not Territory: Studies in the History of Religion*. Chicago: University of Chicago Press.

_____. 1987. *To Take Place: Toward a Theory in Ritual*. Chicago: University of Chicago Press.

Smith, Michael Peter. 2001. *Transnational Urbanism: Locating Globalization*. London: Blackwell.

Smutt, Marcela, and Jenny Miranda. 1998. *El fenómeno de las pandillas en El Salvador*. San Salvador: UNICEF/FLACSO.

Soja, Edward. 1989. *Postmodern Geographies: The Reassertion of Space in Critical Social Theory*. London: Verso.

_____. 1995. "Postmodern Urbanization: The Six Restructurings of Los Angeles." In *Postmodern Cities and Spaces*, ed. S. Watson and K. Gibson. Cambridge, Mass.: Blackwell.

_____. 1999. "Thirdspace: Expanding the Scope of the Geographical Imagination." In *Human Geography Today*, ed. Doreen Massey, John Allen, and Philip Same. Cambridge: Polity Press.

_____. 2000. *Postmetropolis: Critical Studies of Cities and Regions*. Oxford: Blackwell.

Spickard, James, J. Shawn Landres, and Meredith McGuire, eds. 2002. *Personal Knowledge and Beyond: Reshaping the Ethnography of Religion*. New York: New York University Press.

Spivak, Gayatri. 1988. *In Other Worlds: Essays in Cultural Politics*. Edited by Donna Landry and Gerald MacLean. New York: Routledge.

Stanley, Alessandra. 2001. "Make Way for the Vatican's X-Man: Il Papa." *New York Times*, January 7.

Stark, Rodney. 1996. *The Rise of Christianity: A Sociologist Reconsiders History*. Princeton: Princeton University Press.

Stark, Rodney, and Roger Finke. 2000. *Acts of Faith : Explaining the Human Side of Religion*. Berkeley: University of California Press.

Stark, Rodney, and William Sims Bainbridge. 1985. *The Future of Religion: Secularization, Revival, and Cult Formation*. Berkeley: University of California Press.

Steigenga, Tim. 1999. "Guatemala." In *Religious Freedom and Evangelization in Latin America: The Challenge of Religious Pluralism*, ed. Paul E. Sigmund. Maryknoll, N.Y.: Orbis.

Stewart, Charles, and Rosalind Shaw. 1994. *Syncretism/Anti-Syncretism: The Politics of Religious Synthesis*. New York: Routledge.

St. Johns Parish. 1999. "Celebrating Fifty Years of Growth: St. John the Baptist Catholic Church." http://www.omiusa.org/sanjuan.htm.

Stoll, David. 1990. *Is Latin America Turning Protestant? The Politics of Evangelical Growth*. Berkeley: University of California Press.

_____. 1994. "'Jesus Is the Lord of Guatemala': Evangelical Reform in a Death-Squad State." In *Accounting for Fundamentalisms: The Dynamic Character of Movements*, ed. Martin E. Marty and R. Scott Appleby. Chicago: University of Chicago Press.

Stout, Harry, and D. Scott Cormode. 1998. "Institutions and the Story of American Religion: A Sketch of a Synthesis." In *Sacred Companies*, ed. N. J. Demerath, Peter Hall, Terry Schmitt, and Rhys Williams. New York: Oxford University Press.

Stross, Brian. 1999. "The Hybrid Metaphor: From Biology to Culture." *Journal of American Folklore* 112, 445:254–267.

Swyngedouw, Erik. 1997. "Neither Global nor Local: 'Glocalization' and the Politics of Scale." In *Spaces of Globalization*, ed. Kevin Cox. New York: Guilford.

Szulc, Tad. 1995. *Pope John Paul II: The Biography*. New York: Scribner's.

Tagliabue, John. 2001. "On Some Euros, a Face from a Small Place." *New York Times*, August 19.

Tawney, Richard H. 1926. *Religion and the Rise of Capitalism: A Historical Study*. New York: Harcourt, Brace.

Taylor, Charles. 1998. "Modes of Secularism." In *Secularism and Its Critics*, ed. R. Bhargava. Delhi: Oxford University Press.

Taylor, Mark C. 1999. *About Religion: Economies of Faith in Virtual Culture.* Chicago: University of Chicago Press.

Teather, Elizabeth K. 1999. Introduction to *Embodied Geographies: Spaces, Bodies, and Rites of Passage,* ed. Elizabeth K. Teather. London: Routledge.

Thompson, Edward P. 1966. *The Making of the English Working Class.* New York: Vintage Books.

Tiryakian, Edward. 1992a. "Dialectics of Modernity: Reenchantment and Dedifferentiation as Counterprocesses." In *Social Change and Modernity,* ed. H. Haferkamp and N. Smelser. Berkeley: University of California Press.

_____. 1992b. "From Modernization to Globalization." *Journal for the Scientific Study of Religion* 31:304–310.

Tschannen, Oliver. 1991. "The Secularization Paradigm." *Journal for the Scientific Study of Religion* 30:395–415.

Tsing, Anna. 2000. "The Global Situation." *Cultural Anthropology* 15, 3:327–360.

Turkel, Sherry. 1995. *Life on the Screen: Identity in the Age of the Internet.* New York: Simon and Schuster.

Turner, Victor, and Edith Turner. 1978. *Image and Pilgrimage in Christian Culture.* New York: Columbia University Press.

Tweed, Thomas. 1997. *Our Lady of the Exile: Diasporic Religion at a Cuban Catholic Shrine in Miami.* New York: Oxford University Press.

_____. 2002. "On Moving Across: Translocative Religion and the Interpreter's Position." *Journal of the American Academy of Religion* 70:253–277.

Vásquez, Manuel. 1998. *The Brazilian Popular Church and the Crisis of Modernity.* Cambridge: Cambridge University Press.

_____. 1999. "Towards a New Agenda for the Study of Religion in the Americas." *Journal of Interamerican Studies and World Affairs* 41, 4:1–20.

_____. 2000. "Religious Pluralism, Identity, and Globalization in the Americas." *Religious Studies Review* 26:333–341.

_____. 2002. "Historicizing and Materializing the Study of Religion: The Contributions of Migration Studies." Keynote address to the Social Science Research Council meeting, "Immigration, Religion, and Civic Life," March 15–17, University of Texas at Arlington.

Vásquez, Manuel, and Marie Marquardt. 2000. "Globalizing the Rainbow Madonna: Old Time Religion in the Present Age." *Theory, Culture, and Society* 17, 4:119–143.

Vattimo, Gianni. 1992. *The Transparent Society.* Cambridge: Polity..

Veer, Peter van der, and Hartmut Lehmann. 1999. Introduction to *Nation and Religion: Perspectives on Europe and Asia.* Princeton: Princeton University Press.

Velez–Ibanez, Carlos G. 1996. *Border Visions: Mexican Cultures of the Southwest United States.* Tucson: University of Arizona Press.

Venn, Couze. 1999. "Narrating the Postcolonial." In *Spaces of Culture: City-Nation-World,* ed. Mike Featherstone and Scott Lash. London: Sage.

Vertovec, Steven. 2000. *The Hindu Diaspora: Comparative Patterns.* New York: Routledge.

Vigil, James. 1988. *Barrio Gangs: Street Life and Identity in Southern California.* Austin: University of Texas Press.

_____. 2002. "Community Dynamics and the Rise of Street Gangs." In *Latinos: Remaking America,* ed. Marcelo Suarez-Orozco and Mariela Paez. Berkeley: University of California Press.

Vigil, James, and Steve Yun. 1996. "Southern California Gangs: Comparative Ethnicity and Social Control." In *Gangs in America,* ed. C. Ronald Huff. Thousand Oaks, Calif.: Sage.

Virilio, Paul. 1991. *L'ecran du desert: Chroniques de guerre.* Paris: Galilee.

Voye, Liliane. 1995. "From Institutional Catholicism to 'Christian Inspiration': Another Look at Belgium." In *The Post–War Generation and Establishment Religion,* ed. W. C. Roof. Boulder, Colo.: Westview.

Wagner, Peter. 1992. *Warfare Prayer.* Ventura, Calif.: Regal Books.

_____, ed. 1993. *Breaking Strongholds in Your City.* Ventura, Calif.: Regal Books.

Waldo, Cesar. 2001. "From Babel to Pentecost: A Social-Historical-Theological Study of the Growth of Pentecostalism." In *Between Babel and Pentecost: Transnational Pentecostalism in Africa and Latin America,* ed. André Corten and Ruth Marshall-Fratani. Bloomington: Indiana University Press.

Wallace, Scott. 2000. "You Must Go Home Again: Deported L.A. Gangbangers Take Over El Salvador." *Harper's Magazine,* August, 47–56.

Wallerstein, Immanuel. 1974. *The Modern World System.* New York: Academic Press.

_____. 1998. *Utopistics: Or, Historical Choices of the Twenty-first Century.* New York: New Press.

Warner, R. Stephen. 1988. *New Wine in Old Wineskins: Evangelicals and Liberals in a Small-Town Church*. Berkeley: University of California Press.

———. 1993. "Work in Progress toward a New Paradigm for the Sociological Study of Religion in the United States." *American Journal of Sociology* 98:1044–1093.

———. 1997. "Religion, Boundaries, and Bridges." *Sociology of Religion* 58:217–238.

Warner, R. Stephen, and Judith G. Wittner, eds. 1998. *Gatherings in Diaspora: Religious Communities and the New Immigration*. Philadelphia: Temple University Press.

Weber, Max. 1946. "Science as a Vocation." In *From Max Weber: Essays in Sociology*, ed. H. H. Gerth and C. Wright Mills. New York: Oxford University Press.

———. 1958. *The Protestant Ethic and the Spirit of Capitalism*. New York: Scribner's.

Welsch, Wolfgang. 1999. "Transculturality: The Puzzling Form of Culture Today." In *Spaces of Culture: City-Nation-World*, ed. Mike Featherstone and Scott Lash. London: Sage.

Wills, Garry. 2000. "Fatima: 'The Third Secret.'" *New York Review of Books*, August 10.

Wilson, Rob, and Wimal Dissanayake. 1996. *Global/Local: Cultural Production and the Transnational Imaginary*. Durham, N.C.: Duke University Press.

Winant, Howard. 1994. *Racial Conditions: Politics, Theory, Comparisons*. Minneapolis: University of Minnesota Press.

Wind, James, and James Lewis. 1994. *American Congregations*. Chicago: University of Chicago Press.

Witten, Marsha Grace. 1993. *All Is Forgiven: The Secular Message in American Protestantism*. Princeton: Princeton University Press.

Wolf, Eric. 1982. *Europe and the People without History*. Berkeley: University of California Press.

Woodrow, Alain. 1998. "Superstar or Servant?" In *The Papacy and the People of God*, ed. Gary MacEoin. Maryknoll, N.Y.: Orbis Books.

Wright, Robert E. 1996. "Catholic Diocesan Church of Spanish and Mexican Texas." In *The New Handbook of Texas*, ed. Ronnie C. Tyler. Austin: Texas State Historical Association.

Wuthnow, Robert. 1998a. *After Heaven: Spirituality in America since the 1950s*. Berkeley: University of California Press.

———. 1998b. *Loose Connections: Joining Together in America's Fragmented Communities*. Cambridge: Harvard University Press.

Yang, Fenggang, and Helen Rose Ebaugh. 2001. "Transformations in New Immigrant Religions and Their Global Implications." *American Sociological Review* 66:269–288.

Yoshimoto, M. 1989. "The Postmodern and Mass Images in Japan." *Public Culture* 1/2: 8–25.

Zaleski, Jeff. 1997. *The Soul of Cyberspace: How Technology Is Changing Our Spiritual Lives*. San Francisco: HarperCollins.

Zwingle, Erla. 1999. "Goods Move. People Move. Ideas Move. And Cultures Change." *National Geographic*, August, 12–33.

Index

About the Authors

MANUEL A. VÁSQUEZ teaches religion and Latin American and Latino studies at the University of Florida. He is author of *The Brazilian Popular Church and the Crisis of Modernity* (Cambridge University Press, 1998) and coeditor of *Christianity, Social Change, and Globalization in the Americas* (Rutgers University Press, 2001).

MARIE FRIEDMANN MARQUARDT is a doctoral candidate at Emory University, where she teaches sociology of religion. She has published articles on globalization, Marian apparitions, and religion and immigration to the United States.